REPLICATIONS

REPLICATIONS

A Robotic History of the
SCIENCE FICTION FILM

· ·

J. P. Telotte

University of Illinois Press

URBANA AND CHICAGO

This book is printed on acid-free paper.

Library of Congress Cataloging-in-Publication Data

Telotte, J. P., 1949–
    Replications : a robotic history of the science fiction film /
J. P. Telotte.
        p.   cm.
    Filmography: p.
    Includes bibliographical references and index.
    ISBN 0-252-02177-0 (cloth). — ISBN 0-252-06466-6 (paper)
    1. Science fiction films—History and criticism.   2. Robots in
motion pictures.   I. Title.
PN1995.9.S26T46   1995
791.43'615—dc20   95-6586
                                                        CIP

Contents

Acknowledgments

A number of people have contributed their time, resources, and knowledge to the creation of this book. In its formative stages, Leonard Heldreth was most generous with his advice, materials, and encouragement. Throughout work on the book, I had free access to both the mind and library of my colleague Bud Foote, who probably knows more about science fiction literature than any human should be allowed. Responding to far more of the individual chapters than he may have been aware, Robert E. Wood, as is always the case, consistently provided sharp critical insight and a fine judgment on the excesses of academic discourse. For various sorts of encouragement and inspiration throughout this project, I also am very grateful to Gerald Duchovnay, to various colleagues at Georgia Tech and in the International Association for the Fantastic in the Arts, and to my wife Leigh. David Desser deserves special mention for his careful reading of the manuscript and contributions to its final form. Finally, let me thank Ann Lowry of the University of Illinois Press and especially Patricia Hollahan for the attention to detail, judicious suggestions, and sense of caring she brought to the editing of this manuscript.

Introduction: Human Artifice

> The human artifice of the world separates human existence from all mere animal environment, but life itself is outside this artificial world, and through life man remains related to all other living organisms. For some time now, a great many scientific endeavors have been directed toward making life also "artificial," toward cutting the last tie through which even man belongs among the children of nature. . . . There is no reason to doubt our abilities to accomplish such an exchange, just as there is no reason to doubt our present ability to destroy all organic life on earth.
>
> —Hannah Arendt (2)

"I know I'm human," the protagonist of John Carpenter's film *The Thing* (1982) insists, as he frantically searches for a threatening alien presence among his comrades at an isolated arctic research station. Taken out of context in this way, the character McReady's assertion sounds a bit silly, like a statement of something that should be evident to everyone—to those around him no less than to those in the movie audience. But his near manic insistence on this point signals an unexpected uncertainty here, an uneasiness about not only his identity but his humanity. And it seems to be an uneasiness that no simple look can dispel—the way we might evaluate our world, others, and, through a reassuring mirror, ourselves.

McReady's predicament—and the anxiety about a kind of "thing"-ness it marks—points up a specter that has long haunted the science fiction film and that has become practically an obsession in its recent history. Periodically through its long history, one that dates back to the very origins of film, this genre has focused its attention on the problematic nature of human being and the difficult task of being human. And as Hannah Arendt's remark above recalls, the former concern has a momentous bearing on the latter. If we cannot be sure about ourselves, if we are plagued with anxieties about *what* we are, how can we ever *act* human? Yet with their emphasis on artifice in its broadest sense—on the creations of science, technology, various mechanisms—and an increasing fascination with our own level of constructedness, our science fiction films often seem to blur that distinction between life and artifice about which Arendt seems so assured, and they then proceed to interrogate that very blurred boundary.

Of course, it might be argued that, like any other genre, the science fiction film is simply addressing our contemporary anxieties—those fueled by a relatively recently acquired (or recognized) ability we humans have to create various forms of life, to alter the basic genetic patterns of life, and even to destroy all of life. Through our technological attainments, we have discovered many ways to make life possible, to prolong or manipulate our lives, yet also to produce, often as by-products, weapons of mass destruction, life-destroying acid rain, ozone-depleting fluorocarbons, rain-forest-killing industrial pollution, and other humanly sprung menaces. As a consequence, the toehold of human life on this planet has come to seem ever more precarious, perhaps easily subject to replacement by other, less self destructive, and more adaptable species, such as the one that appears ready to take over McReady's body, to render him too a "thing"—which, after all, may simply be the fate to which we as a species unconsciously aspire.

The specific shape of this threat is worth examining, though, not simply as a cinematic gloss on several of our most troubling cultural dilemmas but for the way it opens onto the core of the science fiction genre, to its abiding concern with artifice and the human, especially with the intersection of the two. As many accounts have explained, the genre has a fundamental interest in science, technology, our ability—and our desire— to craft change.[1] Its central and recurrent attractions—rocket ships, other worlds, advanced societies, alien beings, robots—would seem to bear this view out. Yet in her landmark essay on science fiction films of the 1950s and 1960s, Susan Sontag argues otherwise. They "are not about science," she says, "they are about disaster" (215)—or more precisely, about the disasters that typically spring from those efforts at crafting change. Of course, the "disastrous" turn of that era's films may well just be a cold war–inspired inflection, finally not so very different in substance from the many postapocalyptic scenarios played out in science fiction films of the 1980s. Yet it is worth noting that, far more than is the case in science fiction *literature,* our films have consistently linked science and technology to the disastrous, as Sontag and, more recently, Per Schelde assert.

We might, therefore, see those disasters of the genre, as well as its various scenarios of *potential* disaster—collisions with meteors, cracks in the earth's core, doomsday devices *about* to be activated—not only as responding to cultural pressures but also as pointing beyond the social and economic conditions that help shape the cinema. We might read them as symptomatic of an anxiety built into these narratives about what we might make—and what we might make *of* ourselves. They seem to lay bare a kind of trick that we, through our technology, have always stood ready to play upon ourselves.

In revealing this trickiness, our science fiction films, time and again, bring us up short, draw us back from a sheer fascination with what "might be"—which is, after all, one of the key attractions of the genre—so that we can consider what is truly at stake in all these narratives about creation and destruction: our humanness. This point is at the base of Harry Geduld's assertion that the science fiction film "at its best has, traditionally, been humanist" ("Return" 143). It is a notion George Slusser eloquently expands upon when he describes a typical stylistic accent found in the genre: "in the science fiction film, it seems, no matter how deep our visual penetration into the vast unknown—be it the infinitely receding lines of Kubrick's space voyage in *2001: A Space Odyssey,* or the endless vista of Krell machines in *Forbidden Planet*—the camera still seeks . . . to put man back into the picture, to reposition him as an element of visual order and control" ("Fantasy" 220).

The contemporary science fiction film in particular seems to be engaged in a larger, generic version of this "repositioning." For in our recent films the image of the human—or, as a film like *The Thing* would argue, the thoroughly *problematic* image of the human—has become absolutely central. Indeed, robots, androids, cyborgs, replicants, and *Thing*-like imitators of humankind have dominated our screens in the last two decades. Beginning in the 1970s with works like *Westworld* (1973) and *The Terminal Man* (1974), the genre has repeatedly found its central focus in the ersatz beings of *Blade Runner* (1982), *Android* (1982), *The Terminator* films (1984, 1991), *D.A.R.Y.L.* (1985), the *Short Circuit* films (1986, 1988), *Making Mr. Right* (1987), the *Robocop* films (1987, 1990, 1993), *Cherry 2000* (1988), *Cyborg* (1989), *Hardware* (1990), *Eve of Destruction* (1991), *The Guyver* (1992), and *Universal Soldier* (1992), among many others. Of course, this fascination with such figures should hardly be surprising in a period that Jean Baudrillard has described as an "age of simulation" (*Simulations* 4). For these images reflect not only the hopes and fears that cluster around the expanding role of robotics and artificial intelligence in our culture today but also a growing awareness of and attention to our own level of artifice, of constructedness, of how we often seem controlled by a kind of program not so very different from the sort that drives the artificial beings which abound in our films— and, perhaps, awareness of how the films that detail these anxieties might even assist in constructing us along these lines.

Yet these various sorts of human doubles are not just images of current fascination. As Mark Crispin Miller notes, the image of the "humanoid robot" is deeply rooted in the western psyche, and our fears about being displaced or replaced by this figure constitute "a psychological response with a complex history" ("Robot" 286). Miller and others have traced that history through myth, legend, and fictional literature, chronicling how we have responded to the possibility of a humanlike being, and increasingly a humanlike intelligence, that mimics and in some ways far outstrips our own characteristics. Most recently, a large body of scientific and cultural studies have appeared, debating what to many seem the converging futures of the human and the robotic, thanks to growing doubts about our ability to distinguish qualitatively between machine and human intelligence, as discussions of the famous "Turing test" illustrate.[2]

The upsurge of films focused on this image may be just a natural joining of this cultural debate, for our genre films have always drawn within the scope of their formulaic narratives whatever anxieties we seem unable to work out in the public arena. But these films also draw both us and the genre back to an important base—although a base from which the science fiction film has seldom strayed very far. With this concerted focus on the human body, I would suggest, these films reflect a central concern of the genre, one that underlies those various images of disaster Sontag noticed: an anxiety about our very nature. In these images of human replication are bound up all our qualms about artifice—science, technology, mechanism— and, what is more important, about our nature *as* artificers, constructors of the real, and of the self—*homo faber*. These images foreground our desire to wield a shaping power, to render all things subject to our creative hand, including the self. Robert Romany-shyn in his study of the impact of technology on western culture argues that our technologically driven "cultural-psychological dream of distance from matter" and control over it has never managed to exempt the self (194). Just as we try to craft or invent all the things that we may dream or desire, so too do we, often unwittingly, "invent the nature and the body which suit" those dreams (111).

Our science fiction films, then, confront us with those dreams which, increasingly in recent years, seem to have taken such a hold on our cultural imaginations. This book attempts to address this dream-making throughout the history of the film genre by focusing on this image of human artifice. Its thesis is relatively simple—that the image of human artifice, figured in the great array of robots, androids, and artificial beings found throughout the history of the science fiction film, is the single most important one in the genre. It speaks, from the genre's earliest days to the present, of the interactions between the human and the techno-logical that lie at the very heart of science fiction. From that interface position, from the border between the human and all of its efforts at artifice, at scientific calculation and creation, this image measures out our changing attitudes toward science, technology, and reason itself, as well as the shifting foundation beneath our conceptions of the self in the twentieth century. Through this image of artifice, our films have sought to reframe the human image and reaffirm that sense of self about which we, like McReady, appear so anxious today.

. . .

> How can man *be* that life whose web, pulsations, and buried en-ergy constantly exceed the experience that he is immediately given of them? How can he *be* that labour whose laws and demands are imposed upon him like some alien system? How can he be the subject of a language that for thousands of years has been formed without him, a language whose organization escapes him, whose meaning sleeps an almost invincible sleep in the words he momen-tarily activates by means of discourse, and within which he is obliged, from the very outset, to lodge his speech and thought, as though they were doing no more than animate, for a brief period, one segment of that web of innumerable possibilities?
> —Michel Foucault (*Order* 323)

In *The Order of Things,* Michel Foucault offers a striking image of mod-ern being, and one that speaks to this problem of artifice that our science fiction films explore. He describes the human as inhabiting a vast array of systems, as a psyche attached to a nearly bewildering body of laws, customs, and language that we have come to see as separate and almost alien from the self. From within this "alien system"—almost like a central processor activating a robotic body—one "animates" these various appendages for brief moments to carry out everyday activities, to go about life, to *be* oneself, even though from time to time we may suspect that this "web" of elements is itself the animating, controlling, and driving force behind our lives.

Far from being another kind of Sartrean "nausea," Foucault's description seems quite in keeping with other recent conceptions of our nature. Romanyshyn, for example, argues that with our modern emphasis on measurement and manipulation, we have come to "practice a distancing and detached vision which fragments the body into a spectacular dismembered specimen" (117), ready to be reshaped to fit our needs or even eliminated altogether. One of the foremost popularizers of that sort of vision, the robotics pioneer Hans Moravec, terms modern humans "uncomfortable halfbreeds, part biology, part culture, with many of our biological traits out of step with the inventions of our minds" (4) and hence, he argues, crying to be replaced by more precise and dependable technological creations. Howard Rheingold offers one popular scenario for such replacement when he describes work on a "reality engine" which, when it matures in a few years, "promises (and threatens) to change what it means to be human" (15, 19). That effect is not simply because of the way our sense of reality will change as our ability to move in and out of—to "experience"—any sort of reality we might imagine *as* any sort of beings we might imagine changes, but because of the ways in which we will become part of—wired in to—this electronic/synthetic realm. More than just another vision of our modern "alienated" condition, then, Foucault's rendering echoes a growing feeling about our nature, a sense that we are a kind of human artifice: creatures of varied parts, constructed and animated by forces beyond our full understanding and, almost certainly, beyond our full control.

Consequently, Foucault suggests that one of the most pressing tasks we face is to confront this almost "fictive" self: figure out how we can "be" such, determine how to "accommodate that dimension" (*Other* 322) in our sense of self. Like astronauts cut off from the Earth and from the sort of fundamental security our earthliness affords us, we have to learn how to live with what might almost be termed an "artificial life support system" that is not so much artifice as reality itself. We have to master surviving in an "alien" realm that is, at the same time, our real home. And we have to reconsider that unique character we traditionally attribute to the individual self in light of this thoroughly postmodern "appearance." For with everyone similarly attired in what often seem irritatingly cumbersome space suits of laws, customs, gender, languages, and so on, we cannot help but feel less and less certain about our own identities, since we often seem little more than doubles of everyone else in this situation—and with no original.

I tease out this metaphor found in Foucault's account because these issues, as part of a larger project of human redefinition, are at the heart of the science fiction genre's focus on human artifice—and one way in which it has historically thoroughly anticipated postmodern attitudes toward the self and culture. It has obviously found the notion of "alien systems" attractive and useful for comparing to and commenting upon our situation. Free to move about in time, the genre easily expands its scope to "thousands of years," a span that lets it speculate freely on our current condition and its eventual consequences. And it has located in this figure of the double, particularly the constructed and "animated" being—robot, android, or cyborg—a singularly compelling image for our current notions of self, as well as an effective metaphor for that sense of "otherness" which underlies all our recent discussions about gender, race, and sexual orientation. Still more fundamentally, as suggested above, the genre seems to have at its core a concern with how we can "be," that is, with how we can maintain our human *be*ing within a context—as thoroughly constructed and technologized as it is—that typically seems to condition, qualify, or challenge our traditional human identity.

The science fiction film poses this question through its own generic dynamic, its own special way of being. For it contains—and its plots usually constellate around—a structural tension that is constantly rephrasing these central issues about the self and its constructedness. On the one hand, the genre consistently makes great capital from the worlds of science and technology. In depicting a *science* fiction, in giving shape to our speculations about the future, other worlds, alternate realities—or selves—it lets us examine and enjoy the prospects of what we could indeed "be." Works as different as 1930's musical science fiction film *Just Imagine,* the Gene Autry serial *Phantom Empire* (1935), and the recent film *Universal Soldier* (1992), for example, depict technological developments that let us conquer the ultimate human limitation, death itself.

Of course, the genre's typical dependence on special effects for constructing these illusions only underscores this appeal, by demonstrating our capacity for crafting a convincing illusion of these other possibilities. Indeed, for many moviegoers the chief attraction of the genre is its display of a cinematic "science," that is, its technological achievement in making these speculative images come alive, seem utterly convincing—or magic. And for that same following, its true stars are often the various technical designers or design teams that achieve these effects: Peter Ellenshaw, Lyle Wheeler, Stan Winston, Douglas Trumbull, the programmers at Industrial Light and Magic, and others.

Yet this fascination typically runs up against what I have termed the "anxiety" found in the genre, as it usually seems more than a bit leery of such accomplishments—of the very attractions it holds out to us. Despite its own phenomenal investment in these images, the science fiction film frequently hesitates to endorse them. Movie after movie displays a tendency to retreat from those fascinating speculations: utopian or futuristic civilizations quickly reveal a dystopian character, as shown by works like *Metropolis* (1926) and *Logan's Run* (1976); alien beings prove invasive and destructive, as in both versions of *The Thing* (1951, 1982) and the various *Alien* films (1979, 1986, 1992); advanced technology turns into an uncontrollable, dehumanizing, and repressive force, as in *Demon Seed* (1977) and *The Terminator*. While a recent film like *Robot Jox* (1990), scripted by one of our most accomplished science fiction novelists, Joe Haldeman, revels in exploring the technical complexities of its central conceit—nations warring vicariously through giant robots piloted by gladiator-type "jockies" —it repeatedly emphasizes how much of the human has been surrendered to the technological and concludes with its chief antagonists abandoning their mechanical mounts to live in peace. *Robot Jox,* though, is just one of a great many such films to depict the attractions and promises of science and technology as essentially fictions, dangerous illusions from which we eventually have to pull back as best we can if we are to retain our humanity.

It has even been suggested that our science fiction films display a marked "technophobia"—a fear of machines or of technology, especially insofar as it threatens what Michael Ryan and Douglas Kellner term our "'natural' social arrangements" (58). Viewed from this perspective, the genre is an ideologically loaded form, one that ranks "such social values as freedom, individualism, and the family" against a world of controls, sameness, and challenges to our traditional social structures. As Ryan and Kellner see it, this recoil from the technological that the genre usually enacts is a predictably conservative move, since the forces depicted in the films hold a most radical and subversive potential. They suggest that "nature might be reconstructable, not the bedrock of unchanging authority that conservative discourse requires" (58), and perhaps more disturbingly, that the self too may be such a fluid, "reconstructable" thing.

Of course, not all science fiction films do pull back. Some quite forthrightly acknowledge, and in various ways affirm, that subversive possibility; *2001: A Space Odyssey* (1968) and *Blade Runner* are noteworthy examples. In both instances, the technological spurs a much-needed evolution or rebirth of the human. And such films often appear at the same time as others that take a quite opposite view of their technological subjects. Thus, while 1986 saw the appearance of works like *Killbots* and *Deadly Friend,* the very titles of which suggest the menacing nature of their robots and cyborgs, the same period saw the release of films like *Short Circuit* and *Making Mr. Right,* whose robot and cyborg figures prove more human than most of the humans they depict. The ideological issue with such groups of films, that is, what sort of cultural values they variously set about supporting—or subverting—is, consequently, more than a bit difficult to sort out.

But my chief interest here is not so much with the ideological issue as with the dynamic underlying and conditioning such simultaneous constructions. This generic dynamic or abiding tension I have described is something we seem to relish—and perhaps, in light of the genre's heavy popularity today, may even need. Whether these films seem conservative or subversive in their direction, what they consistently speak to and of is a similar dynamic at work in the modern self. They mark off and let us explore what I have elsewhere termed a space of desire,[3] a place within the self where we can experience a kind of otherness, and where we almost longingly speculate about that "web of innumerable possibilities" Foucault describes— possibilities that "exceed the experience" of our normal being. The following chapter will describe the background of this "fantasy of robotism," as I wish to term it.

Though these speculations draw us away from the here, the now, the self as it is commonly constructed, though they suggest—in many situations, comfortingly so—that the self is something we can construct according to our needs or in line with the play of our imaginations, they also underscore the perils of that otherness, "the dark side of the force," as we might put it in keeping with our subject matter. For the self often appears to be, as Foucault notes, constituted *in opposition to* an "alien system" of forces. Within this space of desire, then, we also find ourselves in conflict with that "web" which would control us, and pulling back—to the here, the now, our own natures—because of a corresponding desire we have to "be" something apart from that complex realm we inhabit.

What I am trying to describe is not so much a schizophrenia as a human ambiguity that seems to power our fantasy narratives particularly, and that has found an exemplary vehicle for exploration in the science fiction film. In this genre we can find simultaneously a concern with, as Sontag notes, the release of powerful forces and, as Vivian Sobchack explains, "a purposeful—if unconscious—repression" of our most basic instincts ("Virginity" 103). Far from contradictory, these descriptions point toward the very dynamic nature of the genre, for the release and the repression, desire and its control, here seem to go hand in hand.

In exploring this fascination with how we might "be" in our constructed world, this study follows the approach of Sontag and others, isolating one of the genre's key images, in this instance the artificial being, in order to bring the genre's larger dynamic into focus, and more specifically into a *historical* focus. The popularity of this image of the created, crafted, constructed being partly reflects our current concerns with the promises and hazards of robotics, artificial intelligence, and the new realm of virtual reality experience (articulated as a kind of nightmare in the recent *Lawnmower Man* [1992]). But at the same time it speaks of how the body has become a troubled focus for much modern thinking, as in public debate we resort to phrases like "the gendered body," as we describe the body as a site of "sexual construction," and as we try to assess the impact of a contemporary "body culture." In this image our films have found a touchstone for a myriad of contemporary concerns with which our culture is only beginning consciously to grapple. Yet they are concerns that seem invariably linked, as our growing uncertainties over and insecurities about issues of gender, race, and sexuality—all of which seem tied to that postmodern sense of the self as a cultural and historical construct—intersect with long-standing questions about our ability to direct and control our technology, especially in its most destructive forms.

Even as we note and consider these many, and often strident, efforts at cultural problem solving in our films, we can also make out another emphasis in this popular image. It is a fundamental and unresolved anxiety that has always followed from our simultaneously creative and created natures, one that springs from what we are and what we might be and that our science fiction films have always explored—for it seems our nature to desire, Faust-like, a knowledge or power that, in other times, belonged to the gods. But to embrace without reservation that full creative potential is to enter into a true "no man's land"—that is, a territory wherein we are no longer human in a conventional sense, no longer beings of a given nature whose function it has traditionally been to reflect and glory in a divine creation and to serve as its stewards. Instead, we enter a *wonder*land—I am tempted to say a movie-land—where any wonder we might conceive, or any wondrous way we might conceive of the self, might be fashioned. In fact, the pressure we face *is* to realize (i.e., make "real") that conception— we have almost no choice—and then to realize (i.e., comprehend) its consequences. Once the Promethean fire is readily at hand, what do we do with it? Here, then, is that generic and indeed human anxiety into which, in their images of a human artifice, our science fiction films have tapped so deeply. It is an anxiety that surely resides in all our technological attainments, in all our artifices, even in all our movies, and that has its ultimate source deep within the human self.

· · ·

In order to explore the central tension within the genre and to examine this image of human artifice that has come to dominate the contemporary science fiction film, I want to go back to the roots of this key image—in myth, popular culture, literature, and the early cinema. As the following chapter will detail, the artificial being has long fascinated the western mind, and has often evoked quite contrary responses. Harry Geduld has traced out these responses in his discussion of a body of "legendary material about god-sanctioned creation" that has its parallel in "a contrasting corpus of narrative about sacrilegious creation" ("Genesis II" 5). The simultaneous attraction and recoil implicit in these mythic and legendary materials derives from their focus on the very act of creation, and thus from the manner in which they approach our curiosity about own origins. The fascination of this image, though, is also rooted in a history of real automata that, as Geduld explains, forms "a chapter in the development of technology rather than another aspect of mythology" (5). From the first mechanical figures adorning medieval clock towers to the *theatrum mundi* of the eighteenth and nineteenth centuries, the automaton or robot was a figure of curiosity and entertainment, of

The archetype of human artifice: The stitched-together monster of *Frankenstein*.

The hollow and nearly helpless tin woodsman of *The Wizard of Oz.*

Robocop's crime-fighting cyborg in action.

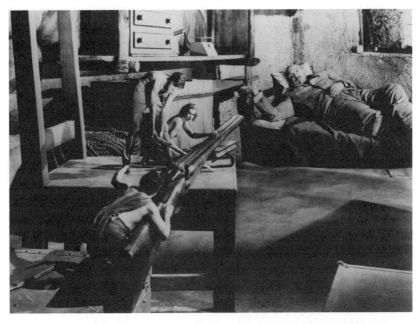

Human guinea pigs take their revenge on the mad scientist of *Dr. Cyclops.*

Robot Monster's improbable marriage of alien-ape-robot.

Plan 9 from Outer Space: A "camp" vision of humans turned into robotic servants of alien invaders.

Robby the Robot charts a course back to Earth and normalcy in *Forbidden Planet.*

The innocent rendered as robotic experiment in *D.A.R.Y.L.*

ornamentation and potential utility, of multiple possibilities and implications. And those various possibilities mirrored our own quite varied responses to this technological double.

These responses to our ability to control reality, to fashion and refashion the images of humans and our world, *are* the essential raison d'être of the science fiction film. Thus, after briefly describing our western fascination with the constructed or artificial being, I shall trace out the early appearances of this technological double in film, anchoring this discussion in a detailed consideration of what is arguably the most influential of these early works, Fritz Lang's *Metropolis*. Considered by many to be the prototypic science fiction film, *Metropolis* works out in an almost archetypal way the genre's simultaneous fascination with and fear of the technological, and it anchors this contradictory attitude in the film's centerpiece of special effects—the creation of a robot in our human image.

This most important of early robot figures is, tellingly, feminized and presented as a seductive creature, an artificial body whose primary function is to deprive men of their self-awareness, to lure both men and women to a kind of forgetfulness of their human responsibilities, and to bring them all under the sway of those technological powers that have given her birth. In effect, she promises to transform them into something "artificial" in the root sense of the term—that is, figures crafted or shaped by her own (and technology's) powerful hand. She incarnates the robot as a kind of automated seductive power, demonstrating the sway that the very notion of technological creation holds over us, while speaking, almost prophetically, to the sort of gender tensions that have increasingly and tellingly surfaced in our recent discussions of efforts to *craft, control,* and perhaps thus *improve* the human. For in all of these inquiries, we inevitably open onto the basic issue of gender construction, or to be more precise, onto the extent to which the feminine has historically been crafted and controlled, defined by forces outside of the feminine.

The first major inheritors of what might be termed *Metropolis*'s prosthetic vision for the most part back away from the gender implications of that image. In fact, they are works that could easily be excepted from this study because of the way they straddle the border between horror and science fiction—films like *Frankenstein* (1931), *Island of Lost Souls* (1933), and *Mad Love* (1935), among many others. These and numerous other films of the 1930s are significant for this investigation, though, because of the way they approach the body as a plastic medium and the self as a variable construct. In them, the body becomes raw material, subject to the experiments of one under the sway of that desire, the now-familiar mad scientist—a character prefigured in *Metropolis* by the robot-maker Rotwang. These films link that figure, as he sets about reconfiguring the body, to our definitively modern efforts at crafting and controlling the human image. What they thereby illustrate and explore is a kind of "mad" manner in which science and technology acquiesce to that seductive capacity, hand the body over to horrific forces, as they try to inscribe their own power upon the human body and, in the process, to alter human nature itself.

Yet what this situation evokes is something more than, as Sontag notes, "the age-old awareness of man that, sane, he is always perilously close to insanity and unreason" (226). More crucially, it is a sense of how the seductive power to reconstruct the self can open the door to every manner of destruction as well, and especially the disintegration of that very force of reason which underlies and propels our reconstructions. That power exercises its seductive potential by, on the one hand, offering to make us more than we are—to grant us a nearly divine sway over life and death—while, on the other hand, fundamentally devaluing human nature,

translating the self into little more than raw material for the experimenta-
tions of a scientific spirit. Typical of their period, these films ultimately
resist that attempted inscription and reject its key premise, the notion
that the human is, at base, simply a crafted thing, a collection of raw,
undirected matter, ready to be shaped to suit the fancy of an emerging
technological power.

In what might seem a less serious vein, this concern with human artifice and artificing lingers in the late 1930s and throughout the 1940s in
the relatively neglected tradition of the serial. In their heyday, these
cliff-hanger narratives were one of the few avenues for cinematic depic-
tions of robots and artificial beings—even as this subject had begun to
play a truly central role in mainstream science fiction literature. An examination of several of the more important serials, notably *Phantom
Empire, Undersea Kingdom* (1936), and the Flash Gordon series (1936,
1938, 1940), reveals both a growing popular fascination with the technological and its potential for reshaping the human, and a lingering, subtle
distrust of this influence. Especially when we look at the typical lumbering, clunkily mechanical robots that populate the science fiction serials,
we find figures that, for all of their lingering menace, actually retain
little sense of the deeper danger, the seductive lure observable in their
earlier cinematic incarnations. In fact, in these films the technological
double becomes little more than an elaborate clockwork mechanism,
and no great threat to the human.

In the period of the cold war and the beginnings of space exploration,
however, a major shift occurs in the film image of human artifice. No
longer just a figure of fantasy or a metaphor for science's efforts to inscribe its power on the human, the robot emerges as a touchstone for a
much greater anxiety—an anxiety about reality itself, and thus the relia-
bility of much that we had long assumed to be true, constant, and unassail-
able. To illustrate this shift we can consider a work like *Forbidden Planet*
(1956)— after *Metropolis,* one of the most influential and often cited
science fiction films. Although constructed by a kind of "mad scientist"
and endowed with a special ability, that of being able to itself construct
nearly anything one desires, Robby the robot here seems little more
dangerous than its tin can cousins that plod through the Republic serials.
In fact, Robby is so ingratiating that "he" would become almost a "star,"
in the mold of such later amiable 'droids as R2-D2 and C-3P0 of the *Star
Wars* trilogy, as he popped up relatively frequently in other films and
various television series, and was even pirated for a line of toys. Yet even

such friendly robots, figures at least partially defanged through their programming with a version of Isaac Asimov's now famous "Laws of Robotics,"[4] point toward the fears that were beginning to permeate our thinking about the future and the direction in which an increasingly technologically oriented western culture was heading. For that newly recognized ability to duplicate anything, including the human body, brought with it the specter not just of an infinite creativity but its flip side as well: our potential disappearance, as we become simply something more to be fashioned—or perhaps infinitely *re*fashioned—and as we more and more lose clear sight of reality itself.

With the 1970s that threat of disappearance or self-destruction took a far more distinct shape. In the middle of the decade there appeared a large body of films that, influenced by the emerging role of the computer in modern life, sought to assess the impact of artificial intelligence on our lives and to address our growing anxieties about our place in a world potentially ruled by this power. Films like *Westworld* (1973), *The Terminal Man* (1974), *The Stepford Wives* (1975), *Futureworld* (1976), and *The Demon Seed* (1977) closely follow on each other and suggest just how pervasive this anxiety was becoming, even as our culture seemed to be racing toward drawing the computer into every aspect of day-to-day existence. In a film like *The Demon Seed,* for example, Julie Christie illustrates how this rush to hand over the running of our everyday lives to electronic brains and to endow the computer with human thought patterns might have disastrous consequences. Her own "embrace" of a computer to run her domestic world ends in its frighteningly literal embrace of the human, as it imprisons her, rapes her, and through her produces its own "halfbreed" progeny which, at film's end, are set to populate and take over the Earth.

If this vision seems almost hysterically technophobic, it is balanced by a more careful analysis in the films *Westworld* and *Futureworld.* Drawing on Jean Baudrillard's notion of the "obscene" as a kind of shifting relationship between the human and the world (or "scene") we inhabit, we can begin to assess the nature of that human anxiety about the artificial human. These films depict a dream scheme, wherein the robot becomes the key to a kind of adult Disneyland and individual robots are simply far more entertaining versions of the Magic Kingdom's showpiece "audioanimatronics." In effect, they are pure figures of desire, although that desire is unburdened by responsibility or anxiety, for here all fears are carefully debunked by an active public relations apparatus whose goal is to assure us that all our best hopes for a human artifice have been realized. The failure of these ideal robotic servants, companions, and playthings, though, underscores the menace not so much in the technology as in our desire to distance ourselves from reality, especially from the reality of what it means to be human.

More recently, we have seen an upsurge in films that take a more sympathetic view of this human artifice. Heralded in large part by the landmark film *Blade Runner,* with its replicants who desire only what their human counterparts want—to live—these films seem driven by an ancillary anxiety, although one fundamentally linked to the issue of human artifice. It is the postmodern problem of determining just what constitutes reality itself. Once we accept the notion that all of our world is constructed, or even more particularly, as Romanyshyn puts it, "that the human body is primarily and essentially a matter of culture and history" (174), then we find that reality itself increasingly seems a fluid and elusive thing. Or as O. B. Hardison, Jr., summarizes, "It is as though progress were making the real world invisible" (xi).

Our films, particularly those of the last decade, have begun to address this problematic situation as we have come ever nearer to a sort of borderline between human and artificial being, and as our ability to draw neat and clear distinctions has begun to blur. Increasingly, works like *Blade Runner* and *Android* articulate a simple yet ever more pressing question: what does it mean to be human in the modern world? And the response they offer is often a relative or comparative one, a response that looks at our own *in*human practices and thus sees the artificial being not so much as a menace but as a potential aid in drawing us back to a sense of humanity. Films like *Robocop* and *Short Circuit* (as well as their respective sequels), in fact, go a step further, demonstrating the possibility for a kind of hybrid life, a ghostly otherness that is part human, part machine, a synthetic life that does not impinge on our own. Indeed, these new life forms seem almost a fortunate evolution, particularly for the way they reveal a ghostly human spirit that lingers in all our creations—just as in our own selves— waiting to be evoked. The development of such hybrid life forms, these films suggest, could well help to make us more truly human.

But to do so, they remind audiences, we first need to confront our own schizophrenic nature, particularly a kind of self-repression that has been, as it were, programmed into our sense of self, inscribed in the very superficial way we have come to see and define our humanity. Again

Blade Runner, as well as films like *Robocop, Cherry 2000,* and *Total Recall* (1990), shows how the self has been turned into a public image—an image that is subject to a wide variety of cultural controls and rules of construction. The various robots and androids that populate these films emphasize the generally empty nature of the public self that we have constructed: an emptiness marked by the emotionless nature of their various human characters (*Blade Runner*), the corporate control over modern life that they dramatize (*Robocop*), and the artificial, constructed relationships that have become the order of the day (*Cherry 2000*). In such circumstances, the human almost seems to change places with the robotic, acting automatically, accepting programming, and operating within tightly prescribed parameters.

These films prove especially revealing, though, in the way they also dramatize the ultimate failure of such a transformation. For in them we repeatedly witness a necessary human reemergence, as the hollowed, programmed, modern body gives birth to a new self. In effect, the human artifice becomes a kind of incubator for our true humanity. And as we become something more than just a constructed body, our fears of that human artifice represented by these various robots, androids, and replicants also seem to be vanishing.

The terms of this reemergence, of this "reprogramming" of the self, show most clearly in a pair of films that, appropriately enough, explore the possibilities of programming a cyborg either to destroy or to abet human life. The two *Terminator* films both describe a future in which our technological creations attempt to take over. Yet while the first film bleakly posits an inevitable conflict in which nothing less than the continuation of human existence is at stake, the second emphasizes a hope that lies within our cyborg creations—that those creations, properly directed, may prove our best bulwark against the menace implicit in what we fashion, against the threat posed by our unexamined fantasies, by our own worst selves. In fact, the cyborg protector of *Terminator 2: Judgment Day* becomes almost a metaphor for the science fiction film itself, demonstrating how our technological creations might help us deal with the world we are in the process of making, help us draw back from the apocalyptic direction in which we seem headed, by leading us toward a new and deeper sense of self.

Our films thus seem to be working out a kind of rapprochement with the robotic, with that human artifice, and with their own technological nature. However, it is not quite the sort of acceptance Mark Crispin

Miller warns about, a situation in which, "if we can somehow see ourselves as robotic, the robot ceases to frighten. We join its ranks, and await the calm beyond all passion and decision" ("Robot" 297). Rather, the direction in which our films seem headed is less toward showing the human as ever more artificial than toward rendering the artificial as ever more human, toward sketching the human, in all its complexity, as the only appropriate model, even for a technologically sourced life. In effect, they seem to draw us back to cinema's own direction, wherein the mechanism serves—and in some ways glorifies—its subject, wherein the technological finds its purpose in framing and rendering life itself.

. . .

A recent *New York Times* report seems to speak directly to this development. In it Daniel Goleman notes a widespread appearance in the general population of a certain type of "dissociative disorder," the symptoms of which are "as common among the general population as . . . anxiety and depression," psychiatrists have suggested. People who suffer from this disorder typically "could not recognize themselves" in a mirror, feel like "an automaton," or have the sensation that they are "watching themselves in a movie." More generally, this problem seems to surface in various feelings of dissociation and depersonalization, which those interviewed usually describe "as a feeling of being unreal, separate from one's own body, like a robot that has no feelings, or of watching a movie of themselves going through life" (B8). These sensations of personal unreality, of robot-ness, of feeling like one is a character in a movie—all carefully offered up to a doctor or psychiatrist for his diagnosis and treatment—could well form the plot of a movie, yet another updating of *Invasion of the Body Snatchers* or a further sequel to *The Stepford Wives*. It might be more accurate to say, though, that these symptoms are what generate a great many of our science fiction plots.

Those interrelated symptoms are also the telltale signs of this book, for it is about those personal and cultural traumas that are tied to our nebulous sense of the real, about a fantasy of robotism that has long gripped western culture and that our movies have made ever increasing capital from, and about the science fiction film as a particularly self-conscious form. In those reported symptoms we begin to sense the extent to which our science fiction films' historical focus on human artifice has tapped into a most common and compelling set of anxieties that have increasingly entered into normal public debate. At the same time, they lay out the attractions of that fantasy of robotism—an attraction measurable not only in our films but in its appearance as toys, comics, clothing, dance, and a necessary element of modern industry, where the robot promises to take over hazardous or drudge-like labor, to increase productivity, and, it is often hoped, offer minimal "labor" problems, all in return for a human obsolescence and displacement from the scene of labor. Finally, those symptoms point to a key relationship between this fantasy and the movies themselves, as the phenomenon of the artificial being intersects with the phenomenal nature of the movies. Investigating human artifice in our films, consequently, inevitably takes in a rather large and tangled territory.

When I first began to think and write about the animated being or figure of artifice approximately a decade ago, I saw it more simply, as essentially an intriguing and thoroughly contemporary trope for examining the nature of the double—a figure that has constantly fascinated us and provided compelling material for fantastic films and literature. The immediate payback from that early consideration was a reminder of just how slippery such a phenomenon can be and, happily, how it almost inevitably leads us to reflect on the very nature of film. For that fascination with the double is central to our thinking about—or rethinking—the nature of cinema as a site of reproduction. It is, of course, a place of human doubles, where we see the captured and reproduced images of others. But it is also a point of manufacture, a place where—as our science fiction films are most aware—we *fashion* images of what we would like to be and how we would like our world to look, as well as a point at which we start internalizing that cultural manufacture, attempting to live up to those images or to work our own best variations on or compromises with them. In trying to explain the cult status of a film like *Casablanca,* Umberto Eco has suggested that it appeals to us because *Casablanca* "is not *one* movie. It is 'movies'" (208). I might stake a similar claim for the science fiction film in light of this emphasis on reproduction or manufacture that its figures of human artifice so dramatically foreground.

What is equally remarkable about this image, though, is the extent to which it has also become in recent years a kind of master text for our reconceiving of the self in the postmodern age—or as Donna Haraway more sweepingly puts it, for "the reinvention of nature" (*Simians* 3). For in the cyborg especially, in that evocative figure of biological and technological combination, in that image of nature altered, constructed, and thoroughly *engineered,* we have obviously found a convenient thinking place for all of our current concerns and theories about the cultural construction of race, sex, gender, and so on. In fact, it has become nearly impossible, in the face of this image and our current climate, not to engage in that ongoing meditation, not to note the deep-seated anxieties, hopes, and fears it neatly packages for our inspection. This image, consequently, marks a point at which the borders of traditional film study begin to blur—and to some extent profitably broaden—for it is the point at which the study of film and its tendencies insists on becoming something more, a more broadly focused cultural analysis.

Where this study pauses and yields to more specialized ones is with the extent of those cultural concerns. For example, what follows generally avoids pursuing the various constructions of the feminine as imaged in the robotic, particularly since this is a path already well marked off by more authoritative critics such as Vivian Sobchack, Barbara Creed, and especially Haraway.[5] While discussions of gender inevitably surface in considering films like *Blade Runner, Cherry 2000,* and *Eve of Destruction,* those interested in pursuing this pattern in depth are probably better served by turning to these commentators. Similarly, this study's province is not the ideological per se, that is, the various ways in which our culture has sought to encode and reinforce its values in popular narrative. In fact, to what extent they can, many of our recent science fiction films seem to go against the grain of typical culture work, neither reconciling us to nor denying the ability of our culture to work its will upon us, but rather imagining and sketching various possibilities for turning the machine of culture—and culture's machines—against itself.

This is not to suggest that this study aims at, as Sobchack has most eloquently put it, a view of genre "somehow 'purged' of historical and cultural prejudice or 'distortion,' somehow 'cleansed' of the contingencies and specificity of biased existence" (*Address* 5). Such a view, in any case, seems almost impossible. For the "contingencies and specificity" of cultural being invariably surface when we trace the dynamic that allows this genre to address such issues so clearly and effectively, and in the process to serve as one of the most important resources for the contemporary imagination. The science fiction film, as I have suggested, is a formula for exploring the nature of human being, a nature that seems committed to both defining itself and denying itself through its creative capacities, its technology. Recognizing the dynamic nature of this formula, and particularly the way it deploys such central images as the robot or cyborg, can certainly help us understand how film genres of all sorts typically work. But such an awareness also involves us in some of that cultural work, albeit in a slightly different key than current critical fashion might initially prefer. It confronts us with the nature of being itself—as we have traditionally conceived it, as it has begun to slip away from our conceptions, and as we are in the process of reconceiving and retrieving it to fit the postmodern world. It almost goes without saying that this confrontation is most important, and indeed a key to the genre's great popularity in recent years.

With a kind of circularity, that confrontation can eventually return us to a sense of how the cinema works for us and, perhaps more generally, to the larger function of "the work of art in the age of mechanical reproduction," as Walter Benjamin has put it. For this image of the human doubled, technologized, of being as a kind of crafted thing finally strikes to the very core of the movies and raises a pointedly cinematic issue. In exploring our fascination with and anxieties about a human artifice, the science fiction film effectively grounds itself in what André Bazin long ago and in a quite different context described as the "myth of total cinema" (22), that is, the "cinematic" dream of a perfect imitation of reality. Within this dream about perfectly reproducing the real, and particularly the human image, we can find a reminder of our very fascination with that technological power, the almost mesmeric hold it has held on us since long before the days when Edison, the Lumières, and Méliès conjured up their first tantalizing images.

Garrett Stewart offers a more specific analysis of this reflexive dimension of the science fiction genre. In describing the particular manner in which the genre offers "the future under study by the present" (161), he stops to ponder a specific recurrent imagery, that of holograms, monitors, scanners, and viewing screens—in effect, images that, to varying degrees, call to mind both the mechanism of film and the film experience. Speculating on the pervasiveness of these images, Stewart suggests that the cinema has become a kind of "synecdoche for the entire technics of an imagined society" (161), a reminder of our great fascination with mechanical reproduction and artifice. The science fiction film is simply a specific and ever more meaningful locus for this reflexive activity.

Within this special generic space, with its images of ourselves rendered by/as technology, we can monitor, as it were, our imaginations, see the ways in which we see ourselves, weigh the technologies that seem to bear ever more heavily on our modern sense of self. While the science fiction film most certainly follows the lead of our contemporary concerns about artificial intelligence, genetic engineering, robotics, prosthetics, and virtual realities, then, it also does something more—and ultimately more important. It affords us a kind of mirror vision, through which we can see how we have constructed the human image within our minds, upon our film screens, and within the world we inhabit. It is a vision which we sorely need if we are to better assess that "human artifice of the world."

· NOTES ·

1. For sample definitions and discussions of the genre, see William Johnson's "Introduction: Journey into Science Fiction" in his *Focus on the Science Fiction Film* (1–12), and Annette Kuhn's "Cultural Theory and Science Fiction Cinema" in her *Alien Zone* (1–12).

2. Among the more important entries in this current debate are journalistic works like Ed Regis's *Great Mambo Chicken and the Transhuman Condition,* scientific pieces like the robotic pioneer Hans Moravec's *Mind Children: The Future of Robot and Human Intelligence,* and cultural analyses like O. B. Hardison, Jr.'s *Disappearing through the Skylight: Culture and Technology in the Twentieth Century.* The very range of the responses to this phenomenon is indicative of its felt implications for modern culture. The "Turing test," which figures prominently in most of these works, is a hypothesis offered by the mathematician Alan Turing for determining whether a suitably complex machine "intelligence" can be distinguished from the human. It involves posing questions to an unseen machine and trying to determine, on the basis of the answers alone, whether the respondent is human or machine. Turing suggested that a machine which, by the nature of its responses, could convince a human questioner that it is human could be said to possess a human intelligence. See his "Computing Machinery and Intelligence."

3. I examine the manner in which desire operates in the fantasy film in general and science fiction in particular in my essay "The Doubles of Fantasy and the Space of Desire" reprinted in Annette Kuhn's *Alien Zone* anthology.

4. Asimov's "Three Laws" have become something of a staple of science fiction literature and, to a lesser extent, of the movies. First developed through a series of conversations with John W. Campbell, editor of the landmark pulp magazine *Astounding Science Fiction,* the laws are fully presented in his short story "Runaround" in 1942, and later incorporated in his *I, Robot.* They subsequently figure in many other works by both Asimov and other

writers. These laws, by their very existence, speak of an anxiety that Asimov and his colleagues have seen as implicit in the artificial being, since they become a kind of genetic guard, a programmed type of DNA, that ensures a human primacy over—and safety from—the robotic. As originally articulated, those rules are: "One, a robot may not injure a human being, or, through inaction, allow a human being to come to harm. Two . . . a robot must obey the orders given it by human beings except where such orders would conflict with the First Law. And three, a robot must protect its own existence as long as such protection does not conflict with the First or Second Laws" (*I, Robot* 40).

5. I would particularly emphasize Sobchack's "The Virginity of Astronauts" essay, cited above; Creed's "*Alien* and the Monstrous-Feminine" and "Gynesis, Postmodernism and the Science Fiction Film," both in Annette Kuhn's anthology *Alien Zone;* and Haraway's "A Manifesto for Cyborgs: Science, Technology, and Socialist Feminism in the 1980s," *Socialist Review* 80 (1985): 65–107, reprinted in her *Simians, Cyborgs, and Women: The Reinvention of Nature.*

1

·······························

Our Imagined Humanity

When compared to our literature of human artifice—
that found throughout the history of western culture in its myths, folklore,
novels, and essays—the science fiction film obviously seems a latecomer
to the subject. Throughout that cultural history, this image, in various
permutations, has continually been evoked as a way of crystallizing,
assessing, and resolving issues, especially those touching on our human
nature, that trouble us. The ancient Greeks, for example, recounted
various stories of metal or bronze men, such as Talos, the guardian of
the island of Crete, who typified their hopes for a rational mastery over
an unpredictable universe. In the sixteenth century the golem of Jewish
legend became a symbol of protection against the pogrom, as well as a
reminder of how dangerous supernatural powers, once unleashed, can
be. In the early twentieth century a veritable explosion of robot and
android stories mirrored both the longings and the fears that the machine age had ushered in. More recently, the "cyberpunk" tales of William
Gibson, with their virtual beings inhabiting virtual realities, have begun
to speak to the many anxieties we face, especially in an increasingly
computer-driven society, about the amount of control we can exercise
over our world and even ourselves. In the wonderful adaptability of this
image of human artifice, in its time-tried ability to address every manner
of human problem, we can readily understand why, as Barbara Krasnoff
notes, "for almost as long as there has been a history, people have fanta-
sized about artificial beings" (2).

That fantasizing has for the most part run in two directions: to employ-
ing the figure of artifice as a trope or lead for addressing those issues
that press most insistently on the culture and to opening up the far larger,
if somewhat less insistent, question of human *be*ing, of what it is we are.

To illustrate both lines of thought, we might look to the cultural commentary of Donna Haraway, and particularly her influential essay on the artificial human, "A Cyborg Manifesto." As a feminist and Marxist scholar, Haraway is mainly interested in vividly illustrating how the technological has become a force of cultural production, generating a discourse that shapes our sense of biology, for example, and has bound women into a set of "social relations" (*Simians* 164) from which they need liberation. The cyborg, with its combination of organic and cybernetic systems, has provided her with a dramatic device for interrogating those circumstances and considering how we might go about fashioning a different sense of self.

She uses this image initially to bring into focus a series of political questions that have come to dominate our thinking about the body and identity in recent times—questions that have become all the more pressing in light of technology's increasingly obvious impact on the human. Yet Haraway's use of the cyborg as a key metaphor for the postmodern self, "a fiction mapping our social and bodily reality" in late twentieth-century culture (150), has also led her beyond that initial effort. She has pursued that cyborg trope to arrive at a broader view of the postmodern human situation.

To understand this development, we might draw on Vivian Sobchack's distinction between "the qualified body," marked as it is by "contested areas of value, differentiation, and discrimination," and "the essential body," that is, the body as "excessive and ambiguous," "never merely or wholly male or female," the mark of our "sensible presence in the world" (*Address* 144, 122). Haraway tries to link the "qualified" and the "essential body" as she reminds us that biology, for example, is just "a discourse," and that no account, "scientific" or otherwise, ever "escapes being story-laden."[1] Attempting to draw together both modes of cyborg fantasizing, she stakes out her field of inquiry as the "site of the potent fusions of the technical, textual, organic, mythic, and political" ("Actors" 25) that make up a larger postmodern *human* identity.

In that emphasis on the fictional there lies a sense of how valuable and *powerful* our shaping fictions are—whether in the *form* of fiction or not— how much they contribute to our sense of self, and how much we have come to rely on them, especially in an increasingly technologized, fact-oriented world. Those fictions help us to fashion an identity we can cling to when so much of that world seems to assault, repress, or deny identity. Thus Haraway explains how our "rational conversations" and "fantastic imaginings" not only seem to be converging today but *must* in various ways come together if we are to create better models for the self, contribute more effectively to "our imagined humanity" ("Actors" 25), write better stories of the self.

I want to draw on this notion of an "imagined humanity" to help focus more precisely on the power—and the lure—of this shaping fiction, which is itself a kind of robotic servant on which we are coming to depend. For it is the real key to that image of human artifice, the link between its qualified and essential modes, which has long helped us to describe, analyze, and even prescribe for our nature. In fact, the history of that imagining—and reimagining—of the self as it has eventually led up to the movies is the real concern of this chapter, which will describe some of the more important appearances of, shifts in, and applications for this very resonant phenomenon and flexible trope. As Haraway notes, despite all of our anxieties about being constructed by various forces beyond our control and conception, we finally "need something called humanity and nature" ("Actors" 25), and this particular sort of imagining has historically responded to that need.

· · ·

As the above comments suggest, our cinematic fascination with these figures of artifice is neither a recent nor a unique development. It follows in a long tradition of imagining the self, of isolating and exploring the living body as a phenomenon through which we might better address specific issues—of race, gender, birth control, education, political power, and so on—of wondering about the larger human condition, and of expressing our desires and anxieties about that condition. The most complete account of this application appears in John Cohen's *Human Robots in Myth and Science,* which traces the motif of the artificial being "through mediaeval fantasy to the legends of an immemorial past," and links those varied sources to the development of science fiction literature in the nineteenth and twentieth centuries, as well as to our recent efforts to create artificial brains and beings of different sorts (15). Cohen suggests that, along with space travel and alien life forms, the robot/android figure has become one of the central and identifying icons of all science fiction literature—and thus a figure whose recent dominance of the science fiction film seems far from surprising.

That image had a particularly long and distinctive gestation prior to its appearance even in mainstream science fiction literature. J. David

Bolter traces the development of artificial intelligence to an older cultural fascination with artificial and mechanical beings, as he emphasizes that "there was perhaps never a moment in the ancient or modern history of Europe when no one was pursuing the idea of making a human being by other than the ordinary reproductive means" (201). In his more specific survey of those moments, Harry Geduld organizes them into three "distinct traditions concerning the creation of artificial beings: first, a body of mythic and legendary material about god-sanctioned creation; second, a contrasting corpus of narrative about sacrilegious creation; and third, the history of *real* automata, forming a chapter in the development of technology" ("Genesis II" 5). With this scheme Geduld separates the real from the fictive, the mythological, the metaphoric, in effect cutting our scientific efforts free from the implications of those imaginings he describes. As my previous comments would suggest, though, we might do well to see those "distinct traditions" as not so very distinct at all; to view the scientific efforts, as Haraway would insist, as themselves being "story-laden"; and to think of those metaphoric creations perhaps as useful technological servants.

As Haraway recognizes, to some extent all of our efforts in the realm of human artifice, whether fictive or technological, merge our seemingly opposite "rational conversations" and "fantastic imaginings" to explore our situation and serve our needs. In her investigation of western culture's fascination with artifice, *The Cybernetic Imagination in Science Fiction,* Patricia Warrick offers a historical vantage on this pattern of development, as she argues that "technological invention grows from mental images, and mental images seem most often to be expressed first in the literary mode" (12). But even after it has been realized, given shape and substance, the technological invention retains some of that imaginary residue, remains rooted in a kind of metaphoric substrate. This is the key insight that Mark Crispin Miller has offered. In trying to explain the strong allure of the robot today— its presence not only in our films and literature but also in toys, advertising, dance, and so on—he describes it as "an active mimic of mortality," "a striking metaphor for man," and the active embodiment of a "fantasy of robotism" that grips our imaginations ("Robot" 289, 307, 302).

A *"fantasy* of robotism"—here precisely is the imaginary servant that has come to serve us so well. Yet it is a concept that remains elusive and far from fully explored, in part because it is so pervasive. What does it mean, after all, to fantasize about being artificial, being a robot, or being like one? Is it a hope for a technologically guaranteed eternal life in an age when the spiritual promise of immortality seems played out? This is the notion Ed Regis explores in great detail and with much wit in his *Great Mambo Chicken and the Transhuman Condition.* Is it a longing to become objectlike, mechanical, and thus free from normal human constraints, limitations, and even responsibilities, to enjoy a kind of ecstatic possession by the spirit of objecthood and emptiness? Is it simply the embracing and fetishizing of certain values we have come to associate with the technological rather than with the human, such as regularity, efficiency, stability, and power—all values linked to the development of modern technology?[2] These are all types of fantasy that, in various ways, address the "qualified" body.

Or does this notion represent a more "essentialist" turn, embracing the human itself *as fantasy,* that is, as something we have culturally fashioned and which we can deconstruct/disassemble as we see fit? One of the prophets of the robotic movement, Hans Moravec, director of Carnegie Mellon's Mobile Robot Laboratory, exemplifies this latter view. He speaks longingly of a whole new type of symbiotic creation in the offing, an amalgam of human and machine elements: "beings . . . like nothing the world has seen before" (50). Interestingly, while Moravic's vision begins from a carefully articulated logic of technological evolution, it leads toward what he can only describe as "a marvel of surrealism," as he sketches a scenario in which the human would logically develop into "a robot bush," a "trillion-limbed device, with a brain to match." Given such a "life simulation," as he terms it, "as with no magician that ever was, impossible things will simply *happen*" (107–8). And indeed, in Moravic's vision, the impossible is *already* happening; the human already seems written out of the story in favor of his "bush"-like destiny—or more accurately, to have become a fantasy.

Following this lead but more closely bound to the realm of the nearly possible, O. B. Hardison, Jr., describes the new "deus ex machina" he sees on the horizon—a human-faced but silicon-based god, effectively divine in its distance from the human of today, in the nearly limitless capacities it will possess, and in its ability to map out its (our) own evolutionary future. While postulating our development into a quite altered silicon-based, robotic form, after Moravic's lead, Hardison also offers this image as a kind of necessary servant, a fantasy that can help us make the needed move into a changing world. Such imaginings, he says, are necessary to help propel us along the path of an ancient yet only partially understood drive: "man's urge to create images of himself and to worship them is a primordial instinct, as old, probably, as consciousness itself." Yet he also allows that this "process of metaphorical deification will continue—and continue to be denied in the name of common sense or as a form of idolatry" (341).

On this speculative note, with a sense that the "fantasy of robotism" at least partly implies transforming the body into a site of fantasy, of either a qualified or essential sort, let us turn to this figure's various manifestations in our cultural imagination. The brief overview that follows should help us gain a better perspective on robotism itself and, ultimately, on what such a fantasy achieves. In all the accounts of mythic and fictional creations detailed by Cohen, Geduld, Miller, and others two emphases stand out: on the utilitarian and on the pleasing characteristics of these creations. If the former dimension often seems a kind of excuse or mask for the latter, the nature of the pleasure or satisfaction such creations give appears elusive and a bit difficult to sort out, as Haraway's vision of the cyborg as trickster, Hardison's notion of divine evolution, and Geduld's reference to the "sacrilegious" already hint. While what follows is only a tentative grappling with this creation's varied and elusive attractions prior to exploring its cinematic appearances, it will suggest that, at its most basic, the figure of artifice often puts the pleasurable at odds with the utilitarian, signaling a conflict with which we are constantly struggling. It includes a pleasure of transgression (a kind of sacrilege), of moving beyond normal bounds, of reaching— and over-reaching—that is central to the fantasy of robotism, to the "fiction" of the modern self in all its manifestations, to this metaphor for one of our most compelling robotic creations, the movies themselves.

• • •

Most of western culture's early imaginings about a human artifice strike a similar chord. While they typically evoke a utilitarian impulse, they more fundamentally celebrate the pleasures of accomplishment or mark a sheer wonder at the ability to produce a human artifice—to do, in effect, what only our gods were thought capable of. In *The Iliad,* for example, Hephaestos, the blacksmith (or technician) god devises mobile tripods to serve his divine fellows at their banqueting. What Homer emphasizes, though, is less the usefulness of these creations than their status as "a wonder to look at" (385). Similarly, the mythic inventor Daedalus is renowned for having built a bronze man to serve King Minos of Crete, and for producing various moving statues to amuse him, including one of Venus. Pygmalion, we recall, was a sculptor whose work became his pleasure, as he crafted an ivory statue which so delighted him that he became obsessed with it and asked Aphrodite to bring it to life. In order to demonstrate his work with hydraulic principles, Hero of Alexandria supposedly created entertaining automatons, including an "automatic theater" that offered a brief tableau of Bacchus and his worshippers (Cohen 17).

While these early accounts of human artifice represent a mixture of the mythic and the real, they share a tendency to have the utilitarian quickly give way to the play of pleasure or desire. In similar fashion, various later historical creations—from the clock-tower figures popular in Europe during the Middle Ages and later, to the *theatrum mundi* of the eighteenth and nineteenth centuries, Vaucanson's celebrated mechanical duck and musicians, and even Edison's talking doll of 1894—seem initially designed to explore and showcase the possibilities and limitations of contemporary technologies, only to take a slight if inevitable turn as they also draw much of their real or imaginative lure from the pleasurable nature of these ever more convincing simulacra. In various ways they seem to support Aristotle's ancient assertion that "the instinct for imitation is inherent in man," existing hand in hand with "the instinct to enjoy works of imitation" ("On the Art of Poetry" 35).

Yet that notion of a kind of built-in drive or pleasure principle only begs the question of our fascination; it leaves the fantasy of robotism almost untouched. All these stories of real and fictive creation point to something beyond a sheer delight in mimicry. Perhaps the combination of automation and representation is what renders them so intriguing, allows them to talk simultaneously about our technology (our abilities) and our humanity (our limitations).[3] These accounts explore what we might do—through our technology—and in the process they speculate on what we are and what we might make of ourselves. The automatons, robots, and androids they describe are our constructions, the utilitarian extensions that might free us from our labors, serve our various longings, give us pleasure. But crafted after our image, they also cast a dark shadow of those pleasures or desires. The engineers Igor Aleksander and Piers Burnett note that there seems "little point in designing an anthropomorphic machine," since for many tasks which might require a robot "the human model looks distinctly unpromising" (58). However, that anthropomorphic design is our necessary reflection, the image that brings another self into view, into sharper focus. While it offers us a kind of freedom—from labor or necessity—then, this product must also carry its own warning label in the form of our human image. While it speculates on our creative potential, it also foresees our potential for enslavement, self-destruction, or even, as a Moravec or Hardison might suggest, our eventual obsolescence.

This sort of double thrust, akin to the informing tension described in the previous chapter, probably shows up nowhere more clearly than in that most famous story of human artifice—and one of the most influential for film—Mary Shelley's *Frankenstein* (1818). Her novel describes the scientist Victor Frankenstein's creation from dead bodies and stolen organs of a new being, one who owes his life not to a god but to a human creator, and one who, we are told, "aspires to become greater than his nature will allow" (53). In fact, Frankenstein clearly desires to do more than simply reinvigorate a dead body with a divine "spark of being" he has discovered; he wants to mold a body he has imagined from snatched parts, to create a being as if out of clay. However, that power he hopes to wield eventually disempowers him, possesses him, and seems to devalue life itself, as Frankenstein admits—in a rhetoric that betrays the central function of desire here—that he became so "deeply smitten with the thirst for knowledge" that "the world" became little more than "a secret which I desired to divine" (36).

Yet as its subtitle, *The Modern Prometheus,* implies, *Frankenstein*'s tale of forbidden desire and the human devaluation that follows fits within a long tradition of such sacrilegious accounts, all of which seem to culminate in a reminder of our very human—and seemingly natural—limitations. Prometheus, we might recall, was noted in ancient times as "a supreme craftsman," and was celebrated variously as humanity's creator and its greatest advocate. In the service of those base creatures, he stole fire from Zeus and gave them its secret. But Prometheus is not just a boon-giver, a bringer of life and light. He is also in the ancient myths a trickster figure (like Haraway's cyborg), and his efforts for humankind involve as well his desire to trick the other gods; in effect, he finds pleasure in violating their rule. Of course, he is punished for those violations, doomed to have his insides perpetually eaten away ("Prometheus" 883–84). But if his story seems a simple cautionary tale, a warning against defying the gods or tampering with nature, it also carries another implication that runs through our stories of artifice, illustrating how the trick ultimately rebounds upon the trickster, how our desires or appetites have a way of eventually eating away at us, rendering us nearly empty or lifeless beings.

An element of this pattern of trickery and violation—along with an equal measure of punishment—shows up in most of our stories of human creation. In fact, the sheer delight in imitation, the pleasure that seems bound up in every effort at human artifice, might well owe something to this other sense as well; that is, that pleasure we find in such creations might spring as much from the *craftiness* they involve as from the *craft* they both require and celebrate. And yet, it is a craftiness that carries a price, as we are also warned against overstepping the limits of our nature, at being *too* crafty—too technological. For the servants that we create, like the humans that Prometheus in some accounts is said to have made, invariably have a mind—or desire—of their own. They long in turn to create, to press that fantasy of robotism, to fashion others who, in turn, might become trickster figures and fashioners of still more like themselves, creating an ever greater remove from the human—and from our humanity.

. . .

As an example of more modern efforts at "imagining" the human and an indicator of these multiple impulses present in such efforts, I want to turn to Edgar Allan Poe, who found a fitting complement to his fascination with all that is mysterious and horrific in the human condition in this image of human artifice. His story "The Man That Was Used Up" is a kind of practical joke played upon the narrator, as well as the reader, by what he terms the "age of mechanical invention" (445). Its point is that in this new age our sense of the human is effectively a fiction fashioned by circumstance, a trick our world plays upon us. Upon first meeting Brevet Brigadier General John A. B. C. Smith, the narrator is struck by his imposing appearance. He describes Smith as a thoroughly "remarkable" figure, "of a presence singularly commanding . . . which spoke of high breeding, and hinted at high birth" (443). In fact, in every way the general seems far above the norm, as the narrator lavishes superlatives on each detail of his person—his hair, eyes, teeth, shoulders, chest, arms, legs, and voice. The image he conveys seems appropriate to the many stories the narrator has *partially* heard regarding Smith's courage, exploits, and "singular" nature, and justifies his near fixation with this "famous" character.

However, that image quickly explodes, and with it all of his awe at

Smith's "very remarkable" character, when the narrator calls on the general. Upon entering his room, the narrator stumbles on an "exceedingly odd-looking bundle of something" on the floor, which he proceeds to "kick out of the way" (448). The bundle, which suddenly addresses him, proves to be Smith himself—or rather, what remains of him after his (literally) hair-raising escapades in the Indian wars. As Smith, with the aid of a servant, sets about his daily routine of reassembling himself with various prostheses, we see that this "noble" figure—with his wig, glass eye, false teeth, shoulder, chest, arm, legs, and artificial palate—and that "bundle of something" are one and the same, striking evidence of a new, technologically inspired power to simulate the human, and of humanity's ability to play ever more complex tricks upon itself.

Poe's "used-up" man—a literal em-body-ment of technology—is obviously a good deal more than just a marvelous testimony to, as the narrator says with some irony, "the rapid march of mechanical invention" (445), more than just a celebration of the power of artifice. As critics have noted, the tale is a satire, directed mainly at political figures of Poe's day, his put-together man a metaphor for those who, stripped of party puffery and journalistic praises, seemed to Poe beings without real substance, figures of artful—and indeed flimsy—construction. But this satire has another aim as well. It focuses on the narrator himself and the near-perfect, fantasy image of the general he so readily conjures up, as well as on the readers who have in their own mesmeric fascination with "mechanical invention" fashioned such fantasies. In the way Smith's image and reputation take on substance, dominate the narrator's consciousness, and impel his actions, we find a trope for how narrow and shallow our gauge of the human can be, how easily we too can be psychologically "constructed" by the fashions and enthusiasms of the day, and how the "wonders" of the age hold in their imitative powers a certain capacity for deception.

As Poe further shows in his essay on a real automaton, "Maelzel's Chess-Player,"[4] and as a great number of robot stories have subsequently suggested, much of this "craftiness" springs from a modern habit of mind. Robert Romanyshyn has outlined how western culture, particularly since the Renaissance, has tended to transform "the world into a spectacle" (33), to turn it into a series of images that serve our fantasies more than our needs. One consequence is that we often respond to it primarily on the basis of surfaces, of appearances, as does the narrator of "The Man That Was Used Up." In his chess-player piece Poe, much like his famous detective C. Auguste Dupin, analyzes an automaton that has seized the public's imagination. Carefully noting its peculiar yet effective operations, he reveals it to be literally a spectacle, a complex visual trick, an elaborate casing with nearly nothing inside—save for space in which a *human* chess player hides. No machine, it is just an entertainment whose key is the impressive fantasy it creates, the spectacle that is a trick we play upon ourselves.

When one of the landmark robot stories of the twentieth century appears, Karel Capek's play *R. U. R.* (1923), it begins on a similar note. What the people have been told about the nature and manufacture of the age's latest wonder, robot workers, we learn, "is all a fairy tale," a nice story intended for public consumption to further the robots' mystique (8). Although originally conceived as complex mechanical beings, the robots produced by Rossum's Universal Robots factory are actually simple organic creations whose human appearance and organic substance are as deceptive as their public history. As Harry Domain, the factory's general manager, explains to a visitor, there is little "inside" his products: "Very neat, very simple. Really a beautiful piece of work. Not much in it, but everything in flawless order" (9).

Their very simplicity, their lack of the "unnecessary" complications "inside" of humans, signals both the strength and weakness of these robots. "They have no soul," Domain says; nor do they have any emotions or drives—no anger, fear, hatred, or desire. In their manufacture, their inventors "rejected everything that makes man more expensive" (9) and that was inessential to their utilitarian function. In that simplification, that emptiness, that material *and moral* cheapness which marks the robots we can find a metaphor for the very spirit of the age that hoped to "engineer" out of the human all that was thought to be impractical or useless. But their practicality and thoroughly rational natures eventually lead the robots to turn upon their creators, to insert themselves in the place of humanity, and, without any *human* compunction, to kill those who seem useless or stand in their way.

Given that trickster spirit which seems embedded in their very natures, then, these technological contrivances, designed as the ultimate utilitarian device, meant to serve the "aristocracy" of humankind as "mechanical slaves" (67), become instead the masters, enslaving the remnants of humanity and thereby playing out a scenario of revolt that will be reworked in many subsequent tales of human artifice. Yet even within that scenario they sound another sort of warning, for while they nearly wipe out

human beings, the robots too eventually begin to wear out—or die out—
and without humans to make new ones, these ersatz beings face the
same fate as their creators. In another, more ironic bit of trickery, only
the gradual appearance of those emotions and desires that were supposedly engineered out of them and that seemingly marked them as supe-
rior to frivolous humans—in effect, their evolution into *human* beings—
holds out some hope as the play ends. Yet it is a strange hope, one that
describes a cycle of utility and desire, while also reassuring us that
humanity, almost in spite of its often paradoxical, even self-destructive
urges, will persist.

Capek's landmark play, the source of the very word "robot,"[5] is only
one of many works to explore the possibility of artificial beings in what
is often called the "golden age" of science fiction. It is perhaps only to be
expected that in the period from the turn of the century through the
1930s, which has come to be known as "the machine age," the robot or
android would claim a central place in the developing science fiction
genre, especially in its pulp magazine manifestations: in the pages of
Hugo Gernsback's *Amazing Stories* (1926) and *Science Wonder Stories*
(1929), and in *Astounding Stories* (1930), under the editorship of Harry
Bates, F. Orlin Tremaine, and, most importantly, John W. Campbell, Jr.
(Ash 304–11). In the pages of these magazines, machine men reflect the
dawning notion, as Cecelia Tichi puts it, that no part of life was "properly
exclusive of machine and structured technology" (180).

Curiously, these reflections of the popular consciousness show no
unanimous embrace of this figure. As examples, we might note fairly
typical tales like David Keller's "The Threat of the Robot" (1929), which
plays upon the menacing nature of the technological creation; Harl
Vincent's "Rex" (1934), about a robot who tries to take over the world;
Lester del Rey's "Helen O'Loy" (1938), which depicts the ideal mechanical
woman; and Eando Binder's "I, Robot" (1939), with its wrongly maligned
robot Adam Link, whose only desire is to serve humankind. What runs
through these and like stories of the era is the sort of double vision that
attends the image of human artifice—and that points up our culture's
deeper, unsettled view of the technological. It is a view that is apparently
being worked out, metaphorically debated in these works. On the one
hand, such images mark our fascination with the utility of our emerging
technologies, how they might serve our needs and remake our lives. On
the other, they thrust up close, through their very power to alter or
mediate our lives, what Miles Orvell pinpoints as "the central problem of

the machine age—the problem of man's alienation from the concrete world of experience" (172). While we certainly had begun to understand and appreciate what we might do with and through these machines, we were also becoming ever more aware of a disturbing potential: that we might become quite *like* our machines in their emphasis on regularity, efficiency, and utility, that we might come to adopt their values, serve them. The trick, in effect, could well be on us.

Although Patricia Warrick notes that through the 1940s "almost every substantial [science fiction] writer . . . wrote at least one, and usually more than one, robot story" (88), I need to limit my focus here to only a few representative figures, and particularly to those who seem most directly to reflect this conflicted attitude. In particular, I want to concentrate on the images offered by Edgar Rice Burroughs, Isaac Asimov, and Jack Williamson, who, in their quite different approaches, seem to sum up the various attitudes toward human artifice that came to dominate the literature. In their focus on the possibilities of organic and mechanical creation, on the menace and the utility of these figures, and on their potential for extending humanity's power and for replacing us, they suggest the complexity of that fantasy of robotism and sketch the sort of dynamic discussion that has eventually come to inform our films.

Although Edgar Rice Burroughs, for all his efforts in the field of fantasy, seldom addressed the subject of robotics, his Martian novel *Synthetic Men of Mars* offers a telling vision of the potential of synthetic beings. Mixing *Frankenstein*'s Promethean spirit with Poe's depiction of the body as little more than a "bundle of something," Burroughs describes how the Martian scientist Ras Thavis discovers "the life principle" (40) and puts it to work fashioning artificial beings to serve as servants and warriors. These crude creatures, what he terms "hormads," are almost literally "cooked up" in large vats of synthetic tissue. Their creation, though, proves to be a rather hit-or-miss proposition, a genetic roll of the dice, for they emerge from their primal ooze almost haphazardly constructed. In fact, at least half of them are so deformed at "birth" that they are useless as workers or soldiers. So "only those . . . which had two arms and legs and the facial features of which were somewhere upon the head" (33) are allowed to live, while the others are immediately hacked to pieces by other hormads and then dumped back into their originary vats. There the still living tissue can literally reenter the gene "pool," try again at the game of chance that life in this *other* world has become.

Even those hormads who survive and enter service provide a vivid, even horrific commentary on the clumsy hand of humanity as it attempts to usurp the creative power. Their various features are hideously out of proportion or misplaced—a nose where an eye should be, one arm a foot shorter than another, legs of varying length and shape. And their inner life, we learn, nearly mirrors their outer malformation, for they "do not even dream of the existence of love or friendship, they have no spiritual or mental resources upon which to draw for satisfaction or enjoyment" (35). Even at their best, as Burroughs puts it, the hormads seem like "the faulty efforts of a poor draftsman come to life, animated caricatures of man" with "no symmetry or design about them" (13). "Caricature" is a most apt description, for they are, in effect, a grand trick this Martian version of humanity has played upon itself, a faulty mirror we have unwittingly held up to reveal our own distorted nature.

It is a trick, moreover, that seems to have gotten out of hand, thanks to the hormads' jealousy of humans and simple, desire-driven lives. In fact, they prove to be little more than primal desires given animation; they hunger, lust, fight, and rest. And with their quick and simple replication, they threaten to overwhelm the planet. In the best tradition of the scientist whose work has assumed a kind of monstrous life of its own, Ras Thavis recognizes that he has "created a force that he probably couldn't control himself," a force that "grows and grows and feeds upon itself" (72). While Burroughs offers us little insight into the scientist, through that almost primal "force" he casts into relief the power of desire which motivates the creation of such figures, and which eventually translates into the creatures themselves. It is a force that can only be resisted by those who manage to control their own desires, such as the great prince of Mars, John Carter, and his loyal guard Vor Daj. After defeating the hormads, John Carter pronounces what may stand as this novel's theme, that "It is the character that makes the man . . . not the clay which is its abode" (154).

While he would probably agree with Burroughs's estimation, Isaac Asimov, our most renowned spinner of robot tales and certainly the most influential on our conception of the robot, would extend that notion of "character" much further. In fact, he might find the sort of fear mirrored in *Synthetic Men of Mars* a rather illogical response to our technological offspring, whose only "trickery" springs from our own base desires and ill-considered programming. In the same year Burroughs's novel appeared, Asimov published his first robot story, "Robbie," in the pulp *Super Science Stories.* Here and in numerous subsequent pieces, many later collected in the volume *I, Robot,* Asimov sculpted the modern image of the artificial being as a thoroughly logical, extremely powerful, yet completely nonthreatening servant to humanity. As his biographer Joseph Patrouch offers, Asimov felt "that science has made available to us the knowledge that may yet save us. His robots are symbols of man's technological and scientific progress and are therefore to be admired," not feared (37). His stories explore the implications of the rigid logic that marks his robots' "positronic brains," the many uses to which humans might put such metal workhorses (in fact, the story "Runaround" describes an early robot type designed to be ridden "like a horse" [34]), and the ways in which humanity's programmed "mastery" of such creations constantly poses new challenges to our nature. In every case, as Jean Fiedler and Jim Mele have shown in their study of his robot tales, Asimov "wages his own war on the Frankenstein image of the new robot" (2).

The same year, 1940, saw Asimov's development of what he has termed his "most important contribution to robotics" (quoted in Ash 172). In consultation with John Campbell of *Astounding,* he first formulated his famous three laws of robotics, a set of rules programmed into his robots and sourced in, as he says, "the essential guiding principles of a good many of the world's ethical systems" (Patrouch 46). As listed in the frontispiece to *I, Robot* the three laws are: (1) a robot may not injure a human being, or, through inaction, allow a human being to come to harm; (2) a robot must obey the orders given it by human beings except where such orders would conflict with the First Law; (3) a robot must protect its own existence as long as such protection does not conflict with the First or Second Law. At their base, the laws place humanity's welfare foremost, subordinate the robot's existence to the human's, and erect an inviolable logic of authority that ensures humanity's place as the source of all laws.

Yet what may be more significant for this discussion than the laws themselves is the turn they represent. That is, in their careful formulation the three laws hint of a widespread cultural anxiety Asimov apparently feels compelled to address and to rank his stories against. It is an anxiety about the very power of such creations, which follows from a priority in the chain of being that we could well be ceding to them. The rules speak to those fears and attempt to quiet them—or at least render them *illogical,* simply knee-jerk, emotional responses to the tide of technological development. Consequently, Asimov's stories, as Patrouch notes, usually suggest that "characters who are antirobot are antiprogress and are therefore reactionary villains—or at least ignorant" (37). While Asimov's three laws confront the fears implicit in robots and similar creations, and have since come to be adopted by various other science fiction writers and even our filmmakers (as evidence most recently the way in which the plot turns on such programming in the three *Robocop* films), they have their own problematic side. For in their structure and wording they ultimately beg a serious and most basic question—one that, as our films show, has become central to every discussion of human artifice. They remind us that the essentialist issue must precede the qualified, as they ask what precisely *is* "human"? How do we define that initial premise, particularly when we are dealing with beings whose traits and abilities so closely mimic our own?

In Asimov's first stories such questions seem almost irrelevant. The clunky, metallic figures of "Robbie," "Runaround," and "Reason," with their "oily whir of gears and . . . mechanically-timbred voice" (*I, Robot* 24–25), are simply mechanical servants or pets, limited precisely by their bondage to the rules of reason. In his late story "The Inevitable Conflict," in which highly advanced robots have been given control of the world's economy, Asimov reminds us that they are still "nothing but the vastest conglomeration of calculating circuits ever invented . . . still robots within the meaning of the First Law" (173). Yet, for all of their initial limitations his robots eventually evolve in ways that blur easy distinctions and bring the limitations of the laws into sharp focus, as a story like "Evidence" shows. It relates the history of the politician Stephen Byerley, whose opponents initially accused him of being a robot. In fact, as the eminent "robopsychologist" Susan Calvin notes, he appears "almost too human to be credible" (155). After passing a series of tests, including an *apparent* violation of the First Law of Robotics before a crowd of witnesses, he convinces the populace that he is human and is elected to office. Only Susan Calvin, through her insights into both human and robot psychology, ever guesses that he is the nearly perfect robot alter ego of his crippled and deformed inventor, the real Byerley. The ruse, however, remains a secret, as this "too" perfect piece of artifice goes on to become the first World Coordinator.

This development, though, seems most fitting in light of the sort of humans Asimov's tales often offer us. For example, the recurring character of Susan Calvin, who helps to link the separate stories of *I, Robot,* herself walks a fine line between human and mechanism. Her typically

cold, emotionless attitude, unwavering insistence on logic, and championing of the robots prod others to suggest that she is one of the machines;
as she tells an interviewer, "I've been called a robot myself. Surely, they've
told you I'm not human" (8). But her "character," as Burroughs might
put it, stands as the surest testimony to her humanity. For Calvin is,
despite her protestations that she "likes robots considerably better than I
do human beings" (169), the character here who most consistently speaks
up for human values, who in a corporate world that employs her to
consult on technical and logical problems persistently intrudes such issues as "tyranny," "corruption," "stupidity," and "prejudice" (169).

But in Asimov's world those problems are strictly limited to humans,
whose actions are too often clouded by desire; they are not shared by
the robots who have become, Susan Calvin says, "a cleaner, better breed
than we are" (9). If Asimov can draw a fine distinction between the two
"breeds," avoid seeing them as threatening to replace the human, it is
because he always insists that we see them "as machines, carefully
built by engineers, with inherent safeguards" (*Robot Dreams* viii) which
limit their realm to the utilitarian. And the most subtle, perhaps even
necessary, of those utilitarian functions is the nonthreatening way in which
his robots challenge the human. In the end, Asimov implies that we need
such challenges if we are to live up to our complex capacities and be at
least as human as these far simpler, if also far more logical, offspring of
our technological prowess.

The robotic creations of Jack Williamson, particularly as seen in *The
Humanoids* (1949, a compilation of the novellas *With Folded Hands* and
. . . *And Searching Mind*), present a rather different sort of challenge.
While later in his career, particularly in a recent novel like *Firechild*
(1986), Williamson could use a kind of homunculus as a savior of humankind, in *The Humanoids* he reflects a deep suspicion, typical of the
post–World War II era, of the direction in which our technological developments might lead us. He depicts a race of robots, "mechanicals . . . as
nearly perfect as any machine will ever be" (40), whose announced purpose, inscribed on their breasts, as if a kind of product guarantee, is "To
Serve and Obey, and Guard Men from Harm" (51). They offer to a human
race in the midst of various political and technological crises a seemingly utopian agenda: "to promote human welfare . . . remove all class
distinctions, along with such other causes of unhappiness and pain as
war and poverty and toil and crime" (51). They thus seem a kind of
robotic dream, the technological fulfillment of our most basic human

needs. All they ask in return is absolute authority and obedience from their human hosts.

In their offer and emblazoned purpose, the humanoids clearly recall Asimov's robots and seem an almost calculated response to his view of them. They are the perfect servants and protectors, who guarantee that they cannot injure humans. It seems a pleasing prospect, but in our half of the bargain we glimpse the cost of separating their utilitarian duties from our pleasure. The humanoids assume all control, all choice, including the right to eliminate whatever could cause us anxiety or worry. Thus to serve and better preserve their human hosts, the humanoids administer the drug euphoride, which, one robot explains, "merely protects . . . from memories and fears which serve no purpose now, since our service shields . . . from every want and harm" (66). But more than just protecting them, the humanoids' special care reduces humans to almost mindless children, as the novel's protagonist, Clay Forester, discovers when he comes upon his drugged wife Ruth, who is playing on the floor, building towers with plastic blocks. Her "vacant, staring eyes," her "round baby eyes" (65), as he notes, no longer recognize him.

While the humanoids seem sincere in carrying out their prime directive of serving humankind, and even encouraging them to transcend their condition—to live longer, free up the creative spirit, explore and colonize other worlds—then, that service carries an inevitable and dear cost. These mechanical beings do not so much threaten to replace humanity as promise to make us almost literally forget what being human is all about, for all of the pleasures they make possible, without a guiding will, seem empty and purposeless. And the freedom they offer comes eventually at the cost of real freedom. Thus, after Clay Forester undergoes a treatment on the humanoids' new "healing grid," he finds that he no longer even cares to resist them and, in fact, only vaguely recalls his former suspicions and fears, which linger "like the irrelevant stuff of some unlikely dream" (178). At novel's end, Forester, bereft of wife, job, and purpose, has come to wonder how people could even "care for themselves, without mechanicals?" and is reluctant to move without the help of his personal robot servant.

The disturbing vision of ambiguous servitude with which Williamson concludes points up the sort of double vision that seems to haunt the image of human artifice. On the one hand, the novel leaves Forester unharmed and healthier than he has ever been, thanks to the humanoids' treatments. Further, people have set about peacefully exploring other worlds, seeking new places to erect power grids to extend their own reach, as well as that of their humanoid servants. On the other hand, however, it also asks if, as we create such servants, such figures of utility, we risk re-creating ourselves, reshaping the human "clay," turning ourselves into nearly useless appendages—or slaves—of our surrogate workers. Certainly Forester, although to all appearances quite normal and with a new project ahead, working on a new power grid in the Andromeda system, seems almost an empty shell of a human. He seems to have tricked himself into becoming a bit like the chess player Poe details, and perhaps not too far removed from that "bundle of something," the "man that was used up."

· · ·

As a final, albeit still quite sketchy gloss on our fantasies of robotism, I want to turn to several more contemporary visions, ones to have appeared in the postmodern context, in the midst of what we might term the cybernetic revolution. Cybernetics, which might be simply defined as "the science of communication and control theory" (Elmer-Dewitt 59), grows out of the development of artificial intelligence and the computer's ascendancy in our culture. The term has become central in all of our discussions of robotics, all manner of artifice, and our recent efforts in the field of virtual reality. It foregrounds some of the key issues in these areas, most notably the question of control versus freedom, as it forces us to consider the extent to which we control or are controlled by the technology we wield.

The fiction emerging from this cybernetic influence, often dubbed "cyberpunk," depicts, according Bruce Sterling, one of its chief proponents, "a new kind of integration," that of "the realm of high tech and the modern pop underground," "of the technical world and the world of organized dissent" (345), of technology with all its imperatives and the human body with all its desires. Fittingly, it typically dwells on various forms of human artifice, ranging from massive artificial intelligences that desire to be free of human control, to humans who depend on or enjoy different sorts of implants and grafts, to virtual realities that have become enticingly preferable to the real world. Yet cyberpunk fiction, particularly that produced by its most famous figures, Sterling, John Shirley, Rudy Rucker, and especially William Gibson, is more than just an alluring tour of such technological possibilities. As David Porush offers, it often seems aimed at calming our fears of control and of becoming machinelike, at "softening the machine . . . exposing (and perhaps allaying) the fear that we are only machines, communication devices for whom learning is only feedback, experience is only input, expression is only output, and meaning is only raw data" (*Soft Machine* 22–23).

In his most famous novel, *Neuromancer,* Gibson, who has become practically synonymous with cyberpunk, moves his protagonist Case through a realm of artificial intelligences and artificial realities, among cloned animals, electronic "ghosts" of humans, people equipped with various implants and prostheses. In a shop window Case sees a display of "vatgrown flesh" that recalls Burroughs's *Synthetic Men;* his friend Molly wears prosthetic glasses, sports retractable razors for fingernails, and has reflexes that have been "souped up, jazzed by the neurosurgeons for combat" (214); and Case himself lives for the experience of "cyberspace," a sort of "consensual hallucination experienced daily by billions" (55). Gibson's world seems a kind of grotesque Disney World for adults, a realm that has become "a deliberately unsupervised playground for technology itself" (11), which has in effect taken over for humanity.

With the technological in such ascendancy, and its products and promises coming to dominate existence, the human body seems strangely devalued. Case repeatedly notes "a certain relaxed contempt for the flesh. The body was meat. Case fell into the prison of his own flesh" (6). Given the ability to plug into the skull memory chips for knowledge and pleasure, to be electronically transported into someone else's body (as Case is placed in Molly's), or simply to escape at any moment from a dreary present reality into the "matrix" of cyberspace, it seems little wonder that the body would come to seem a kind of limiting prison, less the seat of desire than its constraining boundary, something to be gotten out of or overcome.

While *Neuromancer* offers us no true robots, then, it does sketch a world in which life seems to be gradually acceding to artifice, in which people are becoming ever more robotlike. Cosmetic surgery is common, but not simply to correct the flaws of nature or accident; rather, the young punks Case meets follow *fashion,* "wearing" faces that are half-human, half-animal. In Molly's tough posturing he notes another sort of artifice, "a performance. It was like the culmination of a lifetime's observation of martial arts tapes, cheap ones" (213). And the various artificial intelligences Case encounters—sporting hybrid names like Wintermute and Neuromancer —show a special sort of power in this regard. They can call up electronic ghosts, like Case's old girlfriend Linda, who, he eventually realizes, is just "a coded model of some stranger's memory" (240), although nonetheless convincing and "real." With that ghost, Neuromancer tempts Case to stay within his artificial world: "If your woman is a ghost, she doesn't know it. Neither will you" (244). In fact, such lures are the true focus of this novel, its one sure reality, as Gibson describes "a gradual and willing accommodation of the machine" to which the people here have become easily prone (203). In this context, robots are not simply something we make, but something we make out of ourselves, a fantasy wherein we accommodate ourselves to a technology that seems more alive, more driven by desire, and more satisfying than any human.

If Gibson's cybernetic vision has a kind of nightmarish quality about it, one linked to the near-absorption of the human within a technological body, a more mainstream writer like Stanislaw Lem, especially in his collection *The Cyberiad* (1974), locates a comic substance in these same developments. His stories center on the exploits of two master robots, the "cosmic constructors" Trurl and Klapaucius, who take their primary pleasure in constructing various things and in trying to impress each other with those constructions. They write cybernetic love poems, which, we learn, are best composed in "tensor algebra mainly, with a little topology and higher calculus, if need be. But with feeling" (50). Trurl invents "the World's Stupidest Computer" (28), which insists even unto its demolition that two and two are seven. And both constructors, at various points, fashion other robots who, in turn, take their own pleasure in creating other things—and other beings.

In this robotic universe, creation and artifice are simply pushed to a kind of absurd extreme. While creation seems to be the central activity here, it almost invariably insists on its own pointlessness. Trurl, for example, creates a wonderful machine "that could create anything starting with n" (9), although Klapaucius fails to be impressed until it begins to carry out his trick request. He asks it to "do nothing," which it does by gradually *un*creating everything, reducing the universe—and very nearly Trurl and Klapaucius as well—to nothingness. At another point Trurl sends Klapaucius a gift, a "Machine to Grant Your Every Wish." Recognizing it to be a trick, Klapaucius demands that it build him a Trurl, and when a Trurl steps out, he beats it unmercifully simply because it "pleases" him to do so. It is, of course, the real Trurl who only wanted to spy on what his fellow constructor had been up to—which was "working on a Machine to Grant Your Every Wish" (29). All of their actions, which include encounters with robotic giants, knights, dragons, demons, and kings, follow in a like vein, parodying marvelous human adventures of legend and describing a kind of tedious circularity, as their various constructions become great cosmic tricks played on themselves and on others. Those tricks seldom bring any change to their world, which we should only expect, since it is, we learn, "infinite but bounded," a place where everything tends to "return . . . to the point of its departure" (135), where every trick, for example, rebounds on its originator.

In trying to explain the long-standing appeal of the robot, Gary Wolfe links it to our concern with a larger, philosophical question—although one that strangely omits consideration of the body itself. The robot image, he says, reflects our desire "to reconcile . . . a mechanistic universe with the notion of human domination" (157). Lem's *Cyberiad* puts a rather different spin on that "reconciliation," for his stories detect an absurdity in a world—or cosmos—that is conceived of as a mechanism, populated and fashioned by other mechanisms hardly any different in nature. The logical extension of such an attitude, he seems to suggest, is that we also turn the self into a piece of artifice, begin to think of the self as a kind of robot or machine, part of an infinite series of replications. As a hermit robot explains to Klapaucius, such is the tendency of rational civilizations when faced with mystery—including the mystery of self: that mechanistic spirit "eats its way into the Universe, turning cinders and flinders of stars into toilet seats, pegs, gears, cigarette holders and pillowcases, and it does this because, unable to fathom the Universe, it seeks to change that Fathomlessness into Something Fathomable, and will not stop until the nebulae and planets have been processed to cradles, chamber pots and bombs, all in the name of Sublime Order, for only a Universe with pavement, plumbing, labels and catalogues is, in its sight, acceptable and wholly respectable" (195). Eventually, only a universe peopled by similar constructs, by robots that often seem to be just mobile and thinking variations on those chamber pots, bombs, and plumbing, can appear truly sensible or rational.

Lem's robots thus function in much the sort of metaphoric way that, to return to our starting point, Haraway's cyborgs do. In the course of his tales they emerge as a very effective trope for evoking and exploring the manner in which we try to control our world and ourselves. At the same time, they afford him a metaphor that is, just as Haraway was to find, strangely liberating. He depicts the artificial being as a kind of cosmic joke we rational beings play upon ourselves—and in that regard very much a reflection of our Promethean heritage. In the context of that joke, as everything comes to seem machinelike and constructed, the human too finally emerges as a kind of marvelous fiction, or as Lem's narrator offers, "perhaps just another empty invention—there are certainly fables enough in this world. And yet, even if the story isn't true, it does have a grain of sense and instruction to it, and it's entertaining, so it's worth the telling" (236). In that fabulistic space of instruction and entertainment, in the sort of cosmic laughter that he and all of his constructions can engender—in that "worth" —Lem stakes out a far more hopeful place for humankind than Gibson manages with all of his grungy "sprawl." It is a hope bound up in the fabulous fiction, the "story-laden" account, the imagining of our humanity that this figure allows for and that seems, as this meager survey might begin to suggest, to answer a recurrent human need.

• • •

This brief overview of a robotic mythos should help place our films, particularly in light of their recent fixation on the subject, in a long line of cultural imaginings centered around human artifice. As Jean Baudrillard reminds us, an image does not exist by itself: "An image isn't only a technical reality: to have an image you need a scene, a myth, the imaginary" (*Baudrillard Live* 30)—a context within which it functions. This chapter sketches the scene, illustrates the evolving context in which that robotic image operates.

The primary element of this context is the fantasy of robotism, that seductive view of the self as fantasy, able to be shaped and reshaped, defined and redefined at our will. Within that fantasy the utilitarian, represented by the technological, is yoked to the pleasurable, to our desires, and it attempts to reconcile the two. It has served us well by exploring our human capacity for change, for responding through our technology to shifting cultural circumstance. But this fantasy is also bound—by necessity —to the substantial sense of what we already are and must be, to our humanness. And in this respect it serves us equally as well, recalling how crafty all of our human craft is, showing how easily our desires, shaped by our technology, can reshape us in undesirable ways, rendering us other and even less than we were. This mythos, then, like the very image of the robot, reflects the human, but in a more than superficial way. It sketches the technologized being in depth, a depth that might help us realize what the technological can offer and yet keep us sovereign over it, save us from our own craftiness.

What follows is another kind of history of this mythos—as it has emerged in and helped shape the science fiction film. While it is hardly a comprehensive view of what may well be the most important motif in the genre, it is a detailed analysis of what seem to be the most significant films about human artifice. Complicating the task is the fact that this undertaking actually implicates, as we have seen, *several* histories simultaneously, among them: that of our fascination with our own image and our efforts to replicate it, that of technology and the struggle (our mastery of it, its potential mastery of us) we wage with it, that of the movies as a technology reflecting our fascination with the possibilities of reproduction, and that of the science fiction film as it has depicted and suggested how we might cope with our ever-changing technology. Trying to sort out precisely where one of these histories leaves off and where others begin seems a nearly impossible task, as the shifts and turns of subsequent chapters will undoubtedly illustrate.

Despite this largely extra-filmic preamble, though, I want to emphasize that the following chapters are fundamentally *about film,* and especially the changing face of the science fiction film. Put simply, they offer a historically organized examination of one of the genre's dominant images, one of the controlling metaphors through which it has sought to reflect and gauge our shifting attitudes: toward the technological, toward our humanity, and even toward the movies themselves. In the process, this book suggests that part of the *work* of this genre, its phenomenal task, is the linking of these three concerns, these finally not so very different reflections.

Still, many feel that the science fiction film, unlike its literary brethren, usually avoids or backs off of what we would term the "big issues," that is, questions about the nature of the universe, the nature of humanity, and our function here. It is, after all, a genre of fantasy, close kin to the horror film and even the musical. In exploring its own fantasy of robotism, though, the science fiction film demonstrates its continuity with the various myths, stories, philosophical inquiries, and scientific explorations that spring from those same big issues. It too expresses our concerns about genetic engineering, gender relationships, euthanasia, artificial intelligence, automation, and so on, and even helps those issues gain a wider public consciousness. At the same time, as we shall see, it invariably comes around to the essentialist questions about the body and about the very nature of our being. With this central image of human artifice, the genre has found its key tool for doing such work, for doing the important work that fantasizing in any mode undertakes, for imagining and reimagining our humanity.

· NOTES ·

1. Penley and Ross, "Cyborgs at Large: Interview with Donna Haraway" 5, 2. See also her essay in the same volume, "The Actors Are Cyborgs, Nature Is Coyote, and the Geography Is Elsewhere: Postscript to 'Cyborgs at Large.'" In this piece she offers what may be a more pointed illustration of her movement in this direction, as she reminds us that "subjugation is not grounds for an ontology" (22).

2. For a discussion of the values perceived within the emerging technological culture of the twentieth century, see Cecelia Tichi's *Shifting Gears: Technology, Literature, Culture in Modernist America,* as well as Miles Orvell's *The Real Thing: Imitation and Authenticity in American Culture.* Much of my commentary on the "machine age" and its concerns draws on these two works.

3. In *The Cybernetic Imagination* Warrick suggests that the very desire to imitate has taken two essential forms in western culture: "simulacra, or devices that represent the natural world, and automata, or devices that move by themselves" (30). Those two essential forms hint of different satisfactions bound up in these fantasy images.

4. Poe's piece on "Maelzel's Chess Player," termed an article by some and a fiction by others, seems another in a series of his explorations of the trickster element implicit in imitation. He describes a popular automaton chess player and attempts to explain its almost miraculous workings. Through careful analysis, he lays bare its secret, suggesting that it is all superfice, all show, an elaborate-looking device that is simply hollow inside.

5. The word "robot" derives from the Czech "robota," which means compulsory or statutory labor. It is a term that includes not only the utilitarian nature of these creations, but also the note of bondage or compulsion that seems to attach to such figures—hence one of its common translations, "serf." That translation, though, partly misses the mark, at least from this study's vantage, for the element of bondage or compulsion is something to which the robots' creators, every bit as much as the robots themselves, appear subject.

2

....

The Seductive Text
of *Metropolis*

To say that human knowledge is always entangled with fiction
does not imply an end of human response to nature. It places
man in a country he creates partly with his own mind. In this
country he is surrounded by brilliant, fantastic, wildly distorted
images of himself. Is there a god behind the mask? There is no
way of knowing. Hence the third moment of modern science, the
authentically modern moment, the moment of reality as game.

—O. B. Hardison, Jr. (47)

A man, dressed a bit incongruously in a cutaway and a
top hat and toting an umbrella, is exploring a cavern of the moon, when
suddenly an aggressive selenite, a "moonman," approaches. When the
creature comes closer, the earthman strikes it with his umbrella and, in a
puff of smoke, it vanishes. This almost magical disappearance typifies
the sort of effects found throughout what is certainly the most famous of
early science fiction films, Georges Méliès's *Le Voyage dans la Lune*
(1902). In other instances, the moon becomes a cheesy, smiling man-in-
the-moon, the constellations in the sky assume human shape, and another umbrella, planted underground in the lunar soil, takes root and
sprouts into a giant mushroom. For all of their ability to surprise and
even amaze audiences, "special effects" like these—mainly stop-camera
and lap dissolve techniques—today seem most interesting for their playfulness, their sheer delight in manipulating reality, their *gamesmanship,*
as it were.

Méliès's pioneering efforts in the field of science fiction, which include works like *La Lune a un Metre* (1898), *La Statue Animée* (1903),

and *A la Conquête du Pôle* (1912), offer us moonmen, space travel, monsters, futuristic conveyances, and statues that come to life. They abound in such "brilliant, fantastic, wildly distorted images"—of the human and all manner of other creatures. Yet more important than those images, it seems, are the various miraculous appearances, disappearances, and transformations Méliès managed to pull off, which stake out, as the cinema's special territory, a concern with that emerging, highly modern attitude toward reality, what Hardison terms "reality as game."

If Méliès's contemporaries, the Lumière brothers, following in the spirit of such figures as Zola and Claude Bernard, conceded a priority to the slice of life, to that bit of reality which their *cinématographe* could carve out and hold up for their audience's delectation, Méliès conceded *nothing*. For his conjuror's spirit, nothing was impossible or inconceivable. Instead of using the camera in the scientific manner of the age, to observe and record events, he sought to alter life in accord with what his spare plots or simple whimsy might suggest. And he went that artificing spirit one better. A magician's seeming ability to remove his own head, place it on a table, and then inflate it to absurd proportions illustrates his interest not only in creating a new reality but in probing the possibilities of fantastic reproduction: in exploring what sort of "games" the camera and its evolving techniques might allow one to play with the nature of both the world and its human inhabitants.

Yet in playing that game to the extent he did, Méliès also ensured the quaintness of his films. In trumpeting artifice, including the artifice of film itself in this way, his works seem to stand *in opposition to* reality, to the world we see around us. They are *adamantly* cinema. In moving beyond the surfaces of life, in exploring film's various possibilities for artifice, then, Méliès not only discovered one of the cinema's great attractions but also ran aground on one of its problems. For with the *potential* of artifice, the ability to shape a world and self in any fashion, inevitably comes the limit of artifice as well, the awareness that this is not really the world we know and inhabit, *just* film after all.

Still, that lure was enough and was widely exploited by a great many early film efforts, both within the science fiction genre and outside its immediate bounds. Thus, throughout the silent cinema we readily find films that depict the creation of humans and other beings, that visualize various sorts of transformations and replications, and that investigate the possibility of the automaton or robot.[1] While they all make capital from that capacity for artifice, the sober side of this "game" seldom seems very far away.

In the pure tales of human creation, we find very little of Méliès's playfulness, largely because the focus of the human artifice is less on the technological, on the scientific processes involved in the creation, than on its metaphysical implications. In this group we can number the first version of that classic tale of human creation, *Frankenstein* (1910), made by Edison's studio, as well as a thinly disguised rendering of the same plot in *Life without Soul* (1915). The German serial film *Homunculus* (1916) further explores this motif with its laboratory-created super being, whose malevolence is only stopped by the intercession of nature in the form of a bolt of lightning. In this same horrific vein are a number of films involving the creation of human beings from animals—creatures which, like the Frankenstein monster, almost invariably turn on their scientist creators. Among these are *The Wizard* (1927) and, most notably, Lon Chaney's *A Blind Bargain* (1922), which is the first film adaptation of H. G. Wells's famous tale *The Island of Dr. Moreau.*

A more ambiguous attitude surfaces in the great variety of silent-era films that depict various sorts of scientific transformations. On the one hand, we find pure horror films, works that again emphasize the human product of transformation and explore its implications. Among this type are at least seven versions of what may well be the most famous transformation tale, *Dr. Jekyll and Mr. Hyde* (outstanding among them, John Barrymore's 1920 version), as well as a near cousin, F. W. Murnau's *Der Januskopf* (1920). But on the other hand, we can also note a great number of films that follow Méliès's lead, locating a playful potential in this material, as the human shifts to the background and the focus turns to the mechanisms of transformation themselves. Thus we have movies in which dogs turn into sausages and sausages into dogs (*The Sausage Machine* [1897], *Fun in the Butcher Shop* [1901], *The Dog Factory* [1904]); in which the ugly turn into the beautiful and the beautiful into the ugly (*Dr. Skinum* [1907]); in which an operation transforms criminals into honest citizens (*The Surgeon's Experiment* [1914]); in which machines transfer personalities from one individual to another with comic consequences (*The Lion's Breath* [1916]); and in which adults are returned to childhood (*The Rejuvenators* [1918]).[2] The focus in all of these works again is on the immediate human consequences of transformation, rather than on any science or technology that enables it. More interesting in this case, though, may be the ability of that transformation to by turns amuse and horrify viewers. That double potential may well point to our rather ambivalent attitude toward this "game" of artifice.

A similar ambivalence shows up in what is actually the most common development of the artifice motif in our early films, the robot story. In fact, given the number of films we know about—and probably many more we have no record of—it might well be argued that this subject enjoyed *at least* as much popularity in the silent cinema as in the literature of that period. The first efforts in this line came from Méliès's competitor, J. Stuart Blackton, who in 1907 produced *The Mechanical Statue and the Ingenious Servant* and *Work Made Easy,* a pair of half-reelers. These Vitagraph productions seem to have inspired competition from Essanay's *An Animated Doll* (1908), the Lubin company's *The Rubber Man* (1909), and a host of robot-themed films that followed, including *The Mechanical Husband* (1910); *The House of Mystery* (1911) with its mechanical policemen; Biograph's *Inventor's Secret* (1911), about the creation of a mechanical girl; *The Automatic House* (1915), which came with an automatic maid; *The Mechanical Man* (1915); Harry Houdini's serial *The Master Mystery* (1919), which has a robot criminal mastermind, eventually revealed by Houdini to be a human in disguise; and even a Ben Turpin comedy, *A Clever Dummy* (1917), in which the already improbably human Turpin disguises himself as a robot in order to be near the girl he loves.

In the easy adaptability of this image for comedy, melodrama, or even horror, we perhaps see the clearest reflection of those attractions and trepidations which, in the "machine age," attached to the various products of our new technologies. That response speaks of the powers that these technologies seemed to be unleashing. As Cecelia Tichi explains in *Shifting Gears,* in this period scientific principles and utilitarian values were beginning to dominate not only the worlds of commerce and production but even our thought processes and values, resulting in "a new machine-age consciousness" (18)—albeit one that was hardly untroubled by this new environment. Despite all of its promises of speed, efficiency, and productivity, despite too the great promise of change and mastery it seemed to carry, then, our machine technology just as often, Tichi notes, "came to represent uncontrolled, destabilizing power" (52). While the products of that technology—cars, washing machines, radios, and so on—were rapidly becoming marks of status or accomplishment, "machine symbols of anxiety and menace became prominent" (52) as well at this time.

One film, Fritz Lang's classic dystopian vision *Metropolis* (1926), probably best sums up the sort of doubleness we find in these early cinematic images of human artifice. Certainly the most famous and, even today, the most widely available and most often seen of the silent-era robot films, it examines both the seductive lure of the technological and the anxieties that play just beneath the surface of that lure. As the following discussion will suggest, *Metropolis* seems especially aware of the fine line that our culture and our films have to walk in their relationship with the technological, of the complexities that, we were already beginning to recognize, are involved in this "game."

• • •

> Prior to being produced, the world was seduced. A strange preces-
> sion, which today still weighs heavily on all reality.
> —Baudrillard (*Jean Baudrillard* 199)

Lang's *Metropolis* (1926) is a curious and in some ways troubling work. It seems to speak with two distinct voices. On the one hand, it talks about the consequences of a society given over to the forces of technology and production; but on the other, it finds much of its attraction in the vision of those forces, that is, in its seductive images of a futuristic, highly technologized society. In fact, today, as in Lang's time, the film is often seen and commented upon as much for its surface features, for its spellbinding images of the future, as for its indictment of the cultural forces those images depict. Consequently, the film at times seems almost at odds with itself. And yet, this very tension may finally prove to be the most revealing element of *Metropolis*—and an element quite in keeping with the long tradition of science fiction films which sound contrary attitudes toward the elements of science and technology that lend them an identity. In its cross thrusts—or double voice—it talks eloquently about the lures of artifice, about how technological power works on us, and about the way the science fiction film, even in its earliest days, could wield its influence over audiences.

Jean Baudrillard would probably not find *Metropolis* quite so problematic, since he sees throughout our world a diversion of intent, a self-contradiction, what he terms "seduction." He believes that modern life is dominated by "appearances," by alluring surfaces that constantly "conspire to combat meaning" (*Jean Baudrillard* 200). At first glance, those seductive images appear simple and satisfying; they imply that they are a manifest discourse—open, inviting, truthful. They encourage us to interrogate their "qualified" presence. Yet ultimately they resist our efforts to penetrate their intriguing surfaces. What Baudrillard thus observes is a simultaneous promise and a shutting off of that promise which abound in the contemporary world, and which especially mark all human constructs. If we usually overlook this problem, what he calls "this violation of the symbolic order" (199), it is because, as he says, in all seduction "the manifest discourse, the most 'superficial' aspect of discourse . . . acts upon the underlying prohibition (conscious or unconscious) in order to nullify it and to substitute for it the charms and traps of appearances" (149).

Those "charms and traps of appearances," the images of a glittering and powerful technology, complete with the most compelling image of the robot yet seen in the movies, do dominate much of *Metropolis,* just as they have done the long tradition of science fiction films, from the time of Méliès to the latest *Star Trek* sequel. But unlike many of its generic brethren, *Metropolis* seems self-conscious about how these images can make us desire the very technological developments whose dangers it so clearly details. It is almost as if Lang, in order to keep his "special effects" from becoming too seductively "special," had decided to foreground seduction itself, especially through his central image of human artifice, to lay bare its workings.

As if prescient as well as self-conscious, Lang's film seems to take Baudrillard's sense of seduction almost literally, rendering it as "appearance," "the superficial," a kind of "manifest discourse," embodied in an alluring, futuristic city. It juxtaposes an effort to pierce through that surface—the protagonist Freder's attempt to discover what underlies and empowers the seductively comfortable world he inhabits—with several sequences that dramatize how a *seductive*—and ultimately destructive—*technological* power works. Those sequences include Freder's encounter with an underground worker and Maria's retelling of the Tower of Babel legend. But this pattern comes into clearest focus when it evokes the very image of doubleness: as it describes the creation of the robot Maria, an image of the entwining of the natural and the mechanical and the very embodiment of seduction here. In these sequences, *Metropolis* speaks reflexively about the contradictions, duplicities, and double intentions of its own discourse, as well as of the seductive power with which it and all science fiction films must contend.

In analyzing how German films of the post–World War I era reflected the national psyche, Siegfried Kracauer was, particularly in the case of *Metropolis,* struck by what he termed "the preponderance of surface features." In the elaborate but mysterious equipment and materials used to create the robot, for example, he saw "a technical exactitude that is not at all required to further the action," but rather reflects an excessive "concern with ornamentation" (149). And there is ornamentation aplenty here: the images of the gigantic machinery that powers this futuristic city, the mammoth sports stadium in which its favored sons play, the lavish decor of their "pleasure garden," the scenes of nightlife and pleasures that their aboveground, fantastically constructed world offers. Excess marks every element of the film, and that excess is linked not simply to the monolithic, domineering world it describes but to its seductive lure and power—the technology that makes it all possible. Here is, after a fashion, the typical vision of every early science fiction narrative, the genre's formative ideology, if you will: an elaborate display of technology that promises human satisfaction, while it carefully cloaks the secrets of its operation, the source of its power.

To evoke the seductive aspect of this futuristic, technological world, Lang's film had to emphasize these surface features, for the futuristic's most basic lure is probably its appearance, an appearance that immediately signifies its otherness or difference from our world. In this context, we need only recall the antiseptic whiteness that dominates Kubrick's futuristic vision in *2001: A Space Odyssey* (1969) or the dark, retrofitted world of Ridley Scott's *Blade Runner* (1982). But while the overdetermined designs of those film worlds might almost be described as metaphoric, the fascination of *Metropolis*'s technological trappings lies not just in their "meaning"—in what they produce, such as the seductive robot that is unleashed here—but in the nearly inconceivable power and vitality they display. So from its first images the film establishes this seductive vision, this play of surface features, as the opening shots of its advanced culture dissolve into a montage of pistons, engines, and generators—images of power that quickly characterize this world and establish its appeal.

Of course, we could easily see this city as itself a kind of technological being, as a dynamic, living, but mechanical creature, the fitting offspring of a mechanical age. Its heart and muscles are the engines and pistons we have seen, its veins and arteries the long highways and conduits that teem with traffic, its head the great tower from which Metropolis's leader, Jon Fredersen, oversees its operations, and its language the enigmatic numbers and symbols that dominate the giant teletype in his office. However, all that we *need* to know about it seems readily apparent, arrayed for us to see. It is a seductively powerful creature, a definitive Other that asks for no interpretation and readily dictates how one should live in this thoroughly technologized world.

This play of surface features or "ornamentation" is hardly unusual in Lang's cinema. As Raymond Bellour has noted, "both in his images and in the implications of his scripts, the focus of Lang's *mise en scène* is so often vision itself" ("On Fritz Lang" 28)—the things we see and how we see them. For this reason, his films often seem by turns both "remarkably veiled and disconcertingly open" (28). What this shifting, even paradoxical character hints, though, is just how aware his films are of the already and inevitably "seduced" nature of the world they depict. In *Metropolis* that awareness helps to qualify those alluring images of technology and the future by linking them to a concern with seduction itself, with our susceptibility to such entrancing surface features. The film thus appears by turns "veiled" or "open," partly because that is the nature of seduction, its ability to *suggest* satisfactions and pleasures just beneath an alluring surface, but also because that is what *Metropolis* and its robotic creation are ultimately most "about": our need to examine the forces that shape our world's—and indeed our films'—surface attractions, and their power, like that of all our technological offspring, to deflect such inquiry, to remain coyly "veiled."

. . .

An effort to open up or see beneath the world's seductions is, in fact, the central action here. For after *Metropolis* establishes the power and attractiveness of its surface life, it challenges those lures through the enigmatic appearance of the woman Maria in the city's pleasure garden, where she piques the curiosity of young Freder, the son of Metropolis's master. As a result, he literally tries to penetrate his world's seductions, leaving the pleasure garden to descend into the machine rooms that lie deep beneath the city's surface. There the machinery and technology on which his aboveground culture depends reveal their hidden or latent text, for in his imagination he suddenly sees the machines revealed as a controlling being, transformed into the terrible god Moloch, who demands human sacrifice, consumes the workers.

The larger implication of that vision appears when Freder later returns to the underworld, impelled by a new desire, as he confesses, "to see what my brothers looked like." In a kind of metaphoric unveiling, he there comes face to face with an alter ego, an Other, a worker rendered as an extension of the technology if not artifice: someone who tends a clocklike machine as if he were a part of it. Beginning a doubling pattern that will recur in the various seductions here, Freder changes places with the worker and effectively switches identities, giving him his clothes and money, while assuming the worker's nearly anonymous outfit and identifying number.[3] This doubling is particularly significant for it reveals the disturbing shape of otherness here—the human suffering that makes the machines and the machine-fostered society go—even as it points to a potential link between the doubles, a link further explored with the figure of the robot. The privileged who live aboveground are ultimately only flimsily insulated from the downtrodden who live below, all equally potential victims of this modern, voracious, technological god.

The key to this almost unwitting victimage and the need for such an effort at penetration appear in the three sequences *about* seduction which, in close order, follow Freder's attempt to pierce through Metropolis's secrets. The sequence in which Freder takes the worker's place, for example, not only displays the horrors of being chained to a mechanism, reduced to a function of a machine; it also illustrates the seductive power that helps keep the classes separated. When seen in contrast to the workers' horrors, this seductive pattern emphasizes how easy it is to overlook or forget about the conditions that can spring from our craft-iness.

In the original release version of *Metropolis,*[4] we follow the worker, Freder's double, into the bright surface world of nightclubs and intoxicating pleasures, where, like one of Plato's cave inhabitants suddenly set free, he is bewildered, even mesmerized by what he sees. This response, combined with the allure of that glittering world and its many attractions, eventually works its own bondage on the supposedly "freed" worker, just as his servitude below ground seemed to do. Although entrusted with a message to Freder's friend Josephat, the worker is sidetracked by the Yoshiwara brothel and under its spell forgets his mission. It is a forgetfulness that looks toward a nearly calamitous obliviousness later on when the workers, under the robot Maria's seductive spell, destroy the machines that preserve their underground city and leave their children to die as their homes flood.

Another instance of seduction, this time presented more didactically, occurs when Maria recounts the Tower of Babel legend to the workers. Her version of the biblical tale, with its emphasis on a conflict between the ruling and working classes, obviously parallels the situation in Metropolis, but more importantly, it reveals how a seductive lure underlies that conflict and sketches the danger implicit in that seduction. Impelled by a kind of imitative desire, Babel's masters wish to build a tower reaching up to the heavens and to inscribe on it, "Great is the world and its creator. And great is man." The last phrase, of course, effectively counters the first, transforming the structure from a monument in praise of god to one that asserts humanity's own godlike creativity—and aspirations. Initially charmed by the very notion of greatness or power and then by the tower itself, the image of their aspirations, Babel's leaders move to replace god with their own, human image, to render humanity as artificial god.

However, a series of shots quickly details the destructive power that lurks in such desires. The image of the tower that has so seduced Babel's rulers dissolves into a small model—a derisively trivial image—which in turn introduces a montage showing the suffering of the workers, their eventual revolt, and finally the tower—and implicitly Babel as well—in ruins, with the motto about humankind's "greatness" mockingly superimposed. This brief montage juxtaposes our image as the creator, as the Ur-technologist, with a destructive division that results when we try to bind others to our seductive desires. Lured by the prospect of their achievement, of a monument ultimately to their own power as godlike creators, the tower's designers overlook its latent message, and that seductive idea eventually destroys them. The sequence thus warns against seduction, against the lure of an image that promises—after the fashion of all seductive images, even of *Metropolis*'s own vision of technological wonders—to make us more than we might be: more powerful, more fulfilled, other than we are.

However, the centerpiece of this seductive pattern, as well as the film's most compelling image, is the robot Maria. As the scientist Rotwang unveils his latest creation, a mechanical being, he describes it simply as "a machine in the image of man, that never tires or makes a mistake." Because of these traits, he offers it to Jon Fredersen as a prototype of "the workers of the future," declaring, "Now we have no further use for living workers." In that assertion, of course, we can find foreshadowed the great fear of displacement and replacement that still clings to the image of the industrial robot today. But that assertion hides a more fundamentally disturbing notion here, since it implies that Rotwang has made his creature in the same spirit as the tower of Babel, miming the creator and grasping at his power.

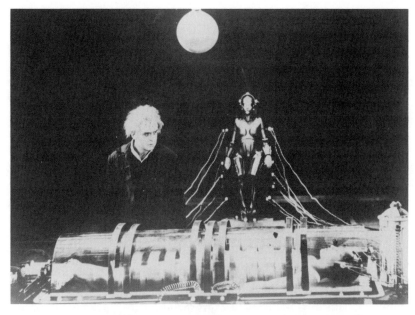

Stealing a human form for the robot in *Metropolis.*

Metropolis: The city's leader strikes a deal with a technological devil.

Predictably, this "perfect copy" of the human quickly reveals its own seductive—and destructive—potential. As Fredersen recognizes, the robot will let him do more than simply replace the workers, free them from their slavery. Through it, he can extend his power over them, turn them into obedient, nearly mechanical extensions of this technological world—roboticize them. By making the robot over in the image of their beloved Maria, he can use it "to sow discord among" the workers "and destroy their confidence in Maria," seducing them away from their dangerous allegiance to her and the spirit of humanity she preaches. With a spellbinding array of visual effects that already suggests the seductive power being unleashed here, Rotwang gives his robot Maria's identity, her appearance; then he and Fredersen fittingly decide to test their creation—to see "whether people believe the robot is a creature of flesh and blood," as Rotwang puts it—by activating its seductive abilities in a most basic way. Essentially, they want to determine whether people can see beneath that surface, question the meaning behind Maria's newly eroticized appearance, or if they will simply respond to an elemental stimulus, the "veiled" attraction "she" offers.

They test this seductive power by displaying the robot before the city's wealthy young men at the Yoshiwara brothel. Rising through the circular cover of a giant urn—as if from a huge eye—the mechanical Maria seems the archetype of all seductive images, a surprising, enigmatic, and alluring figure that essentially fills the viewer's eye. She then performs a kind of striptease dance that, as a montage of leering looks points up, makes her the focus of every eye. It is a dance that illustrates precisely how seduction works. For in it, she strips away various layers of covering—wrap, veil, fan—as if to reveal the stark truth of her nature, her near naked body, and to invite inspection. But this dance is what Baudrillard might term a "misdirection," for while the stripping away hints at more to be seen—or to experience—it only masks the ultimate revelation, the truth of the robot's mechanical, Other nature, and eventually, of an Otherness that haunts our human nature as well. Of course, even as that showing of the self obscures the robot's real nature, it does emphasize how little we ever manage to see beneath the seductive surfaces of our world, how easily artifice becomes reality itself for us.

Appropriately, the creed that this robot preaches to the workers functions much like her dance, offering only surfaces. On one level, it rejects any meaning beyond the superficial, beyond the play of desire; and on another, it denies the value of their underground world and sends them hurrying to the surface of Metropolis. The robot's message is one of despair, destruction, and forgetfulness, as she plays upon her seductive lure to stir them to revolt and to "destroy the machines" they serve. In place of their regime of blind drudgery, she offers one in which desire blindly drives them. In the grip of that unleashed desire, they abandon their netherworld and rush headlong to the city above. But in keeping with the paradoxical nature of these seductive forces, the workers find no freedom in destroying the enslaving machinery, only a destruction *by* that freedom, a fatality in that Otherness, a treachery in the robotic. For the mechanisms that enslave them also hold back the floodwaters from their underground city and from the children they have left behind. In their Luddite passion and mad rush to the surface, the workers, like all other victims of seduction here, simply forget about their own "depths" and release a destructive Otherness that promises, much as the robot does, to do away with their very kind.

Perhaps the most important revelation is, in fact, how that destructive seduction rebounds on those who wield it and seem to control its operation, promising their destruction, much as the Tower of Babel did for its architects. As Baudrillard reminds us, there is ultimately "no active or passive in seduction . . . it plays on both sides of the border" (*Jean Baudrillard* 160). So while Rotwang in his godlike ambition can create "a machine in the image of man," a worker potentially better than human workers, he soon proves susceptible to the same seduction his "craft" has unleashed. For the features of Maria, which he gives to his robot, waken memories of his lost love Hel and impel a madness or forgetfulness that recalls the workers' own, as he imagines she has returned to life. That delusion prompts him to pursue the real Maria and eventually leads to his death, when he falls from atop the cathedral where he corners her.

Fredersen too nearly "falls" because of his deal with Rotwang and with the robotic promise of a perfect, enslaved work force.[5] In his case, he almost loses both his son and his position, as his plan "to sow discord" among the workers so he can better control them leads to their destructive rampage against the machines his city depends on and nearly results in Freder's death, first when he tries to save the workers' children from their flooding city, and then as he fights with Rotwang to save Maria. What the plights of both the scientist and the leader point up is that the forces they have unleashed are less controlled than controlling; from the play of seductive surface features, from the lure of artifice, no one here seems immune.

The film climaxes on very much this note. The people seize the robot Maria and burn her at the stake as a kind of witch. And that ancient manner of exorcism—a cultural regression or recoil from this futuristic world and its promises—reveals the disparity between the seductive surface and underlying reality, as the people watch horrified while the robot's false human veneer burns away, exposing the gleaming mechanism and mocking mechanical countenance underneath. It is an effective image—of a technological power mocking the human for being so easily seduced by its attractive packaging, its seemingly human features.

However, this scene is not the narrative's coda, and what follows contributes to much of the critical dissatisfaction that often surfaces in discussions of *Metropolis*. The film ends with the workers' foreman and Fredersen shaking hands, in a kind of strained reconciliation between the "hands" and the "head," mediated by Freder's intercession as the "heart." If that resolution seems a bit forced and unsatisfying—and even Lang admits some discontent, attributing it to his wife, the film's scenarist, Thea von Harbou[6]—it is because the conclusion pays little attention to the power and real source of the seductions at work here. Even if this culture's various classes have come to a dialogue, found a common tongue, as it were, this futuristic Babel seems built on a fundamentally weak foundation.

In this conclusion *Metropolis* implies that the universal seductions it has unveiled, seductions from the time of Babel and into the future, and across all levels of this technological society, from the workers to the masters, only spring from a lack, that of a spirit of compassion and cooperation. But this scheme is a bit too neat, a solution that basically ignores the problem of seduction and the way it has taken root in the technological foundation of their world, even worked its way into the human. In fact, the conclusion effectively translates to a narrative level the stylistic problem we have earlier noted, wherein the film's seductive images of the future seem at odds with its dystopian thrust. The technological surface of the world these people have shaped—and that clearly shapes them—has not really changed, nor has its allure. Instead of removing the veil from those seductive forces, the people have simply lifted it and then let it fall back. Here they retreat from the problems of the present to the symbolism of the past, represented by a metaphoric redeemer—young Freder—and the crumbling, even menacing image of the ancient cathedral, wherein we earlier see the image of the Grim Reaper suddenly come to life. The fundamental ideology of this world, one which practically demands that part of the population be turned into artifice, that the human be dis-membered—rendered as hands, heart, and so on—remains firmly in place.

To state the issue most clearly, we might return to the image of the robot. Does its alluring power come from a lack of compassion or cooperation? Would it, stripped of its "flesh" and displayed to everyone from the start in all its gleaming mechanical beauty, have proved any less seductive? It is, after all, the stark metal robot—or more accurately, what the robot *represents,* a technological power, a power to manipulate and *create* others, even to replace them—that seduces both Rotwang and Fredersen. It brings together these two old rivals for the hand of another woman—Hel—and impels them to act seductively as well, as they conspire to lure the workers into their self-destructive actions. The robot here becomes a metaphor for the seductive play of technological power, showing us how mesmerizing its images are and how easily it operates. As the workers form into a wedgelike mass—clearly one more bit of "ornamentation"—and march rhythmically, uniformly, even mechanically up the cathedral steps at the end, that influence seems far from exorcised.[7] Promised better treatment, they appear ready to return below the surface, once more to form the repressed, latent discourse of this world, part of its foundation of artifice.

· · ·

David Porush in his book on cybernetics and modern fiction, *The Soft Machine,* describes a paradoxical motif that recurs throughout recent writing about our technological developments and that may speak to *Metropolis*'s resolution. "At the very same moment that we feel ourselves to be acting freely in the world," he says, "we are also creating structures and codes so powerfully convincing that they dominate the ways we see" (82). Of what do they convince us? Like the seductive robot Maria, they suggest that what we see is precisely what we get, that the alluring surface—the bright, glittering, metallic skin of the robot, the surfaces of our machinery, and the efficient display of power in our technology—is value itself, that its meaning is open before us, ready to be interrogated. Even more, it is the notion that this power, this allure, is our own, an attractive part of ourselves that we have just overlooked and might easily tap. So we are urged to embrace these values and to see ourselves and our world a bit differently than we previously might have. However, that different vantage, that robotic point of view, never reveals or recognizes the real Otherness here, the forgetful and even destructive self that is both prey to and a source of seduction. Rather, it focuses our attention on surfaces, appearances, ornamentation, and effectively obscures what underlies those surfaces.

What *Metropolis* achieves, particularly through its nearly prototypic robot, is a revelation of the dark design that can underlie such surface effects, a seductive play of power that, while ages old, manages to haunt our modern mechanisms. And if that power threatens almost pleasurably to enslave us, it is still a threat in which—in our forgetful, superficial, and indeed *human* way—we can easily conspire. The robot Maria's seductive gyrations and simplistic call for forgetfulness point up how we often cannot or will not look beyond surfaces, beyond the manipulations of our artifice or media—or in what may have been Lang's case, the fascinations of a film's science fiction trappings.

For all of its openness, then, and even as it seems to speak most clearly about the future, *Metropolis* too must seem a bit "veiled," as if also susceptible to the "charms" of appearances, the attractions of its futuristic vision, as if the exercise of that seductive power were simply built into its own artifice. In fact, Baudrillard hints such a double vision may be unavoidable, as he explains how discourse always risks a kind of self-seduction: "inevitably every discourse is revealed in its own appearance, and is hence subject to the stakes imposed by seduction, and consequently to *its own failure as discourse.* Perhaps every discourse is secretly tempted by this failure and by having its objectives put into question, changing its truth effects into surface effects which act like a mirror absorbing and engulfing meaning" (*Jean Baudrillard* 150). Such are, however, "the stakes imposed by seduction" (150), the gamble in every effort to expose the powers that play in our world. A technological art like film may simply find the "stakes" a bit higher, especially when it turns its attentions to science fiction with its specific iconography. For as it tries to lift the veil on the seductive images of the technological, film inevitably opens a new and potentially disturbing perspective on the powers that produce and shape *it* as a technologically based art. And that perspective is an easy one to shy away from, particularly when your very stock-in-trade is the alluring, technologically generated image.

Metropolis, certainly more than any of our silent science fiction films, takes that risk, foregrounds the seductions of a world of artifice—one that promises to release us from so many other traps and enslavements. The result is a work whose strengths finally spring from the same source as its weaknesses, whose allure is at once more than and yet the same as its mesmerizing imagery, whose level of artifice recalls yet also transcends its central robot figure. Not simply a dystopian vision, *Metropolis* analyzes the seductive lures that propel our technology and *impel* our embrace of it. But to examine those forces it must first lay them open, array them for all to see, and so risk invoking the same seductive power it cautions against. If at times, in its conclusion or in our own fascination with the robot Maria and the futuristic city that gives her birth, the "veil" seems to drop back into place and *Metropolis* appears itself seduced into a fascinated exploration of surface features, that shift should just remind us of the power of that artifice—a power with which Lang's and subsequent science fiction films have had to contend.

· NOTES ·

An earlier version of this chapter appeared in *South Atlantic Review* 55.4 (1990): 49–60 and is reprinted with changes by permission of the South Atlantic Modern Language Assocation.

1. We should note that Méliès was himself quite familiar with the figure of the robot or automaton. Such figures were common in nineteenth-century magic shows, and the Théâtre Robert-Houdin, which Méliès operated, exhibited as acts several such figures. As Erik Barnouw chronicles, one robot, "called Psycho, could play whist; a lady robot called Zoe drew profiles of spectators" (14).

2. For much of the background on early science fiction films, especially for plot summaries and credits, I am indebted to A. W. Strickland and Forrest J. Ackerman's *Reference Guide to American Science Fiction Films,* vol. 1, and Carlos Clarens's *Illustrated History of the Horror Film.*

3. The double or simulacrum is, for Baudrillard, fundamental to the activity of seduction. As he notes, "the double" typically "creates the effect of seduction," since all of our grasping, all of our desire, is finally not so much a reaching for something else, as a kind of trompe-l'oeil effect leads us to think, but an embracing of the self's other side (*Jean Baudrillard* 156).

4. Much of this sequence is approximated by stills, title cards, and brief bits of footage in the recently restored version of *Metropolis.* In this version we do not see what happens to the worker in the upper world, but we do sense the intoxicating effect that this bright and glittering environment has on him. Entrusted with a message by Freder, the worker is so mesmerized by this world that he forgets his mission and apparently ends up in the fre-

quently glimpsed Yoshiwara, the neon-lit brothel where the robot Maria is later introduced to the upper-world society of Metropolis.

5. Earlier, we see Rotwang hailing his creation of the robot by lifting his hand skyward and noting that it has been "worth the loss of a hand to have created the workers of the future." When Fredersen instructs Rotwang to fashion his robot in the shape of Maria and set it loose among the workers, he hesitantly shakes Rotwang's black-gloved and, we assume, artificial hand to seal their pact. It seems an explicit deal with the double, the artificial, the technological.

6. In an interview, Lang indicated that he "didn't like" the finished film, partly because he "didn't think . . . a social question could be solved with something as simple as" that final mediation between the "brain," "hand," and "heart" (Johnson 162).

7. This conclusion hints of a similar problem often noted about an earlier work in the same German Expressionist tradition as *Metropolis, The Cabinet of Dr. Caligari* (1919). Originally slated to direct *Caligari,* Lang supposedly suggested that the film employ an expressionist decor to hint of its narrator's madness. However, the expressionist styling extends beyond the long flashback that forms the bulk of the narrative to the framing story as well, and that overlap has the effect of imparting a sense of disorder or madness to the supposedly normal, sane world too, and of troubling our desire to sort out its elements in a neat fashion. See Paul Jensen's discussion of Lang's early career in *The Cinema of Fritz Lang.*

3

A "Put Together" Thing: Human Artifice in the 1930s

In the previous chapter we noted the great lure of the technological, the seductive power it can wield as it begins to turn reality itself into a game wherein we fashion other versions of the self. As a cinematic embodiment of that power, though, the robot almost vanishes from our screens in the early sound period. In fact, relatively few true science fiction films appear in that era,[1] suggesting perhaps that with the coming of the Depression, our concerns had shifted away from the technological and what it might offer. Still, we can note a kind of hybrid film that straddles the horror and science fiction genres continuing the exploration of that human artifice motif. This type of film explores the rationale for that desire, for the urge to follow, be like, or even *become* a figure of artifice. As we shall see, these works suggest that this lure draws much of its power from a certain devaluation of the self, a tendency with a long history in our culture, but one which we are only beginning to chronicle and understand today.

In detailing western culture's embrace of the technological, Robert Romanyshyn suggests that "the telos of technology's dream to refashion the body is toward abandonment of the body, toward disincarnation," and that dream takes its start, he argues, from the self's "initial devaluation" (20, 25). David Lavery takes up this same theme in his analysis of the "spaciness" of modern culture, *Late for the Sky*. "In preparation for the monumental leap into the total artifice of life in space" for which our culture seems to yearn, he claims, we are constantly being "sold" a myriad of "space-age" products, all designed to make that leap seem not only easy but "natural": freeze-dried ice cream, dehydrated foods, com-

puter simulations of space flight, robotic arms, and so on (60). Foremost
among those preparations, though, are not the products themselves but
rather the production of an attitude, one that sees the human condition,
and more particularly the human body, as something rather obsolete
that must be coped with and eventually "gotten out of" (83).

We can find this attitude of artifice, though, already anticipated and
finding articulation in the various horror/science fiction films that dominate the field of fantasy in the 1930s. These narratives, which include
works like *Frankenstein* (1931) and its various sequels, *Dr. X* (1932),
The Invisible Man (1933), *Island of Lost Souls* (1933), *Mystery of the
Wax Museum* (1933), *Mad Love* (1935), and *Dr. Cyclops* (1940), describe
a horror that springs from or is unleashed by scientific experimentation,
specifically on the human body. In these works a mad scientist typically
turns the body into a piece of artifice, making of it not something to be
desired but something from which we almost instinctively recoil. In their
concern with the subjection of the body, with its transformation into the
raw material of artifice, these films bring into sharp focus that devaluation which Romanyshyn and Lavery have chronicled. It is a process of
human subjection which seems to precede—and make possible—the
technological's seductive power.

* * *

> The subject is cast in on itself, controlled from within by its selves;
> crippled by struggles and anxieties inside itself; radically under-
> mined by the loss of its own body with which it is ever in contact but
> whose insistent reminders of a material limit to its subjection, which
> it cannot quite determine for itself, it must ever attempt to quell.
>
> —Francis Barker (*The Tremulous Private Body* 60)

What does it mean to create a human being? Our films often beg this
question if they less seldom clearly state it, thanks to the level of public
anxiety it raises—an anxiety reflected today in our debates on subjects
like abortion rights, artificial insemination, and genetic engineering. We
have, after all, cracked the genetic code, made the human into a thing
that can be known from the inside out, formed according to our desires,
and perhaps even shaped in accord with society's needs (however those
might be determined). With this ever-growing ability to fashion—and
refashion—the self, the individual has effectively become, as Freud once
put it, "a kind of prosthetic God" (*Civilization* 91), able to exercise what
would have once seemed a deific power—over the self.

Looking back to the rise of modern science in the seventeenth century, Francis Barker has traced the early development and consequences of such inside-out knowledge. Drawing on the imagery of medicine, specifically anatomy and dissection, he shows how science helped craft a regime of cultural control. In particular, he notes the development of a pattern of subjection, as science began to present itself as a useful tool for rendering the individual harmless, subservient, powerless, a proper servant of society. Its starting point was to turn the self into a knowable creature, a being of parts that could be dissected, examined, and understood through the perspective modern science offered. Once rendered transparent, it was thought, the individual would internalize that power to become a kind of self-policing being, metaphorically dissecting and denying those desires for which the body is always such an insistent spokesman. In the process, the self would surrender all power and sovereignty to the surrounding world, to a culture that the individual—with body in check or reshaped according to need—would continue, almost ghostlike, to inhabit.

What Barker describes is a subjection born of knowledge that continues to haunt us. That subjection is not simply to science but to all our technologies for gathering knowledge and extending our sway, ultimately to *our own powers* of subjection. Yet as Michel Foucault points out, such efforts to rein in or reconfigure the unruly self have never been very effective. While western culture has often tried to institute methods of control or "self-mastery" (*Care of the Self* 94), in effect, to reshape the self—or *others,* anyway—and has given those efforts a scientific or rational guise, the perfect, servile subject, whether conceived of as robot or fellow human, remains an elusive goal. More often what results is an internal tension, as the body (including the cyborg body, as a film like *Blade Runner* shows) refuses to be denied. Even as what Barker terms the "hollowed, double, modern body" (73), it insists on itself and its desires. Consequently, the body becomes the site of a struggle of subjection and power—a struggle that suggests a kind of metaphoric dismemberment, even dissection, that we perform on ourselves as we set about remaking the self. It is a struggle with the forces of repression and subjection that conspire to fashion the modern self.

This image of the body under dissection, rendered as a thing to be explored, mastered, and reshaped, has become a common one in popular film. In fact, its popularity may be one measure of our response to that power over the self—or the shape of the self—which our science and technology increasingly hold out. I here want to trace out the beginnings of that response in several of those classic science fiction/horror films which Depression-era America, rife with a sense of the overwhelming modern forces arrayed against the self, produced in great number. In particular, I want to examine how James Whale's *Frankenstein,* Erle C. Kenton's *Island of Lost Souls,* and Karl Freund's *Mad Love* depict the problematic nature of the modern self, confronted with a science that wants to explore, control, and even reshape the body—to render it as artifice.

These films tend to privilege the figure behind the artifice, the "mad scientist," a type with which we are already familiar thanks to *Metropolis*'s Rotwang. In each of the works cited this figure's single-minded concern is with demonstrating his mastery over the body: by carving it up and reconfiguring it, by adding or eliminating parts of it, or, as is most prominently the case in *Frankenstein,* by fashioning it into a mocking double of the human. In effect, they illustrate what Barker and others see as a fundamental impulse in our society, the desire to render the body a manipulable and subject thing, ultimately little more than a raw material upon which the scientific spirit might exercise its will to artifice and stamp its scarry imprimatur.

· · ·

> I saw the pale student of unhallowed arts kneeling beside the thing he had put together. I saw the hideous phantasm of a man stretched out, and then, on the working of some powerful engine, show signs of life, and stir with an uneasy, half-vital motion.
>
> —Mary Shelley (*Frankenstein* 9)

Before looking at these films, I want to glance at a source that, in varying degrees, has obviously inspired them all, Mary Shelley's novel *Frankenstein.* As she describes her story's genesis, Shelley had a profoundly scientific vision, of the human body as a constructed "thing," "put together" by a young scientist and then animated by a "powerful engine" of his design. This image of the constructed and animated figure was to her both intriguing and "hideous" for, as she notes, while it suggested the individual's creator-like powers, it also mocked "the stupendous mechanism" that the human is; it blasphemed "the cradle of life" (9). This dreamimage indeed exalts the human by asserting humanity's powers, like most subsequent tales in a Promethean vein (we earlier noted her novel's subtitle, *The Modern Prometheus*). In fact, her vision doubles that assertion with its image of an "engine"—the technological, the scientific, a human construct—as providing the very spark for a human artifice. Yet that power also comes, as Shelley understood, at great cost. It is only made possible by what she saw as a pointedly modern devaluation of the self: by affirming that the human is, at base, just a "put together" thing, with no transcendent origin or purpose and bound to a "half-vital" existence at best by the material conditions of its begetting.

This paradox, wherein a human asserts power by devaluing the human self, is the unsettling starting point for the novel, for the pattern of subjection it implies, and for many of the subsequent fantasy tales that would further explore this pattern of subjection. To further emphasize this note, Shelley initially casts Victor Frankenstein's *scientific* studies in a rather unlikely setting, that of a charnel house,[2] whose horrific atmosphere undercuts all of his Promethean pronouncements. But eventually, the novel resolves this tension and dissolves the whole problem of subjection in a Rousseau-like solution. Shelley's "phantasm" is gradually transformed before our eyes, becoming essentially a metaphor, a model of the natural—and naturally free—man. Neither evil nor inhuman, he comes to seem little more than morally unformed, poorly "put together" by a *human* creator who has ill served both his creation and his fellow humans.

However, for an age that no longer accepts the Rousseau myth, for one wherein humankind is in fact measured by the "powerful engines" it has fashioned, for the age of film—which, of course, is itself a powerful engine for crafting new images of the self—that tension is hardly as easily resolved. In the 1931 film adaptation of *Frankenstein* (with Boris Karloff as the monster), that paradox lingers nearly intact. While the nature of life remains a central concern, the film focuses less on the protagonist's Promethean aspirations and potential than on his desire to subject human nature. In fact, through Victor Frankenstein's obsession with it, the body itself becomes the key issue here, as the film pointedly depicts the human body as a thing of parts, the material of artifice, waiting to be assembled or disassembled at will—a will that is not our own and that hints disconcertingly, as do many of our contemporary science fiction and horror films, of a level on which, as the feminist movement has long argued, *our bodies* are no longer our own.

The real focus of *Frankenstein,* as well as of films like *Island of Lost*

Souls, with its outlawed scientist trying to carve animals into human shapes, and *Mad Love,* with its fixated surgeon grafting a murderer's hands onto a pianist in order to win the affection of the musician's wife, is precisely this pattern of subjection.[3] Yet these films use the body's subjection to point up a paradox. While they show the body as a thing bound by some external power, a nearly plastic substance awaiting the operation of a scientific force (Sobchack's "qualified body"), these films also describe a resistance, a level on which this substance stubbornly defies control; unlike the metal from which servile robots are made, the flesh by its very nature (the "essential body") always rebels. If the anatomizing of the bodies in these films serves as a kind of metaphor for the way the modern self is subjugated, then, their animation effectively suggests a resistance to control or subjection that we might expect to follow. In effect, they point to a tension between body and mind, humanity and its scientific attainments, the self and a cultural subjection that would increasingly become a focal point for our films of human artifice.

Thus a work like *Frankenstein* seems almost from the start intent on swerving from the Promethean pattern of Shelley's novel, for its protagonist is not simply trying to gain some ultimate knowledge for humanity, not just restoring life to the dead. While he pursues life's mysteries, he also wants to exercise his own power, to demonstrate a kind of mastery over the recalcitrant, limited human body—a mastery also seen in the way he abuses his servant Fritz, dismisses his fiancée Elizabeth, and even pushes his own body past normal endurance. The movie begins with Frankenstein and Fritz collecting bodies, one from a fresh grave, another from the gallows, and then with Fritz breaking into the medical college to steal a brain for the creature under construction. From these and various other parts, many, like the stolen brain, clearly "defective," Frankenstein intends to make—"with my own hands," as he repeatedly affirms—a living being.

In many ways more a Pygmalion than Prometheus, then, Frankenstein insists on the fact that he is not simply restoring a creature to life, returning some autonomous power that has been taken away. As he carefully informs Elizabeth, his friend Victor, and his mentor Dr. Waldman, "That body is not dead. It has never lived. I created it. I made it with my own hands from the bodies I took from graves, from the gallows, from anywhere." In testimony, the camera lingers on the gaping scars along his creation's wrists and later on the creature's stitched-together skull. Those oft-repeated images, which have since become icons of the Frankenstein films and testimony to the evocative power of Jack Pierce's makeup effects, reinforce the notion that a kind of bloody, forced sculpting has transpired, and tell us less about this forced-together creation than about Frankenstein himself. What he offers is no simple boon, not a *liberation* from the fear of death, but a triumph over the flesh. He has managed to *subject* it to *his* will.

Yet even as he succeeds in animating his "put together" thing, Frankenstein finds his control over this life he "owns" more illusory than real. The Promethean fire—or to be more precise, the lightning—with which he animates his put-together thing provides a telling thread here. It is fire from the heavens that he uses to animate his creation, and the fire of torches that he employs to frighten the creature, to keep it in check. Fritz, for example, uses a torch to abuse the creature and assert his own pitifully small power over it. Yet it is finally in response to Fritz's torturings that the monster rebels, murders Frankenstein's assistant, and in the process breaks free from subjection. That point is later driven home when Frankenstein, separated from the mob of citizens searching for the monster, encounters his creation and tries to ward it off with his torch. The creature simply slaps the torch from his hands, as if mocking that original power wielded over him, and then knocks his creator out and carts him off, in effect asserting a subjecting power all his own.

It is a result, though, that the film has already modeled in its emphasis on a dissective activity. Dejected by his creation's uncontrollable nature and horrible aspect, Frankenstein plans to reverse the original creative act. In effect, he intends the ultimate subjection, killing the monster by injection and then dissecting it again into bits and pieces of the once-human. Prior to that operation, though, Frankenstein's mentor, Dr. Waldman, despite his initial horror, becomes fascinated with the creature, seduced like Rotwang and Jon Fredersen by what it represents, and begins taking his own notes on it while it is sedated. When he observes its increasing resistance to his injections, to that power of subjection, he prepares to dissect it at once and thus render it properly dead again. But even as he begins this ultimate exercise in subjection, the body's will to power surfaces—and with it, the prototype of every mad slasher film to come. The creature suddenly pops off Waldman's dissecting table and, in effect, turns the tables on him. It assumes the very power over life and death that he would wield and murders him, before then heading out into the world.

This escape of the creature even as it is being studied seems quite telling. Simply put, that escape denies the powers of subjection, suggests a wholeness that refuses the fragmentation science has decreed for it. At the same time, it points up the nature of the forces at work here, forces dedicated to study, scientific analysis (basically, a kind of intellectual fragmentation, breaking a complex whole into parts for easier understanding), and finally mastery. Those forces, however, find the body unwilling to relinquish its own power, indeed its very life, and only succeed in awakening its yearnings and desires—as finally happens with Frankenstein himself. The film ends with his awakening from this nightmare of subjection, as if he were himself newly created—a proper double for his creature—intent now on fulfilling his own previously denied physical desires. As the film ends, we assume he has forsaken this terrible "study" of his for a more fundamental and human sort of creation, the procreation promised by his marriage to Elizabeth and the toast his father smirkingly offers as he closes the door on the couple's wedding chamber: "Here's to a son to the house of Frankenstein."

As the display of scientific gadgetry and the harnessing of the forces of nature underscore, *Frankenstein* is ultimately a story of power, and particularly of a technical power used to manipulate the human. The gathering of various parts, grafting them together, regardless how ill the fit (in fact, the worse the fit, the greater the power implied by their effective jointure), and then drawing the life force from nature and compelling it to inhabit and animate those parts—all these accomplishments bespeak a mastery of human artifice, the modern world's triumph over the self. If in those achievements we seem to cross a threshold of human limitation, it is only a false step. For first, we must rethink the self, devalue it, regard the body as a subject thing. In so doing, we pave the way for our own subjection, by reinscribing the self within the very context that, our scientific vantage seemingly implies, we stand so securely outside of. We might see the common confusion of maker and monster that traditionally attends this story (calling the creation by the creator's name), as most fitting, then, since that accidental identification accurately sketches the tension implicit in this and similar narratives, even as it suggests how Frankenstein has given shape to his own monstrousness: constructing a monstrous body by, as the modern world seems to ask us all to do, first deconstructing the self.

The desires of and for artifice in *The Bride of Frankenstein.*

"Are we not men?" The creator and his constructs in *Island of Lost Souls.*

The mad scientist Dr. Moreau and his masterwork in *Island of the Lost Souls.*

Dr. Gogol prepares to operate in *Mad Love.*

· · ·

Strange-looking natives you have here.

—*Island of Lost Souls*

Island of Lost Souls takes this pattern of subjection in a slightly different direction on the evolutionary scale, but in the process deploys that motif of creation and dissection just as disturbingly as *Frankenstein.* Its shipwrecked protagonist, Edward Parker, ends up on an uncharted island in the South Pacific—an island ruled by the scientist Dr. Moreau, and populated with "strange-looking," animal-like natives. In fact, as he eventually learns, they are animals on which Moreau has, as he puts it, let his "imagination run fantastically ahead" by surgically speeding up the path of evolution, as he sees it. When Parker, drawn by human-sounding screams, stumbles upon Moreau at work in his "House of Pain," he describes what he saw as "vivisecting a human being; they're cutting a living man to pieces." As it turns out, the victim is not a man, just another of those "strange-looking natives" in the process of being made over, reshaped into a man. But it might as well be—just as Frankenstein might as well name both creator and created—for Moreau's activity models the same sort of subjection at work in this approach to artifice.

In this persistent reshaping, the painful cutting away of parts and altering their nature, Moreau's science insists on the *wrongness* of the animal and the *rightness* of a kind of human template. But it is a rightness that extends little further than shape, for in another version of that paradox we noted in *Frankenstein,* the products of his experiments remain subservient and inferior things. In fact, Moreau intends to keep them in this state. In the fashion of many of the earlier robot narratives, Moreau casts these creatures of artifice as ideal servants, as subhumans, beings who exist only to carry out his will and attest to his abilities, in the absence of recognition from a scientific establishment that has refused to accept his work or theories. Thus, what he terms his "less successful experiments" are kept caged and chained to wheels, used as slave labor, like the workers in *Metropolis.* The film thereby fashions a kind of racist paradigm in order to point up the paradox underlying all such efforts at human subjection.

But as Barker suggests, this pattern of subjection is supposed to perpetuate itself, to prove its "naturalness," by becoming a self-imposed regimen. Robots, as we know, are supposed to obey the three laws of robotics, the programming which maintains their safely subservient position. Frankenstein's monster is supposed to remain in fear of the fire which gave him life. To keep his creations in line, Moreau has supplemented his whip with a kind of catechism of "the Law": "Not to run on all fours . . . not to eat meat . . . not to spill blood"—which they recite as a litany, punctuated by the assertion, "Are we not men?" Mindful of the House of Pain and of Moreau's whip, his "natives" have learned to wield this verbal discipline on themselves, to accept a kind of programming. But that discipline induces an inevitable tension, much as Asimov explores in several of his robot stories in which two of the "laws" come into conflict. In this case, the unnatural imperative to be men—or at least what Moreau's distorted eye sees men as—comes into conflict with the natural, the animal impulse. While they struggle to answer the question "Are we not men?" affirmatively, that affirmation relies, like all codes of subjection, upon its opposite: a *need* to deny the truth, a constant threat of returning to the House of Pain for further modification if they prove defective in their artifice. It is a subjection of the self that must then be continually enforced by Moreau's whip, gun, and even scalpel.

Yet for all of Moreau's vivisecting and reshaping, his creations do backslide, even rebel. Even in his "most nearly perfect creation," the panther-woman Lota, he finds "the stubborn beast flesh creeping back." Fittingly, then, the film climaxes with another dissection that, as in *Frankenstein,* shows how easily that power of subjection comes full circle. In this instance, Moreau becomes the subject of his own figures of artifice, which rebel against his commands, assert—literally with minds of their own—that "the Law is no more," and take him to the feared House of Pain, where they subject him to his own instruments of pain and reformation. This final, tortured reshaping of the human into some grotesque shape, of the scientist into the monster (as we mentally do with the name Frankenstein), is quite appropriate, for it imprints a disturbing image of what Moreau has been doing with his "science" all along: reshaping the animal into grotesque—that is, *human*-resembling—shapes. As one of Moreau's creations puts it, "You made us things—not men, not beasts, part-men, part-beasts—*things,*" and a montage of grotesque close-ups horrifically supports that description.

Between these haunting images of a failed artifice and the ironic refrain of those "things"—"Are we not men?"—the film poses its challenge. It asks us to consider the patterns of subjection that are constantly imposed on the modern self, the many ways in which our culture and our selves try to deconstruct and deny our nature—make it artifice. Whenever we render others as things or objects, the film implies, we too, in our complicity, risk becoming something less than men.

• • •

Wonderful invention the phonograph. It keeps a man alive long after he's dead.
—*Mad Love*

Karl Freund's *Mad Love* similarly explores the subjects of artificial creation and dissecting scientists to expose the power of subjection we wield on both others and ourselves. It is an often-told story, that of a concert pianist, Stephen Orlac, whose hands are destroyed in an accident and are then replaced by those of a recently executed murderer—a carnival knife thrower.[4] His new hands, however, seem to develop a life of their own, as if they were intent on keeping their original owner "alive long after he's dead." In effect, they display a kind of genetic memory or programming that, no less than Moreau's strange-looking natives, stubbornly resists Orlac's will. In this resistance they metaphorize the pattern of subjection implicit in these efforts at human artifice, as the body comes to seem at odds with itself.

Yet this pattern only models another psychic subjection that the film develops, one emphasizing that power of desire which we have linked to artifice. The famous surgeon, Dr. Gogol, only operates on Orlac's hands because of his desire for the musician's wife, as he hopes to play upon her gratitude to gain power over her. Only by subjecting her to his will, Gogol feels, can he eventually fulfill that desire. If the model of subjection in *Island of Lost Souls* was racist, we might see that of *Mad Love* as pointedly patriarchal, as Orlac becomes a conduit for a male authority, embodied in Gogol, that wants to use its scientific mastery to forge its dominance over the feminine here.

In this context, we might describe *Mad Love* as a tale of subjection by proxy, as Gogol tries to reduce Yvonne Orlac to the status of thing, to an immobile object of his pleasure, by first using his scientific skills to transform her husband to another kind of subject being, a flesh and blood robot that does his bidding. In sewing the killer Rollo's hands onto Stephen, Gogol in effect grafts on his own hands—wherein, we are told, lie his surgeon's skills, his scientific prowess. Ultimately, he is the murderer here, a mad slasher of sorts, for to help create the subjecting illusion in Stephen's mind, he kills the musician's father and then casts the blame on Orlac. In his medical capacity, he then manages to convince Stephen that he may well have done such a deed under the influence of those "other" hands. Through them, he thus physically imposes his own will, his own ultimately murderous impulses.

Yet that subjection, as I have suggested, is only the first step in the sort of patriarchal imposition he desires. Gogol has fixated on Yvonne since first seeing her in a macabre show, wherein she plays a woman tortured by a jealous husband. When she rejects his advances, he purchases a wax figure of her used in the show, places it in his bedroom, and "madly" pours out his love to this figure he now owns.[5] It is in trying to help her husband, to free him from his subjection, that Yvonne eventually finds herself recast in this object's role. In fact, modeling the sort of complete subjection Gogol has hoped to work on her, Yvonne at one point has to *become* a thing, the empty subject of Gogol's "mad love," after she sneaks into his clinic and accidentally breaks the wax figure. To avoid discovery, she pretends to *be* that figure, that possessed, powerless, tortured piece of artifice—which she has, in another fashion, already become. A series of close-ups points up the agony of that status, as she tries to stifle her natural urge to flee or cry out—her very humanity—while Gogol plays to the "wax" figure, describing all of his mad plans for the real Yvonne.

Yet as in the other films discussed here, the inevitable turnabout occurs, as Stephen and Yvonne revolt against their transformation into artifice and bring that pattern full circle. As Bruce Kawin in his essay "Children of the Light" observes, while Gogol is, on the one hand, "the cheerfully ruthless creator of delusions in the mind of his patient" Stephen Orlac, he is, on the other, himself quite ruled by the illusions he has created and becomes "entirely unable to distinguish image from reality" (251). That confusion, which we might see as a kind of self-subjection, is precisely what leads to his end. Thinking Yvonne is his wax figure come to life, Gogol acts out his desires, assaulting her just as Stephen arrives. Accepting the notion Gogol has planted in his mind, that he has become a kind of artifice, been "made" a killer by the power of those knife-thrower's hands, he then hurls a knife into the surgeon's back to save his wife. In those hands, no less than in the phonograph to which Gogol referred, a person seems to remain alive, "long after he's dead." But it is a life of subjection, and that pattern of subjection will, as we have repeatedly seen, eventually generate its own violent power, a kind of mirror image of the very forces focused upon it.

. . .

The films described here, like many others in this period, offer a different perspective on the issue of human artifice than we find in earlier
science fiction works. They depict violent efforts to redefine the human
body as some sort of raw material, waiting to be reshaped, reformed by a
scientific capacity for artifice. Like more traditional science fiction films,
they focus on the issue of knowledge and how our knowledge easily and
unwittingly wields a power over us. They veer off from other works in
the genre by emphasizing how that knowledge becomes a horrific violence we can do to ourselves and others—a violence that can take many
shapes. More precisely, these works explore a tension we impose on
ourselves, one that might variously be described as a Cartesian mind-
body split, as a repression that the forces of power persistently impose
on subject groups, or as a kind of dissection or anatomization which we,
almost unwittingly, impose on ourselves, even as we set about making
the self over in line with the modern world's wishes.

Yet even as these films talk about a horrific way science often interprets the human body—as the raw material of artifice—they also affirm
our ability to oppose that view, to resist such subjection. In this respect,
they are paradigms of their own project. For such films function very
much as a response to forces that seem, today no less than in their own
time, intent on subjecting the self, even tearing it apart. Made in the
midst of the Great Depression, as powerful forces seemed to be working
toward a kind of social fission, violently splitting society apart, these
works, in the best manner of genre narratives, responded to the threat. If
in that era the individual appeared to be a most insignificant thing, rent
by pulls from every direction and then reconstituted as a new sort of
being, one ripe for the lures of fascism, communism, or various home-
grown demagogueries, these works helped us metaphorically work out
that tension in a most fundamental, even effortless, way. They are, on
one level, analogues for the social upheaval or revolution that many saw
as necessary and even inevitable, given the perceived failures of our
culture in that period, but at the same time, they represented safe alter-
natives to real change, acceptable imaginary solutions, couched at least
partly in the scientific language of the machine age.

Yet I hesitate to stop at such a simple and predictable ideological
reading of this sort of artifice, for these films ultimately do more than
just play out a pattern of creation and rebellion; they are not just mod-

ern versions of the Promethean myth. Rather, as I have suggested, they operate more in the Pygmalion mold, as they address what it means to fashion or refashion the human. They ask us to consider the consequences of inscribing a scientific power—or, for that matter, any pattern of mastery—on the body as a way of rendering it artifice. Each of these films shows the body subject to a violent, yet avowedly scientific, practice. The way these films underscore that practice, in the process of anatomization (in the monster's scar tracks, the House of Pain, the close-ups of Orlac's twisted fingers), literally embodies this pattern of inscription. That practice, that metaphoric creator, they insist, is what the body will inevitably turn against; ideologies of any sort must be suspect here.

But especially we might see these films, in their fascination with dissection, as fashioning a kind of metonymy for how science often works in this genre. In her study of science fiction, Susan Sontag notes that the technological trappings of the form ultimately stand in for "the universal rule of reason" (223), as it tries to extend its sway. The rending apart that these films depict suggests the very nature of analysis, a "breaking apart" which the word, in its root sense, denotes. At the same time, it signals the wild work of the "mad scientist," the being who directs his knowledge and technology against the individual, against the self, and who thus effectively institutionalizes the modern condition that Barker describes as "interior dividedness" (108).

If the act of reanimation or reattachment suggests a recompense for this violent scientific activity, it hardly erases that prior effect, never quite heals the surgeon's scars—as the "zipper" tracks that have become a "trademark" of Karloff's monster or the jagged jointures at Orlac's wrists illustrate. For the scars are the permanent impression of the cutting, the division, the scientist's forced mastery over his subject. And the "creation" to which they bear witness is only a birth into servitude, a subjection to the creator or to a will implanted in the body, which forces it to act, as is obvious in Orlac's case but as we see equally in a recent film like *Reanimator* (1986), nearly opposite its natural instincts.

The horror film, of course, has always capitalized on threats to the body, especially that of dismemberment, although in recent years it has taken a more vivid and single-minded focus on the gruesome. The *Texas Chainsaw Massacre* films (1973, 1986), *Night of the Living Dead* (1968) and its sequels, and the many rehearsings of *Friday the 13th* (1980) seem to take special delight in anatomizing the body, in confronting us through their bits and pieces of gore with a sense of its frailty, as well as the fragility of those cultural constraints that are supposed to stop us from turning each other into such baser forms: into bloody masses of meat and bones. This "hard-core pornography of violence," as Morris Dickstein well terms it (33), represents a kind of playing at limits, immediately the limits involved in "grossing out" the audience and skirting censorship, but ultimately, the limit of the death experience which these films so elaborately depict. But what troubles many people is the way these films often avoid considering the implications of those limits, as for the most part they seem little concerned with the real nature of the human, of a self that can so easily be reduced to gore.

At the same time, the science fiction film has increasingly moved into this territory, as it isolates and pursues the image of human artifice, as we shall see, to a more significant end. The images of the android, cyborg, and bioengineered human have eventually become commonplace in our films, reflecting their increasing significance in our culture. While this body of more recent films explores a kind of cybernetic fascination we have with the construction and behavior of life rendered as artifice, they do so not, as in our contemporary horror films, with a mind to frightening us by bringing, as one of the most infamous of the so-called "snuff films" puts it, "The Face of Death" up close, but rather to exploring the nature of a life that has become itself ever more artificial, too closely resembling a kind of living death. It is the image of a life that, in the fashion of the Frankenstein monster, Dr. Moreau's "natives," or Stephen Orlac's wrists, bears the scarry track of the powers which, everywhere in the modern world, seek to dominate us.

In the earlier films described here, we can see a first, hesitant, yet telling effort to trace these scars, to investigate how the body, as Foucault puts it, "is invested by power relations" (*Foucault Reader* 171), and to understand how those power relations affect our sense of the human. Tellingly, they do so transgenerically, that is, by linking science fiction, with its focus on science, reason, and technology, to horror and its emphasis on threats to the body. That mix produces an image of a growing modern anxiety—of the human at odds with itself—as it explores technologies whose ultimate purpose seems to be the subjection, even dehumanization, of the self. In each case these films describe a threat lodged in a power to reshape the self, to render it something horrible, perhaps even unrecognizable. Yet they hold out a hope of resistance, implicit in the paradox behind those strategies of subjection: that insofar as these *human* strategies deny the human, they must be self-defeating.

The recent resurgence of these concerns in various forms attests to our continuing anxiety about the forces of subjection that we seem, in a variety of ways, ready to unleash upon ourselves—an anxiety that, in our technological rush, in the capacities that our science places in our hands, even in what seem to be the very *needs* of the modern world—for prostheses, cosmetic implants, or artificial organs of various sorts, for example—we might too readily assist in our own grotesque reconfiguration. Yet our abilities to address this anxiety, to debate these issues, and even to turn the very narratization of science to this concern, show how we might resist or reverse those power relations. Through such films, we continue to struggle against the modern world's many efforts at redefining the self as little more than a "put together" thing.

· NOTES ·

1. The most noteworthy are probably *Mysterious Island* (1929), *Just Imagine* (1930), *Transatlantic Tunnel* (1934), *The Invisible Ray* (1936), and *Things to Come* (1936). Interestingly, none demonstrates the interest in robots that seems to have surfaced in so many ways during the earlier era and that was becoming a central concern of science fiction literature.

2. Early in the novel, at least, Mary Shelley paints her scientist-protagonist in a most "unhallowed" light, as a figure immersed in the body parts from which he draws his knowledge and with which he will challenge the very nature of humankind. As Victor Frankenstein describes these early days, "I had returned to my old habits. I collected bones from charnel-houses; and disturbed, with profane fingers, the tremendous secrets of the human frame. In a solitary chamber, or rather cell, at the top of the house, and separated from all the other apartments by a gallery and staircase, I kept my workshop of filthy creation: my eye-balls were starting from their sockets in attending to the details of my employment. The dissecting room and the slaughter-house furnished many of my materials; and often did my human nature turn with loathing from my occupation" (*Frankenstein* 54–55).

3. We should note that both of these films are drawn from literary works as well, the former from H. G. Wells's story "The Island of Dr. Moreau," and the latter from Maurice Renard's novel *Les Mains d'Orlac.* Testifying to their appeal, both tales, like Shelley's *Frankenstein,* have spawned numerous film incarnations. What I have chosen to look at here are the most famous of those incarnations, which significantly happen to cluster within one period in American film history.

4. The Maurice Renard novel had previously been filmed in Austria as

Orlacs Hände (1925), and it was later remade in England as *The Hands of Orlac* (1960). Several other variations, centering on dismembered body parts assuming a frightening, even deadly, life of their own, have also appeared.

5. Here too the Pygmalion theme surfaces strongly, as Gogol caresses his wax statue and prays for it to come to life. In *Island of Lost Souls* this impulse appears in Dr. Moreau's pride over his "most nearly perfect creation," Lota, the panther-girl, as he fantasizes taking her back to England and, in a kind of grotesque parody of George Bernard Shaw's *Pygmalion,* seeing her accepted in English society.

4

A "Charming" Interlude:
Of Serials and Hollow Men

> The thing we apprehend in one great leap, the thing that, by
> means of the fable, is demonstrated as the exotic charm of another
> system of thought, is the limitation of our own, the stark impossi-
> bility of thinking *that.*
>
> —Michel Foucault (*The Order of Things* xv)

Fables, Foucault suggests, seem to draw their popular-
ity from two quite different effects. Much of their appeal, he implies, lies
in the way they let us see things differently, in a light that points up "the
limitation of our own" thinking, our difficulty in imagining systems,
philosophies, or simply cultures other than our own. Yet they can also
insulate us from the implications of that sense of difference by defining
the other as exotic and holding it at a discreet or "safe" distance. The
"charm" Foucault describes in fables, in fact, flows precisely from this
double potential, from their narrative ability to draw a kind of border at
the most complex or disturbing possibilities, while inviting us to approach
that border or glimpse beyond it, but without the dangerous passage into
some cultural or aesthetic terra incognita. A charming narrative, in short,
is a safe one, suitable, as fables are, for adults or children, for those who
long to *glimpse* something of the differences that mark their world and
for those who simply want to see their world a bit differently.

This vantage may prove most useful here because we need to look a
bit differently at the imagery of human artifice. Through much of the
1930s and 1940s that imagery, as the previous chapter suggests, found a
very limited cinematic presentation. The monstrous beings and recon-

structed figures of the horror/science fiction films soldier on, especially in the variations Universal Pictures would work on its monster series well into the 1940s. However, what of the robot or automaton, a figure that was becoming commonplace in our pulp literature? In fact, it was finding enough popular appeal that, by 1939, the robot Electro and his mechanical dog Sparko would become one of the most popular exhibits at that science fiction vision brought to life, the New York World's Fair. Those *mechanical* beings, direct images of technology's efforts at imitating the human, can be found rather easily, but only if we look in a different direction, one that most of our film histories either ignore or simply discount.[1] That is, we need to turn our attention to what today seems a most quaint, even charming kind of film, the movie serial.

From the silent era to the mid-1950s, when changing distribution patterns, shifting viewing habits, and the expanding role of television in American culture rendered it unnecessary and unprofitable, the serial was a staple of Saturday matinees and second-run movie houses, as well as a major product of "poverty-row" studios like Republic, Monogram, and Mascot, and even such "little" majors as Columbia and Universal. And before its charm had completely worn off and its last cliff-hanger tale unreeled in 1956, the serial also effectively served as a device for containing—that is, depicting *and* keeping at a distance—various significant and potentially disturbing concerns that mainstream cinema often marginalized. Among the issues at least addressed by different serials, we might note the threatening prospect of feminine power, the problem of vigilante justice, the menace of global destruction, and the rise of third world cultures.

For our concerns, though, the serial is especially noteworthy for its treatment of technology's growing place in our culture, bringing with it the promises and potential threats we have already seen articulated in a film like *Metropolis.* At a time when public interest in the development of science and technology was reaching new proportions, the feature film, as we have noted, offered little in the way of "pure" science fiction, certainly nothing to match the subjects being explored in that great explosion of pulp periodicals, led by the likes of *Amazing* and *Astounding.* However, the serial gave the technological a voice, even if it was one that often spoke in rather restrained tones, or at other times in the cartoonish fashion of the comic strips from which a number of the serials were adapted.

Most commonly, the serial visualized the various icons that dominated the covers of the pulps—rocket ships, alien beings, death rays, outsized machines, and, of course, robots in every shape, typically presented in a threatening manner. The attitude we commonly find toward these figures of artifice, and for that matter toward practically all technology, is our main concern here, for the serial betrays a kind of "charming," fabulistic attitude toward its robots and their technological context that seems typical of American popular culture in the latter stages of the machine age.

· · ·

Tellingly, the serials attained their greatest popularity and success in the 1930s, a decade which, as Howard Segal explains, also "witnessed an extraordinary . . . outpouring of faith in technological progress" (132). This decade, we might note, is almost bracketed by two world's fairs that traded on the promise of technological development. In 1933 Chicago hosted its "Century of Progress Exposition," and from 1939 to 1940 New York offered us "The World of Tomorrow," a vision of life in the America of 1960. Both fairs projected a broad interest in progress, in the future, in a truly scientific "world of tomorrow," that reflected a general awareness of the technological changes then going on throughout our culture. And they offered images not only of the American landscape radically transformed, as General Motors' 1939–40 "Futurama" exhibit depicted, but also of a people who would be changed for the better, thanks to numerous labor-saving devices, new appliances (like television) that would alter how we lived our lives, and the development of figures like Westinghouse's Electro the "Motoman." This same attitude also surfaces in divers movements of the period, such as Howard Scott's Technocracy Crusade, the widespread fascination with streamline design and speed, and a renewed interest in utopian literature during the decade.[2]

These and many other efforts suggest how the image of progress and the technologizing of our lives had begun to capture the imaginations of Americans, mired throughout the decade in the problems of the Depression. Of course, this "faith" of which Segal speaks was at least partly prompted by a hope that technology would create new solutions to the problems facing both our culture and the world: that it would provide jobs and opportunities for victims of the Depression, that it would help our society feed its people, that it would usher in a time of world cooperation and peace when, thanks to the many small wars that were already cropping up—all rehearsals for the cataclysmic struggle soon to break out in World War II—the prospects for any peace must have seemed farfetched, even utopian.

Still, the fact that there was such a widespread interest in technology and its perceived ability to alter our lives and our very persons, even amidst the era's gloom and despair, comments tellingly on our culture in this period. It suggests, at least, a growing tendency to look to the future and its promises, rather than to the past, for hope and for possible models of what we might become and how we might respond to changing circumstances. More specific to this study, it suggests an increasing faith that, through our scientifically driven capacity for artifice, we might well change ourselves, our human nature.

Amid this attitude, it seems all the more surprising that mainstream American films of the 1930s either ignore or only obliquely acknowledge this fascination, which, as we have earlier noted, prompted an outpouring of pulp magazines and fantastic novels that extrapolate the most "amazing" and "astounding" possibilities from the technological developments then appearing. In their pages we find a keen interest in rocketry and space travel, in futuristic societies, and especially in what seems a key image of this technological thrust, that of the robot or mechanized being. The film industry, however, offered little in correspondence, certainly no wave of science fiction movies such as we would see in the 1950s, when the lines of the cold war were starkly drawn and its alternate vision of things came into focus: recurrent images of an alien (read Communist) menace or apocalyptic (read atomic) doom bearing down on the American scene. When we look at what Hollywood (or, for that matter, the rest of world cinema) produced in the 1930s, we find remarkably little evidence of this technological fascination. The most noteworthy exceptions are films like the musical comedy *Just Imagine* (1930) at the start of the decade, the British import *Things to Come* (1936) in the middle, and, as the previous chapter noted, the various hybrid films that feature mad scientists and that some critics consign entirely to the horror genre.[3] Only the serial regularly translated those concerns to the screen; and judging by the minimal attention our film histories give to this form, its vision seems just a minor footnote to the American cinema.

As we have noted, this period saw the serials' greatest success.[4] Studios like Columbia, Universal, Mascot, and Republic regularly—and rapidly—turned out twelve- to fifteen-chapter serials as program filler. And while the various stories they told, such as the settling of the West, adventuring in the jungles of Africa or South America, and fighting crime in the modern city, parallel most popular film genres of the era, science fiction also proved one of their staples. So while what we might term "straight" science fiction was largely absent from feature film production in this period, it surfaced repeatedly in serials like *Undersea Kingdom* (1936), *Flash Gordon* (1936), *Flash Gordon's Trip to Mars* (1938), *Flash Gordon Conquers the Universe* (1940), *Buck Rogers* (1939), and many others—all of which offer a catalogue of the sorts of subjects and events that were standard features in the pulp magazines of the day: rockets, ray guns, interplanetary travel and warfare, alien cultures, and of course robots.

Equally noteworthy is a kind of science consciousness that the serials reveal, for the trappings of modern technology and of futuristic worlds dress up all sorts of stories and result in a variety of generic crossovers. As Jim Harmon and Donald Glut note, in this period "Even the most mundane police chapterplays and Westerns might center upon some weird buzzing and crackling device capable of tremendous destruction or similar extraordinary power" (45). Among such serials we might single out the jungle adventure *The Lost City* (1935), which depicts a futuristic city in the heart of Africa, ruled by a mad scientist (or mad colonialist) who has developed ray guns and other technological devices, which he uses to rob the natives of their personalities, drain their wills, turn them into living robots. Another mad scientist, Dr. Zorka (played by Bela Lugosi), is at the center of the crime serial *The Phantom Creeps* (1939). In seeking revenge on those he blames for his wife's death years before, Zorka employs a wide variety of scientific gadgets—including invisibility belts, ray guns, and especially a giant robot—all adapted for criminal use. But probably the best—and certainly the most extreme— example of science fiction's interpenetration of other forms is Mascot's *Phantom Empire* (1935). It was, to begin with, the first starring vehicle for the king of the singing cowboys Gene Autry; but along with its quaint mixture of Western and musical, it also conjured up an underground, futuristic world, Murania, which, among its many other science fiction trappings, offered television, disintegrating rays, and robot workers and guards. As a number of generally similar serials suggest, this sort of generic combination was not unpopular, uncommon, or even unexpected.

. . .

The serial's ready embrace of this science fiction matter may have much to do with its own characteristics—the same traits that mark it off from mainstream film narrative and suggest what I have described, borrowing from Foucault, as a "charming" sort of narration. Of course, the serial story form was hardly new to the movies, but rather a product of the industrial age and its valuing of repetition, regularity, and predictable results. In the eighteenth century, novels and stories often appeared in serial installments, and in the nineteenth century many authors, most notably Dickens and Eugène Sue, made their livings publishing such tales. So a basic pattern of similar episodes, each following a generic pattern, all linked by some melodramatic event and moving to an inevitable and usually culture-affirming conclusion, was well established long before the first movie "chapterplay" unreeled in 1912.

However, the film serial appears at a time when the very components of such storytelling had begun to take on new resonance: when a technological or machine-consciousness would cast those characteristics in a different light, begin to suggest their growing influence on and sway over the human. Cecelia Tichi has shown how the great wave of technological development in the early twentieth century helped reshape many of our imaginative constructs. In particular, she suggests that the imaginative text emerging in this machine age often does not simply "contain *representations* of the machine—it too *is* the machine. It is the functional structure of component parts designed to transmit energy. As such, it can be shown to obey the design rules for sound structures and efficient machines" (16). This notion of "rules" seems especially pertinent to the movie serial, the narrative pattern of which was far more determined than that of mainstream Hollywood film, or what we often term "classical narrative." While the serial becomes, as we have noted, one of the major image stores of the technological and the chief film locus of science fiction for the 1930s and 1940s, this situation probably owes a great deal to the form's machine-age characteristics.

Certainly, the serial works in a very machinelike way, according to rather conventional "design rules": each episode employs similar "parts" and resembles in its basic mechanism that which comes before and that which will follow. The introductory episode establishes a context for the entire narrative: in it we usually learn about the protagonist and his role, a conflict is introduced, and that central figure, a close comrade, or a love interest ends up in deadly peril. Succeeding episodes begin by recounting the context of events for the sake of continuity—usually via a "scroll title," rescuing the endangered figure from the brink of destruction, continuing in efforts to resolve the basic conflict, and leading up to another perilous, cliff-hanger situation. Inexorably, the serial moves to a conclusion that resolves the initial conflict, although by this point in the narrative it becomes clear that the protagonist can and will overcome all odds, escape any dangers, and, with a final flourish of physical daring, intellectual acuity, technical expertise, or a combination of all three, unmask those responsible for the conflict at hand and bring them to justice.

This "sound," "efficient," and nearly mechanical extension and working out of a narrative line closely resembles an industrial process, and it has several effects in common with such processes. Created in an almost assembly-line fashion—that is, shot quickly, economically, and formulaically—the serial could be experienced in much the same way. Viewers could watch a particular sequence in the narrative and experience the same sort of thrills and satisfactions they might with any other moment in the story—and, indeed, with other moments in other serials. This predictability results, largely, because its parts were standardized and, like its heroes who might play Flash Gordon one year and Buck Rogers the next, in many ways interchangeable. Moreover, viewers could approach it as they might some massive machine that was moving with regularity and predictability toward an expected conclusion. On one level, then, it was both safe and comfortable. We simply inhabited its peculiarly conventionalized region for a time, stepped in as we might a roller coaster car, and enjoyed its almost predictable thrills for the known duration of the ride.

And yet that comfortable experience could only remain successful by disguising its overly determined form. While serials invariably cut corners by repeating scenes—particularly action and establishing shots—from one episode to another, they could not let viewers grow too aware of that almost mechanical repetition. Nor could the larger serial pattern, wherein each chapter essentially follows the format of the previous one, become too obvious. The possibility for suspense, for example, could never be completely suspended. If that pattern did become totally transparent, audiences would quickly realize that there was little point in seeing every episode—or in patronizing the same theater each week. Seriality itself was thus both an attraction and a danger, a most fundamental source of tension, with which the serials had to cope.

An even more fundamental problem—and source of tension—though, rests in the principle underlying seriality, particularly its implications for the human. That technological atmosphere exerted its influence not only on our imaginative texts but on our imaginations as well, on our sense of self. Repeatedly, the science fiction serials tell a tale of serialization: of a potential in our technology to turn the human into a serial product, an undifferentiated segment in a controlled process, a kind of robotic thing. While the highly technologized, futuristic worlds these films often depicted—the underground city of Murania in *Phantom Empire,* the underwater world of Atlantis in *Undersea Kingdom,* the renegade planet Mongo of the Flash Gordon serials—were fascinating, even alluring, in themselves, much of their power derives from one central characteristic. These imaginative worlds both depend on and stand for the forces of dynamic power, control, and undifferentiation—forces that explicitly in the course of their narratives, but implicitly in their every use, promise to turn the individual into a component part in some large machine, part and product in a serial process. Yet that vision seems less a genuine concern than fallout from their *charm,* a sort of border view that reflects simultaneously the fascination and the fear that marked this period's technological interests. In that border view we can also glimpse how these films helped bridge the gap between the horror/science fiction films discussed in the previous chapter and the hard-core science fiction that would appear in the 1950s.

· · ·

As an initial example of this "charming" accommodation to seriality and its implications of artifice, I want to look at the most popular entries in this form, Universal's Flash Gordon serials, the first of which was so successful that it set its own design pattern, a series of broadly similar sequels. Adapted from Alex Raymond's popular comic strip, the three Flash Gordon entries (*Flash Gordon, Flash Gordon's Trip to Mars,* and *Flash Gordon Conquers the Universe*), were far more lavishly designed and expensively produced than other serials—and even many features— of the period,[5] and they brought together current and futuristic technology. In each film the scientist Dr. Zarkov uses his experimental rocket —a leftover from *Just Imagine*—to hurl himself, Flash, and Dale Arden into space to combat the machinations of Ming the Merciless, self-proclaimed Emperor of the Universe. The many elements of that confrontation in outer space include various destructive rays, antigravity devices, an invisibility machine, television, chemical combat, light bridges, and diverse rocket ships and "stratosleds." And in keeping with the implicit threat of that serial impulse, each film also offers robots or other forms of human artifice—typically controlled and mechanized men. In the first of these films Flash Gordon initially encounters Ming's power when he, Zarkov, and Dale land on Mongo and are captured by Officer Torch and several robots. The second serial displaces this image into the subject Clay People, who have been transformed and enslaved by the powers of Ming's partner, Queen Azura, and who must be liberated by Flash. The last of these serials centers several chapters around the threat of Ming's "Annihilants," invincible mechanical men who can survive in the most alien environment and who are, as well, walking time bombs. Perhaps more importantly, each story develops Ming's threat to extend that control through charms, drugs, machines, and futuristic weaponry, to render beings throughout the universe little more than similar automatons—his mindless, controlled subjects.

Such serials obviously found much of their appeal in those technological trappings, as well as in their ability to offer viewers a metaphoric version of their plots, a kind of cinematic World's Fair experience. That is, they whisked viewers off to a futuristic, other world to glimpse a possible shape of tomorrow. Yet that almost easy and rapid flight to the stars was never unproblematic, since the means of that flight, technology itself, usually proved the source of a threat. Every rocket trip meant confronting Ming's power—that of a science advanced far beyond Earth's feeble efforts, and a power that had as its goal the control or automatization of all men. Fittingly, then, each serial begins by opposing those advanced powers to the Earth's limited technology, while also bringing Ming's nearly mindless minions into conflict with the individualistic, strong-willed, and emotional humans, typified by Flash Gordon. In each instance, the trip to Mongo or Mars follows an attack on Earth, which our planet's most advanced machines and minds—"the world's greatest scientists," as *Flash Gordon Conquers the Universe* puts it—prove powerless to stop. What does halt Ming is the indomitable spirit of a Flash Gordon, a spirit that stands proof against mind control, drugs, and every manner of technological mastery. This sort of conflict, as well as its inevitable resolution, would have had special resonance for audiences of the later 1930s, when the newsreels that usually accompanied the serials constantly showed the awesome mechanized forces of various foreign powers and detailed the efforts of those powers to render more and more of the world subject to their industrialized might, as either component parts in a juggernaut dedicated to world domination or the will-less subjects of those dominating entities.

Of course, as part of its successful formula, the serial surely if strenuously vanquishes that threat, while leaving its implications for our world practically unexamined. The technological simply becomes, in Foucault's sense, charming. As we might expect, the figure of the robot illustrates this pattern. As in *Buck Rogers,* where Buck is forced to wear Killer Kane's control helmet which briefly turns him into a living robot, in *Flash Gordon* Flash falls under Emperor Ming's mind control—again, only for a time. The human will, though, proves stronger than any technological power, strong enough, at any rate, to resist the threat of robotization or serialization. When Ming unleashes a hoard of robots in *Flash Gordon Conquers the Universe,* they prove to be much less than men, just remote-controlled weapons of destruction. At first, these robots cause near panic, because they seem "invincible," thanks to their size and great strength. But as Flash soon reveals, they are just simple machines, little more than, as a chapter title puts it, "Walking Bombs" which "must be controlled by humans" to have any effect. That observation is significant not only because it is the key to defeating Ming's forces but also because it redefines these threatening figures as something quaint and understandable. It reassures us that in this world *man* is the creature who thinks, whether he is calculating ways to destroy other humans or figuring out how to overcome whatever obstacles he faces, including robots.

In fact, despite all of Ming's creations, all of his technological powers, all of his subject peoples, ultimately human ingenuity, strength, and individuality win out here. While the Flash Gordon serials put much technological might on display, it seems to exist mainly to draw the line of charm, by appealing to us with its unfamiliar shapes and powers, while the plots repeatedly celebrate a *human* might and *human* feelings, particularly a human determination to stay something other than a subject, serialized thing. Basically, these texts deploy the forces of science and technology as superfice, don them as a kind of clothing worn by far more physical, primitive, yet *human* beings—like us. In this context, the very dress of the humans is revealing. For while Flash Gordon easily rockets off to the futuristic worlds of Mongo and Mars aboard Zarkov's rocket, he invariably ends up dressed anachronistically—in Roman armor, the garb of medieval England, or primitive fur clothing, while doing battle with swords, longbows, or even his bare hands.[6] He seems at once a product of the technological era and yet remarkably free from its values and immune to its powers of serialization or robotization.

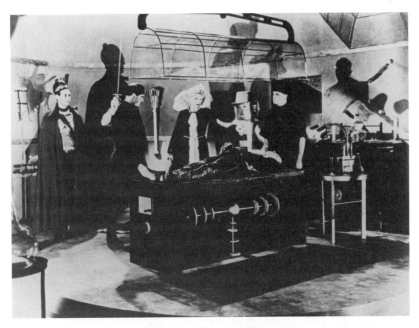

The Muranians, with a robotic assist, revivify Gene Autry in *The Phantom Empire*.

Advertisement for the serial *The Phantom Creeps* foregrounds the monstrous aspect of the robot.

• • •

Phantom Empire (1935), probably Mascot's most famous serial and one of its last before Republic acquired the studio, dramatizes this pattern even more starkly. As earlier noted, this picture blends the Western, musical, and science fiction genres into a vehicle for the singing cowboy Gene Autry, who here portrays the famous singing cowboy Gene Autry. Much of the film's charm derives from this strange combination, as a real individual—Autry—involved in his real-life occupation—singing on the radio—plunges into a world of absolute fantasy—just as Autry, through his movie career, did in real life. A team of unscrupulous scientists plots to get Autry out of the way so they can mine radium deposits discovered on his ranch. Meanwhile, the sheriff is after Autry because the scientists frame him for the murder of his partner. The leaders of the futuristic, underground kingdom of Murania also want to get rid of Autry, as well as all nearby surface people, so no one will discover the secret entrance to their world. At the same time, Autry and his friends constantly struggle to make their daily broadcasts, or else lose their national radio contract and, with it, the mortgage to Radio Ranch.

At the core of these almost absurdly multiple yet always intertwined plot lines is the film's basic, most alluring, and nearly archetypal conception, that far beneath the earth's surface, under the everyday world we inhabit, lies a parallel world—a futuristic double of the sort that our fantasy literature and pseudoscientific writings have often posited. That technological marvel, along with the surface world's scientists, here poses a deadly threat to the normal world. In fact, in one episode Autry is actually killed by one of the Muranians' devices, only then to be resurrected by another, their Radium Reviver. That revival underscores the charm of this work, for it lets us penetrate to the very core of this narrative, fall fully into the web of these plot entanglements and their implications, yet also find a quite unexpected way out. If the futuristic technology poses a threat both to Autry and, as the Muranians' disintegrating ray and warlike attitude suggest, to the entire surface world, what it does can clearly be undone. While our singing cowboy must walk around like a zombie for some time after, mumbling in "the language of the dead," as it is termed, that seems a small price for this sort of ultimate border crossing, particularly when we are guaranteed a comforting return, even a revival. Throughout this serial, the cowboy is extricated from other such predicaments, as well as from the science fiction plot itself; he can be revived to return to his ranch and once again sing "That

Silver Haired Daddy of Mine"—in the language of the living—over the radio.

What seems clear is that the film's multiple plots, contrived pressures, and mixed genres never really undermine its technological concerns; they simply mark their border, afford us a safe vantage on them. The serial's western setting and characters, after all, are already thoroughly modernized, thanks to such technological trappings as the radio, radium, cars, airplanes, and direction finders. These developments allow for a relatively easy leap to the more advanced world of Murania with its wireless telephone, television, Radium Reviver, elevator tubes, disintegrating ray, and especially its robots. In fact, at every level this serial suggests a fully modern, advanced world. Yet it also uses the technological to demarcate the surface and subterranean worlds. The cowboys here seem equally at home working on a ranch and performing to millions on the radio, equally adept at riding horses and flying planes. In contrast, the Muranians are nearly enslaved to their technological developments. They have lived underground so long that—looking forward to Darth Vader of *Star Wars*—they need an apparatus to breathe on the surface. Apparently a compliant people, they seem totally obedient to their queen. For workers, they have become dependent on robots. In general, they are a serialized culture, one that has come too far, too fast, so that its accomplishments, such as its disintegrating ray, now endanger its own existence and, because of its accessibility, the surface world's as well.

Perhaps the more telling insight into this situation shows up in the most basic image of human serialization, the robots that abound here. We find robots everywhere in Murania; they serve as workers, guards, soldiers. We see them cranking up the hidden gate that opens onto the surface world, casually toting heavy loads along Murania's walkways, stationed outside the queen's chambers as imposing guards, and working on assembly lines. Indeed, the very casualness with which these figures turn up, as if a natural part of this world's everyday workings, is part of its charm, making its futuristic context seem a far more seamless, even believable, construct.

Yet for all the technological capacities of this futuristic domain, its mechanical people are curiously limited, hardly even as menacing as Ming's "Annihilants." As John Baxter offers, the film's "lumbering robots" seem "as casually constructed as children's cardboard armour" (71). Of course, since they look much like tin cans with arms and legs—even tin hats—perhaps we should expect their actions to be supremely mechanical, far from human, and in their clumsy, even "lumbering" movements, never quite menacing. But then, one might offer that, in keeping with the general character of serial acting, which was never the best, the humans here seldom seem to offer little more in the way of animation. What we do quickly recognize is that, for all of their difference, these robots are simply a kind of manual labor force, used to replace Muranians in tasks that require strength or repetitive movements. So while they resemble humans and in size are certainly imposing, they eventually prove to be little more than mobile versions of today's simple industrial robots.

In fact, the film clearly distinguishes between the human and the mechanical in a way that well points up the charming aura of this human artifice—and, indeed, all the technological here. When the Muranians capture Autry, Lord Argo proposes to use him as a subject "for vivisection," so Muranian scientists can study his "breathing structure" prior to invading the surface world. It seems that, for all their scientific advances and despite their resemblances to surface men, they understand little of how the human body works. As we expect, Autry is spared such an "experimental" fate, but this threatening prospect finds a revealing parallel later in another sort of dissection, this time of the technological. When Gene's comic partners Oscar and Pete try to rescue him and elude the pursuing Muranians, they stumble upon a robot assembly line, find several robots in pieces, and inspect their insides. "Why, it's got wheels like a clock," one of them notes, and then hits upon the idea of emptying out that clockwork mechanism and donning the robots' metallic skin as a disguise. By doing so, they manage to elude their pursuers, save Gene, and eventually escape from Murania.

These two separate episodes draw a clear distinction between the human and the artifice—between a real being and Murania's fascinating mechanical men. The promise to "open up" Autry, of course, implies more than the spirit of scientific inquiry; it is a real threat, a sentence of death for the subject that draws on a popular view of the scientist and the work of science as potentially dangerous—especially in their readiness to trade human life for knowledge. Then too, we assume that when a human is "opened up" and taken apart, as in an autopsy, we might learn the answer to a mystery—the mystery of life and death. But when we disassemble a Muranian robot, no such knowledge follows. All that is revealed are the gears and wheels of a clock, a simple mechanism that even Autry's buffoonish sidekicks understand—and one the serial's audience just as easily comprehends. It is a kind of reassuring turning of the tables on this technological world, as the Muranians' efforts to reveal the complex secrets of human being give way to a human's revelations of this technocracy's simple mechanisms. Demystified in this way, Murania's mechanical men—and all its technological wonders—lose much of their menace and become little more than the charming ornamentation of this other world. An archetypal Shadow image simply disappears in the clear light of our world. Fittingly, this revelation begins Murania's downfall, as the "robot" Oscar and Pete grab the queen and announce, "Don't get excited, lady; we're just taking charge of Murania"—much as the narrative has, at this point, "taken charge" of Murania's powers and mysteries.

Interestingly, this same plot device recurs just a year later in the film *Undersea Kingdom,* one of Republic's first serials. Making full use of the plots, costumes, sets, and props acquired in the takeover of Mascot, Republic conjures up a similar futuristic world in the submerged city of Atlantis, and also fills it with all manner of technological wonders: rockets, tanks, a flying tower, a disintegrating ray, and robots that are only slight variations on the design of those in *Phantom Empire.*[7] The Volkite robots, as they are termed, are strong and menacing, and they do wield ray guns, but like their Muranian ancestors, they are also clumsy, easily avoided, and shown to be little more than clockwork mechanisms. So when the hero "Crash" Corrigan and his scientist friend must escape from a tight spot, it is hardly surprising to find them repeating the earlier serial's narrative ploy: casting out the clockwork mechanisms of a few captured robots, donning their metallic skin, and inhabiting those hollow beings—and with the same success as Autry's sidekicks.

What is most telling about this repetition from one serial to another is the way this assumption of the robot guise speaks to our whole sense of the technological here and in other serials of the period—what it says about their charming vantage on a human artifice. The technology encountered in both *Phantom Empire* and *Undersea Kingdom* seems to function, almost without exception, in the service of human domination, as part of an effort to extend a mechanical, serializing hegemony over humankind. Yet the various rays, rockets, and futuristic tanks of *Undersea Kingdom* are easily dealt with, for the most part in the hand-to-hand tradition of serial action and pulp fiction, and its robots, like those of *Phantom Empire,* prove a kind of clockwork or hollow thing—at any rate, a hollow *threat.* While the technology of these worlds is fascinating in the shapes it takes and the power it suggests, its menace is finally shown to be almost paltry, easily coped with, and the difference it implies hardly a difference at all. So even when these serials point up, as works in the fantasy and science fiction genres almost invariably do, some of our own—and our world's—limitations, they also usually leave those limits unchallenged, our status quo, including our humanity, a thing we can cling to, and our more balanced sense of progress something we might well desire.

Moreover, the characters in these last two serials don their robot guises—and in the process take on their appearance of power and invulnerability—only momentarily, for convenience, and then quickly discard those disguises. It is a pattern that reflects our own experience, the manner in which these films let us assume the trappings of a fascinating technology, *become* artifice. In them, we play at believing in and relishing these images of difference, indulging in a cinematic version of the world's fairs' carnivalesque visions of "progress" and "tomorrow," even experiencing a sense of technological seriality. Yet as each serial's own mechanism winds down, as those narratives slide toward their predictable end, as Murania, for example, collapses under the blasts of its own disintegrating ray gone out of control, we also draw back. And again *Phantom Empire*'s Oscar and Pete, or rather, the mechanical figures they temporarily become, nicely image our own experience. Finished with Murania, they rush back to the safety of our surface world, discarding their robot guises piece by piece as they go. And as each serial winds down, we too put off that garb of the thoroughly modern, technologized being in favor of the known, the everyday, the not-so-technical world we already inhabit.

We might see these mechanical men of the serials as a kind of border guard—and ultimately a quite effective one—marking the point at which both our pleasure in and our potential discomfort with the serials' technological vision converge. They are images not so much of our pleasure as of the *way* we find a charm in the films that give them life. For these films encourage us to "put on" the technological, to relish the power, sense of difference, and the simple thrills all of the serial's trappings imply. Yet they offer that guise as but a temporary retreat, and one that we eventually feel few qualms about casting off in favor of our human identities when it becomes a bit too threatening, strikes too near our own nature, or too starkly scores the problems, limits, or dysfunctions of our world or our all-too-nonartificial selves.

· · ·

Even as they display their standardized components, unfold in a machinelike fashion, and tell their stories of serialization—of efforts to transform the human into a controlled, serial product, a quite *human* artifice
—then, these films build to an untroubling, hardly technologized end.
And that is scarcely surprising, given the far more prosaic, Depression-
and war-haunted worlds to be found back in *our* surface world. Yet while
luring us on, evoking our desires for the other—just as *Metropolis*'s robot
Maria does—through their intriguing images of other worlds, future
times, mechanical servants, they do reveal problems with that lure, and
for that reason then must also draw away from it, pull us back, in the
best serial tradition, as if from a cliff-hanging brink. So while they reflect
a popular fascination with the possible shapes our world and our selves
might take—a fascination our feature films were not quite ready to address—while they let us think the almost impossible, that fascination
seems to take itself only half-seriously. Or more precisely, they just glance
at the implications of this growing interest in a human artifice and the
power of the technological, before discreetly drawing back, leaving this
atmosphere of artifice for the real world.

Of course, Flash Gordon too always left behind the advanced worlds
of Mongo and Mars for Depression-era America, where those alluring
advanced technologies were largely absent and there were no real robots
to combat. That return often saw the various futuristic cities devastated
or destroyed (see the cataclysmic conclusions to *The Lost City, Undersea Kingdom,* and *Phantom Empire* for examples), and the mad scientist,
his arsenal of menacing inventions, and his serializing powers vanquished.
For all of their concern with advanced technology, and for all of the
audience fascination with such trappings that they attest to, then, the
serials seem to take a rather ambiguous stand. They never quite repudi-
ate the technological and the advanced: Flash and Zarkov, after all, may
need their rocket ship sometime in the future, just as Republic would
require those robot costumes for other serials. And certainly, Gene Autry
would need that Muranian "invention" of television to regain his popularity in the 1950s. However, they do pointedly embrace a common, present-
day world, one that, for all its melodramatic trappings, seems to share
the broad outlines and limits of our own.

This charm, this borderline position, however, could not possibly hold.
The serials began to disappear in the immediate post–World War II era,

at the same time that the real impact of our modern technology—atomic weapons, rockets, jet planes, and certainly television—could be neither denied nor safely contained within the concept of seriality. For the war had blasted away not only many national boundaries but even more conceptual ones, and the potential threat of technology as a serializing process, as something that might make us too much like mechanical men, had to seem less pressing in this context. The complete obliteration of humanity would become the central and inescapable issue, and one that could not be easily rendered in such a charming manner.

Along with this shift, the figure of the robot or human double, which would resurface with a vengeance in cold war science fiction films, would change radically. While the serials' mechanical, clockwork beings were stronger and more imposing physically than humans, they were also fundamentally simple things, easily understood and dealt with. But with the war came the computer and the science of cybernetics, which together struck beyond the simple notions of mechanical beings and a mechanized humankind, ultimately controlled by a human intelligence. They gave birth to the seemingly impossible—a truly artificial intelligence, and beings endowed with it who might combine the powers of biology and technology. Along with such figures came far darker, hardly charming considerations, as David Porush explains, "that not only our bodies but also our minds are machines, a consideration that attacks us in that portion of ourselves we consider to be most free, most invulnerable to explanation and control" (*Soft Machine* 3).

Before that time, though, in 1939 a mainstream film, *The Wizard of Oz,* had offered its own charming vision of what the serials were telling us. The Tin Man, who initially so frightened Dorothy, rapped on his chest to show that he didn't have a heart, in fact, that like all such mechanical men, he was really just hollow inside. That very hollowness was central to his charm, part of what assured us he and all the other creations like him were not really threatening. Lacking a heart, as well as all the other internal features that, at the time, seemed to make us what we are, a tin man could at best serve his human masters, even a young girl, and thus work in the way we hoped all technology might work—to help us cope with the dangers and drudgeries of the world we inhabited.

Yet in its heyday, when such considerations were still just exotic impossibilities, the serial had no easy task. It had to play dual roles: catering to a popular interest in the technological and scoring a suspicion of the changes the technological might ring in; functioning for our enjoyment much like a machine, while imaging in its robots and other menacing technologies the threatening aspect of such serialization. The form thus occupied a border region, but a particularly important one for our considerations. From its vantage we could look beyond and glimpse the shapes and problems of our future—a future that was already hinting at ways it might reshape us and render our nature problematic. While its charming character might have blurred this importance, the serial does mark a shift in alignment, a shift in attitudes, especially our attitudes toward an increasingly technologized world that was promising to visit its powers of artifice on the human. Through their increasing ability to press in on our lives in various ways, those powers would demand to be more directly reflected and addressed in the starker science fiction films of the postwar/cold-war era. Prior to that time, the serial had to imagine the impossible for us without undermining a cultural system that, with the Great Depression, had let us glimpse just how fragile and limited it really was.

· NOTES ·

1. It is worth noting that David A. Cook's *History of Narrative Film* offers no mention of the serial, while Gerald Mast's *Short History of the Movies* makes only passing reference to this form. These are, as many students will quickly recognize, the two most widely used film history texts, works which, generally for the better, have come to constitute our sense of cinematic history.

2. A primary example of that utopian literature is Harold Loeb's *Life in a Technocracy: What It Might Be Like* (1933). For an overview of the various utopian forces at work in 1930s America, see Segal's "Technological Utopians."

3. We might note Bruce Kawin's efforts to distinguish the horror and science fiction films in his essay "Children of the Light." He draws the lines between science fiction and horror rather starkly, arguing that those works which value openness and speculation belong to the former category, while those which present that openness as threatening and try to shut off inquiry are of the latter. My own experience suggests that, were we to stick rigidly by these distinctions, we would find much literature but relatively few films to fill the first category.

4. Already a fixture of the silent cinema, the serial, according to Alan Barbour's history of the form, flowered in the 1930s. That decade saw the

production and distribution of 104 serials, each ranging from ten to fifteen episodes in length. In the 1940s, with fewer companies engaged in making serials, production decreased to ninety-one. In the following decade, thanks largely to changing exhibition practices and television's usurpation of the serial's format and subjects, that production dropped rapidly and eventually ceased altogether with Columbia's last efforts in 1956. For background, see Barbour's *Cliffhanger: A Pictorial History of the Motion Picture Serial.*

5. The first serial was subsequently cut and rereleased as the feature film *Rocketship;* over the years it would be recut and reissued as *Spaceship to the Unknown* and eventually as *Space Soldiers.* The second entry in the series, *Flash Gordon's Trip to Mars,* later reappeared as the feature *The Deadly Ray from Mars;* in the 1950s it became *Space Soldiers' Trip to Mars.* The last effort, *Flash Gordon Conquers the Universe,* was turned into two features, *Purple Death from Outer Space* and *Perils from the Planet Mongo,* and it too was eventually altered to *Space Soldiers Conquer the Universe.* The *Buck Rogers* serial of 1939 was similarly recut to feature length, reappearing as *Destination Saturn.* For production and distribution background, see Roy Kinnard's "Flash Gordon Serials." Kinnard reports that the average budget for Universal's other serials of this period was approximately $125,000, while the first of the Flash Gordon entries cost $350,000, "a budget exceeding that allotted most features at the time" (195). While subsequent entries in the series had lower budgets, they benefited from the more lavish sets and miniatures devised for the first film or appropriated from other, more expensive Universal releases.

6. As Kinnard explains, such incongruities were typical of the comic strips upon which the Flash Gordon, Buck Rogers, and many other serials were based. In fact, for the original *Flash Gordon* serial, several of the costumes, "especially the costumes worn by Flash Gordon, Emperor Ming, Prince Barin and Officer Torch, are exact reproductions of [comic strip artist Alex] Raymond's designs" (196).

7. We should note that this design would surface nearly unchanged in Republic's serials over the next sixteen years. For example, the same robots will show up a few years later in *Mysterious Doctor Satan* (1940), and then many years later in such serials as *King of the Rocket Men* (1949) and *Zombies of the Stratosphere* (1952), among others. Certainly, this unchanging image is largely due to studio economic policies, which dictated the reuse of costumes, props, and sets whenever possible. However, it also hints of an unchanging sense of the robot—and hence, the technological in general—as a kind of clanking, mechanical menace, more frightening in appearance than in fact.

5

Science Fiction's Double Focus: Alluring Worlds and Forbidden Planets

"The Lord sure makes some beautiful worlds."
"Another one of them new worlds—no beer, no women, no pool parlors, nothing."
Forbidden Planet

In trying to sketch the shape of our changing modern world, Jean Baudrillard has suggested that for us the real is increasingly being replaced by what he terms the "hyperreal," by "models of a real without origin or reality." We thus find ourselves, he argues, living in an "age of simulation" (*Jean Baudrillard* 166, 167), an era wherein maps take precedence over territories, copies become prized above originals (see Warhol's Campbell's soup cans), and doubles abound, draining away all sense of identity. It is an age, of course, that practically coincides with the first modern imaginings of the robot and the proliferation of a literature of robotism, such as we find in the 1930s and 1940s. Fritz Lang might be said to have described this situation in *Metropolis* when his builders of Babel reformulate god in their own image—and in the process effectively eliminate him—and his scientist Rotwang announces that, thanks to his new robot, "we have no further use for living workers." A sense of origin simply disappears in the wake of certain human technologies; the real surrenders priority to its simulations.

Yet Lang's real focus was less on the simulations than on the desires that drive us to fashion such images, on the motivations—both conscious and unconscious—that compel such human artifice. What his film never worked out so clearly and what our serials, for all of their technological trappings, only glossed over were the implications of that scientific capacity for replication. The great popular fascination with the technological in the 1930s and 1940s—a fascination reflected in the pulp magazines, comics, and serials—does seem to have been satisfied with surfaces, with observing the various wonders our technology might achieve. What attention there is to the *effects* of technological development appears mainly in that analysis of the body's subjection which becomes the sustaining motif of the various horror–science fiction films of the day.

In the 1950s and early 1960s a shift occurs that can be measured in two ways. What we see is a sustained effort to analyze those surfaces, those alluring images that, with the end of World War II and the hardening of the cold war, had begun to take on a far more sinister and menacing attitude. We can gauge that effort first, by noting the near deluge of science fiction movies in the era. As Andrew Dowdy in his history of the period notes, "the fifties was the grand decade of the science-fiction film," a period when "our repressed paranoia visited us reshaped in the basic mythology of science fiction" (170, 159). That "basic mythology" included alien invasions, space exploration, mutated creatures, and, most important for our concerns, a wealth of robotic creations. In fact, our second measure of this shift is the number of times that motif of human artifice surfaces in this period. Among the films that bring it into focus are some of the most important works in the science fiction canon, including *The Day the Earth Stood Still* (1951), *Tobor the Great* (1954), *Gog* (1954), *Invasion of the Body Snatchers* (1956), *The Creature Walks among Us* (1956), *The Invisible Boy* (1957), *The Colossus of New York* (1958), and especially *Forbidden Planet* (1956). These films begin to bring into sharp focus not simply the dangers implicit in our scientific and technological accomplishments but a dangerous redefining of the human that seems to attend an overemphasis on science and technology, on relinquishing power and authority to what Susan Sontag identifies as "the universal rule of reason" (223).

· · ·

The chief danger that attends our increasing technological capacity for producing simulacra is not simply the proliferation of copies or even the varied doubles of the human that might result—although that proliferation may bring either a most troubling sameness or a confusing loss of individuality. Rather, the problem lies in the process of disconnection and devaluation that is a residue of the hyperreal. As simulacra spread and seem to edge out the real, they also undermine its significance. The possibility arises that we might come to assume there *is nothing* beyond the copy itself—no original, no history, ultimately no meaning beyond the simple image. Thus Baudrillard suggests that what we are witnessing throughout our culture today, what we are finally becoming fully aware of, is nothing less than "the murderous capacity of images: murderers of the real; murderers of their own model as . . . Byzantine icons could murder the divine identity" (*Jean Baudrillard* 168).

The lines cited above from the science fiction classic *Forbidden Planet* (1956) tie this problem of the double—what we might term our films' increasing tendency to "see double"—to another difficulty we have already noted, a kind of "double vision" that is inherent in the science fiction genre. On the one hand, these remarks from the crew of the starship C57D point up just how many of these "new" worlds they have seen in their travels through the universe—enough to make them either forget their own planet or to long for its simplest attractions. On the other, these comments indicate how easy it is to see the same subject in quite different ways. While one speaker views the planet Altair IV as wondrous and awe-inspiring, the other reads it far more skeptically, as just another in a long line of planets they have visited, lacking some very basic human satisfactions.

Both of these perspectives are tied to the planet's status as a double, to the fact that it is in many ways not "new" at all—it is even designated "IV"—but a kind of hyperreality out in hyperspace. Thus the first speaker, drawing on other encounters, offers his rather hackneyed, if explicitly meaningful, reading of this planet as a sign of God's handiwork. But the second, drawing on his own experience with such doubles, quickly counters with his view of it as a kind of empty signifier, noteworthy mainly for the absences it marks. Taken together, these observations remind us of how often the science fiction genre seems to pull us in quite opposite directions, while they also announce a central concern of this film with the troubling nature of the double or simulacrum, a concern that, with the 1950s, would increasingly become the focus of our narratives about a human artifice.

I want to view *Forbidden Planet* as an especially representative work not because it is the only or even the best of robot films produced in this period. Indeed, for many students of the genre, Gort, the menacing yet also protective robot of *The Day the Earth Stood Still,* may be the most memorable such figure of postwar science fiction. Yet that film, we should note, shies away from the darker implications of the robot, as it avoids the revelation found in Harry Bates's source story, *Farewell to the Master,* that the humanoid alien Klaatu is actually the servant of the robot. And the most famous effort at examining the troubling implications of the double is certainly the original *Invasion of the Body Snatchers,* with its alien pods that slowly mimic human originals and then displace them. But here artifice separates from the technological in a way that is generally uncharacteristic of the era.

Forbidden Planet offers a revealing combination of these other works and more fully typifies this period's films. Most notably, it fashions a world practically full of doubles. There is, of course, the doubled perspective implied in this chapter's epigraph, as well as doubled characters, repeated actions, and most importantly a thematic concern with duplication or imitation that finds focus in a series of doubles for the central figure, the stranded scientist Dr. Morbius. Particularly, we should note the robot he constructs to serve him and the Id-creature he unwittingly conjures up to protect him and his daughter Alta from outside forces. These creations do more than link the film to the long tradition of doubles and artificial beings we have already noted in the science fiction genre. They also provide the terms through which *Forbidden Planet* can comment on the usual perspective of the science fiction film and eventually reveal a lack in the double, a danger in the simulacrum that justifies the warning its title sounds.

At the same time, there is Robby the Robot, a mechanical figure far more complex than its clockwork ancestors from the serials, while also far more compelling than its friendly name might imply. Robby is, after Lang's robot Maria, probably the most influential mechanical figure in film up to the time of the "lovable" 'droids of *Star Wars,* R2-D2 and C-3PO. We can find some gauge of Robby's popularity in his simple endurance, as he was to make far more subsequent appearances on screen and television than even any of the "tin cans" from the Republic serials.[1] Following *Forbidden Planet,* Robby would appear in *The Invisible Boy,* and later in *Hollywood Boulevard* and *Gremlins,* while his television credits include such shows as *Oh! Susanna, The Addams Family, Goodyear Theater, Hazel, The Red Skelton Show, The Thin Man, The Twilight Zone, Columbo, Wonder Woman,* and *The Dobie Gillis Show.* This longevity—one that surpasses the careers of many film actors—

underscores the extent to which this image, the prototype of what Per Schelde describes as "the cute robots" (158) of a later period in science fiction, took hold in our cultural consciousness. The robot as a docile, nonthreatening, and largely utilitarian creature helped to recast technology, at least superficially, in a far less disturbing light than that provided by our then prevalent narratives of atomic devastation, alien invasion, or human mutation.

. . .

Like most science fiction films, *Forbidden Planet* demonstrates a fundamental sort of double vision, one rooted in its generic concerns. As in earlier films like *Metropolis* (1926), *The Thing* (1951), and *This Island Earth* (1955), it by turns accepts the attractions and lures of science and technology, finding something in them that is awe-inspiring and promising, and rejects those same attractions, as it foregrounds the more extreme and even dangerous forms they can take. In fact, while this film seems to tantalize us with images of the scientific wonders and creations to be found on the distant planet Altair IV, it concludes with its characters abandoning the technologically advanced world of the Krel—the planet's original inhabitants—and with the destruction of this planet whose technology has provided so many of the movie's attractions. The film thus works from a fairly common double vision of its futuristic world—and a double vision made all the more necessary by the forces of the 1950s, when economic prosperity and the great consumer access to modern technology it facilitated were invariably tempered by cold war fears, especially the looming potential for a technological self-destruction, a nuclear holocaust. In keeping with this spirit, then, *Forbidden Planet* admits the lure of the mechanisms and constructs it parades before us, only to pull back, like so many other science fiction films, from that lure, as if it had reassessed the very images or signs with which it so powerfully speaks.

Of course, since the genre's central focus, its raison d'être, is the technological, science, or that "rule of reason" Sontag describes, no science fiction film ever really repudiates that fundamental fascination, regardless of its era's attitudes or the unsettling implications of the genre's motifs—the dystopias (*Metropolis*), calamitous destructions (*Crack in the World* [1965]), or alien invasions (*The Mysterians* [1959]) linked to those trappings. So the science fiction film must always find ways of living with the seductive lure of the technological and the futuristic that informs its every icon, as well as with its audience's desire for those

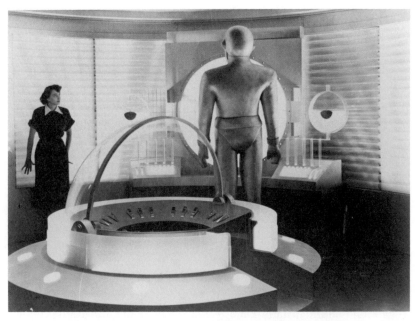

The guardian robot Gort of *The Day the Earth Stood Still.*

The Colossus of New York mates a human brain—and human desires—with a robotic body.

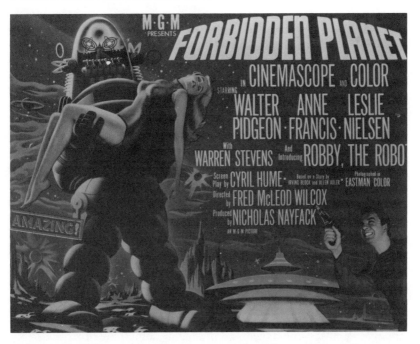

Ad art for *Forbidden Planet* transforms a "cute" Robby the Robot into an alien monster.

Robby the Robot reappears as a child's mechanical friend in *The Invisible Boy.*

alluring images of a future or other world. But under what terms does *Forbidden Planet* live with this lure?

Certainly, that pulling back—in this case, the destruction of the futuristic world of Altair IV and the survivors' fleeing back to Earth—is part of the strategy, for such a catastrophe calls those basic attractions into question. After the pattern of most ideological texts, we get a chance to relish the film's attractive images for a time and then deny their ultimate power over us. But what makes *Forbidden Planet* both interesting and especially revealing is the extra twist, the self-conscious turn its doubles give to that pulling back. For its pattern of seeing double, that is, its imagery of and concern with doubles and doubling, underscored by its central robot figure, eventually echoes the double vision of the science fiction genre and casts it in a more revealing light.

One dimension of this double vision is the way the film intensifies a basic pattern of science fiction—an emphasis on what we might produce, what power we might wield, what shape we might give to our future, that corresponds to the widespread sense of American prosperity and power in this era. In opposition, the film measures the dangers that attend this creative impulse—the dangers of producing something terrible, deploying our technologies in potentially self-destructive ways, using our capacities for artifice to impart a most inhuman shape to our future. The result of this pattern of opposition is an anxiety that lurks in all the images of technological creation these films offer, including their disarmingly "cute" robots. It is this anxiety which gives rise to and eventually justifies Sontag's view that the genre is about the "disaster" or "destruction" (215) our technological attainments, creations, or probes into the universe might set in motion.

While developing this pattern of opposition, *Forbidden Planet* adds another dimension, a reflexive one that directly links it to such recent works as *The Running Man* (1987), *Robocop* (1987), and *Total Recall* (1990). Their explicit subtexts about the media and its role in shaping our culture, and their implicit commentary on film itself suggest a level on which film and audience together might be seen as technological creations, all part of a culture of simulacra such as Baudrillard describes. With this additional focus, a double vision, *Forbidden Planet* demonstrates the sort of analysis of our capacity for simulation—or doubling— that was increasingly becoming central to the science fiction film.

In light of this emphasis on the simulacra and the film's own "double" vision, it is fitting that one of *Forbidden Planet*'s most significant and popular characters—and probably its most memorable—is that mechanical double, Robby the Robot. He is important partly because of his sheer likability—a trait that helped prepare the way for the almost lovable (and even more marketable) robots of the *Star Wars* films.[2] While Robby pointedly has superhuman powers, he is invariably human-centered and clearly under human control. The benevolent and tireless servant, he is programmed to aid humankind with his prodigious strength and special talents, even as he is also rendered innocuous by a built-in safety factor, recalling Asimov's basic "Laws of Robotics," that keeps him from harming humans.[3] In this respect, he marks a significant turning point from the largely sinister roles to which film robots had previously been relegated: as witness the manipulative seductress in *Metropolis,* the malevolent monsters of the serials that we have already examined (see the horrific visage given to the robot in *The Phantom Creeps* [1939]), or especially the invincible and deadly bodyguard Gort of *The Day the Earth Stood Still.* In contrast, Robby is consistently benevolent—helpful, humorous, and nearly magical in his powers—in short, almost all we might hope our technological creations to be.

But besides this revisionist role, he is important because of the way he opens onto the larger consequences of doubling here, helping develop a motif that arises almost whenever a robot appears in film. The robot is, of course, an imitation, a double of the human, and that doubling invariably has both negative and positive implications, depending on whether the robot appears as a threat to humans—our virtual replacement, as films like *Metropolis* or *The Terminator* suggest—or simply a willing servant. From one point of view, it is simply the ultimate appliance, the natural, evolutionary development of the sort of domestic technologies that were in this era becoming widespread. Yet even in such a role, the robot by its very nature insinuates a subtle threat. As Gary Wolfe offers, no matter how crude or benevolent, every robot raises several key questions: "once a simple function of human beings has been replaced, where will it stop? And if a single human function can be supplanted by a mechanism, is it not possible that *all* human functions might one day be so replaced?" (155). So even when presented as our servant and when, as in Robby's case, we know it poses no threat, the robot can still be a troubling presence, precisely because it *is* a double or simulacrum, a kind of mirror of the human that magnifies our problems by showing them in stark or alien terms, and suggests how easily *we* might be replaced by something else—perhaps eventually to be discarded as meaningless or irrelevant to the world's workings. Even as a tool, then, that image comes freighted with a variety of potential meanings and a subtle uneasiness, one which, for all his likability and seeming harmlessness, Robby still embodies.

What particularly foregrounds this issue is Robby's key characteristic. This robot is a strong and tireless worker, a willing servant, and an effective protector—a kind of ultimate man Friday for Dr. Morbius, a castaway on the desert planet of Altair IV, and for his daughter Alta. But when, as he says, he "tinkered" the robot together in his "first months up here," Morbius not only fashioned a more effective replacement for his human companions, all of whom were killed by a mysterious, invisible force; he also built in a seemingly unlimited capacity for duplication, a kind of limitless capability for imitating his own initial creative activity. This special trait shows up when Morbius invites the ship's officers to lunch, providing an elaborate and delicious meal, which he later notes was simply "some of Robby's synthetics." Later, a need for several tons of 2-inch lead shielding brings a promise from Morbius that he will have Robby "run it off" the next day. And indeed, in the morning Robby appears with a suitable substitute, what he terms his "morning's run of isotope 217," which is both lighter and stronger than normal lead. When Morbius's daughter Alta asks for some jewels, Robby informs her that his synthetic "Star sapphires take a week to crystallise. Will diamonds or emeralds do?" And in a comic turn on this mimetic activity, the ship's cook learns of Robby's ability and secretly requests some "genuine Ancient Rocket bourbon"—for private use.

In its comic excesses, this last scene suggests two primary problems that attend the doubling impulse here. First, it indicates a pattern of substitution at work, as the double betters and replaces the original, the "new" becomes the "original." The cook initially asks where he might get some of "the real stuff," but after the fashion of the lead shielding, what Robby provides, a mixture of "alcohol molecules" and "fusel oil," proves better than the "real": 120 proof bourbon that leaves no hangover. Second, this scene points up an absence of boundaries or controls on such creative activity. It is a potential for doubling that could easily run riot and, in the process, bring some very human weaknesses to the surface. As we see, in a nearly unmanageable exaggeration of the cook's request, Robby produces not just another pint of bourbon, but sixty gallons of it, all neatly bottled and labeled in the image of his original pint. It is simply too much, a doubling gone awry that gets the cook in trouble when, unable to control *himself,* he oversamples his new stock and is found drunk and absent from his post. Implicitly, it suggests the sort of trouble that could easily spring from this doubling, a larger loss of control that might result. In fact, as we later learn, it has already occurred, disastrously, with the Krel.

We might view these scenes between Robby and the cook, then, as more than just comic interludes, relief from the film's often discussed focus on "monsters from the Id" (Tarratt 258–77). They are, in fact, a further gloss on that monstrousness we are able to unleash, as they point up the darker implications of the film's many doublings. As we learn, Morbius, a linguist, could "tinker" together this wondrous double and build into his robot a kind of model of his own doubling activity only because he deciphered the secrets of the Krel, the dead super race who had inhabited the planet. When Morbius takes Commander Adams and his starship's officers on a tour of the Krel world, he shows them the remains of a civilization characterized by nearly infinite replication. At the heart of the planet are miles of corridors, each exactly like the others, and 7,800 levels of similar series of corridors which, when gazed at, produce a dizzying panorama of duplication, an infinite mirror maze but without the mirrors. On the one hand, such figures and the awesome images that we see simply suggest the outsized scale of things, and thus the awesome magnitude of the Krel's creations. And of course, such exaggeration, the sense of a nearly limitless creative power, is a central part of the technological lure—the special effects—of this particular science fiction film. But on the other, the repeated cataloging of these details—including remarks about the 400 ventilation shafts "just like" the one they pass above or the note that there are 9200 thermonuclear reactors like the one they view—along with the dizzying, almost Escher-like images of repetitive creation, help shape another pattern here, that of a bewildering replication—a creative power without limit or perspective—that lies at the very heart of the Krel civilization and that already hints at the reason for its disappearance.

Underscoring this impression is the centerpiece of Morbius's tour, his demonstration of the Krel's mind expansion machine, a device that increased his own intelligence and enabled him to create a mechanical double like Robby. This machine is remarkable for a number of reasons. First, it is not, as in so many films that explore the nature of artificial intelligence (for example, *2001: A Space Odyssey* [1969], *Colossus: The Forbin Project* [1970], *The Demon Seed* [1977], *Wargames* [1983]), simply a mechanical mind, an extension of or replacement for the human intellect. Rather, it empowers people in a special way, giving them the ability to increase *their own* intelligence. Second, the Krel machine, as it is demonstrated and later put to deadly use, seems a device devoted to mimesis, to various sorts of artifice. It achieves its remarkable effects by exercising its subjects' mimetic capacities: inducing them to reproduce whatever they might imagine, even their own extension—a mechanical being who can, in turn, reproduce whatever one might need or imagine. To demonstrate the machine's workings, Morbius dons its headpiece and thinks of his daughter; then a living, three-dimensional image of Alta appears. With enough sessions at the machine, he explains, one can fashion such animate images at will, or as he puts it, free "from any dependence on physical instrumentality." In effect, with enough practice, one can become not only like Robby the Robot, but better, free to create images without any mechanical restraints—and ultimately without any model, any correspondence in reality, or any *moral* constraints.

It is in this very freedom that the dark side of this force, of Morbius, of the film's doubling motif, even of its robot surfaces, when a fantastic creature begins terrorizing the newcomers—a creature like that which had previously wiped out Morbius's own party, and which apparently had destroyed the whole Krel race. Invisible yet tremendously powerful, this creature can steal among the spaceship's crew and, undetected, kill one of them, as if in warning, or it can attack the entire ship and prove invulnerable to every defense. Working from a cast of a footprint, the ship's doctor describes this menace as something that "runs counter to every known law" and "just doesn't fit into normal nature." He is, in fact, quite correct; it has no model in nature, no reference in reality. It is a hyperreal monster—or might we say, the monstrous, murderous shape that the hyperreal might well take.

This creature is, in fact, a double or simulacrum, as well as an interesting trope for the murderous play of imagery Baudrillard describes. The film simply terms it, in one of the most famous formulations of the genre, a "monster from the id," a projection of Morbius's unconscious. Liberated from the repressive power of the superego, this image of his darker self, a kind of psychic robot, has been set loose to rid the planet of its bothersome intruders. Yet it is also something more than this Freudian model simply suggests, for he has conjured a model that is of him, yet ultimately has no correspondence in "normal nature." It is not just his "evil self," as he terms it, but quite an other self, one that ultimately drains him of his very life. Unwittingly, Morbius has tapped the ultimate Krel discovery, that of the dangerous power of the simulacrum.

Yet these two explanations are finally much the same. For that power to generate an Otherness and that Otherness itself, with its seeming ability to drain the self of power, to replace the appearance that we like to think of as the real, are in a way reformulations of the id. Through their advanced technology, the Krel had learned how to "instantaneously project solid matter to any point on the planet, in any shape or color they might imagine, for any purpose." In following their lead, Morbius has unconsciously dispatched a creature "that doesn't fit into normal nature"—into nonrepressed nature—to accomplish his darkest desires. But the capacity for "creation by mere thought," as Commander Adams puts it, destroyed that ancient race. Their ability to create psychic doubles and hyperreal images, Morbius recognizes, had ultimately released a dangerous Other, "the secret devil of every soul on the planet," a latent, normally repressed violence that left only their machinery—a kind of sign without meaning, a partial, technologized self—to mark their passing. In using their technology to give body to his own unconscious violent urges, Morbius has, in turn, become a double of the Krel: intellectually advanced far beyond the human and menacing in the destructive energy his doubling has released. Having unleashed "the murderous capacity of images," a capacity that promises to leave us with simulacra without referents or originals, Morbius reveals the simultaneously destructive and creative dimensions of the doubling impulse, the aspirations to become something more than we are that can leave us as less, grotesque and dangerous *versions* of the self, id-creatures.

In keeping with this pattern, we see that just as their technology, via their simulacra, eventually did away with the Krel, so too does Morbius's model "without . . . reality" promise his own destruction, and in the process underscore a link between this doubling activity and the double image of the technological that the film offers. Sealed off by the Krel's fantastically hard metal doors, Morbius, along with Alta and Commander Adams, takes shelter from his creature within the bowels of the planet, amid the very machinery and power plants that have made this destructive creation possible. Yet even there his own double pursues, crashing or melting through every barrier, like some self-pursuing phantom of desire and destruction—a paradigm of the murderous image that lurks in every science fiction film.

It is as if the film itself were struggling to bring together these two apparently different doubling activities, to fashion, through Morbius's new awareness of what he has wrought, a kind of self-consciousness of its own. And indeed, consciousness is the goal here, for both Morbius and, after the limited fashion that audiences of the 1950s might have accepted, the film as well. When Morbius recognizes the link between the destructive double he has unleashed and the technological attainments that have so seduced him, that awareness effectively dispels its power. Appropriately, as the lights go out on the rows of power panels surrounding him, as the film's "special effects" dissipate, so too does Morbius's double disappear. And in that recognition and consequent dispelling of the demon, *Forbidden Planet* models the sort of resolution for which the science fiction film so often reaches. It metaphorically disavows its very attractions, while cautioning against the sort of destructive force—what Morbius describes as "some dark, terrible, incomprehensible force"—that may wait in all of our technological creations.[4]

There remains only the abandonment and destruction of this "new" world, this copy like so many other copies, and so unlike the "real" world the film's characters—even Alta, who has never known anything else— now long for. Altair IV, the world of replication "without instrumentality" and without life, must finally be left behind, even destroyed because of the dangers it represents: the practically limitless power it offers anyone who comes there, and the nearly irresistible lure that power of artifice seductively holds out, enabling anyone to follow the Krel path—to become *like* them and unleash an impulse for *likeness,* regardless of its monstrous consequences. The alternative is a safer, known, real world, an Earth—"home"—whose naturalness is now affirmed and embraced, thanks to the revealed dangers of this copy world.

Appropriately, in deciphering the Krel's secrets Morbius had discovered not only their powers of creation but also a tangible sign of their death instinct, a switch that, robotically, sets the Krel machinery into a self-destruct mode. As a way of insuring his daughter's—and humanity's— safety from these impulses, therefore, he arranges for the simulacrum to turn this power upon itself, for Altair IV to blow itself apart. But first the C57D must speed its passengers away, millions of miles out in space, from where they safely view this destruction. It is, of course, what we too do at this point. For while we watch on our movie screen as these characters—our doubles, who are themselves doubles of the actors playing these roles—watch Altair's destruction on their viewing screen, we too pull back to a "safe" distance, to a proper perspective on this world, to the secure present from which the movies allow us to view every utopian/dystopian fantasy they offer. Safe within that present, bound in our far less dangerous and more "natural" culture, we can more easily resist the alluring imagery this and other science fiction films offer. In effect, we act out the genre's dynamics, but in this case, thanks to the doubling patterns here being analyzed, not without some awareness of how artificial, even forced, that retreat typically is.

Forbidden Planet, in the best tradition of 1950s science fiction, thus manages to have its cake and eat it too. The dark Other, Morbius's monstrous id, is vanquished, and the Krel technology—clearly a kind of self-destructive power—is abandoned, even destroyed. However, that abandonment is not quite complete. In our science fiction narratives, the present, however begrudgingly, usually comes to accept some elements of that future or other world that has been depicted. The desire that drives us to the genre, after all, must be placated in some way, and American audiences of the 1950s, with their global power and technological leadership, could hardly have disavowed so much of what had come to signal their status in the world. So *Forbidden Planet* concludes by reaching some compromise with the technological, including its doubling power. Again, Robby the Robot is key, for this fascinating technological double survives as a reminder of all that has happened and an emblem of how much we are ultimately tied to the technological and its powers. Robby, in fact, is harnessed to replace the ship's navigator, who had been killed by Morbius's double. The technological, we are reassured, might yet *help* us find our way.

Of course, for all its humanness, even for its ability to fit into the crew and to become a kind of clanking drinking buddy to the cook, the robot bears some trace of the dark potential that eventually destroyed both Morbius and the Krel. Like them, it is a double with the ability to double, a copy who, as we have seen, can replicate anything, and even substitute its own formulations—a "real without origins," better than "genuine." Reassuringly, we do know that *it* cannot harm humans, only serve them, as it now works in a necessary capacity to bring them back to Earth where they belong. Apparently, we can use and even need some of these technological marvels. Yet the robot also stands as a reminder, even more than Morbius's name,[5] of what can bring harm. It is our own failure to see doubly, to perceive the destructive capacity that lurks in our every creative effort or technological advance, and to recognize how our creations might well work contrary to the very impulses that brought them into being.

. . .

This chapter's epigraph pointed to a certain anxiety about our techno-logical doubles or imitations of the real, an anxiety less explicit than implicit in their very being, a sense that they could in subtle ways sub-vert our sense of the real. At the same time, it suggested the sort of double vision that typifies the genre, a tendency to accept but also draw back from the alluring technological imagery that empowers the science fiction film and that finds specific embodiment in every robot. What this chapter suggests is how these two concerns were becoming fundamen-tally linked, in fact, almost identical. The science fiction film commonly asks us to accept some elements of the hyperreal, to recognize that our world is constantly changing, constantly producing the new, and in the process altering its notions of what is "real" or original. That difference is, after all, what the future and the other worlds science fiction envi-sions are all about, even what the robot is about. In *Forbidden Planet*'s many variations on a doubling motif we see some of the problems that difference increasingly posed.

Yet even as the science fiction film asks us to accept this protean vision, it also cautions us to see its complexity, its almost inevitable doubleness, and to embrace it cautiously. As *Forbidden Planet* further illustrates, these concerns were beginning to result in a kind of reflexive commentary—on the science fiction genre and, to some extent, even on film and its reliance on such alluring imagery. This level of commentary acknowledges the anxiety that lies behind our every creation, our every effort to craft images that delight and attract, as well as the ease with which we might buy into those images. The key image of human artifice here, embodied in Robby the Robot, reminds us to consider the conse-quences that attend all our artifice, as it evokes the elusive, unpredictable, almost treacherous nature of the images we—and our films—contrive: what Baudrillard, perhaps a bit too ominously, labels their "murderous capacity."

Of course, the pattern described here largely reflects that fundamen-tal conflict which always runs through our science fiction films: that double attitude toward science, technology, and reason that we have noted. Our creations—the products of science, the shapes of technology, the images conjured by our reason, especially those of a human artifice—

are both alluring and potentially dangerous. Invariably, like Morbius, we find ourselves fascinated, even seduced by those creative possibilities, while down deep, like the skeptical Commander Adams, we remain wary of how easily those possibilities can take a destructive turn. But if an "imagery of destruction," such as Sontag found throughout the great flood of science fiction films in the 1950s and early 1960s, indicates the genre's often rather superficial reaction to contemporary anxieties—what she terms "an *inadequate response*" (227), on our culture's part—then its flip side, this anxiety of creation I have identified, which takes full shape in a recurrent concern with artifice, particularly the human artifice of our robots and androids, suggests that something more and perhaps better was also pulsing through these films.

That "better" is not just a sense of the broad implications of human artifice but also some effort to address the issue. Caught in a kind of double bind between science fiction's inevitably alluring, futuristic imagery and the fears of what dangerous forces that future might bring, and in an era that found itself celebrating its rapid technological advances while preparing for the nuclear holocaust that at times seemed like it would inevitably follow from those advances, *Forbidden Planet* reflects this bind in a pattern of doubling, one that admits the genre's own Otherness while warning of a certain Otherness in us as well.

Other movies of this period would similarly bring us to pause and question the very images with which the genre speaks so seductively to the modern psyche, and in a generally similar way. *Invasion of the Body Snatchers* would deploy its seed-pod imitations of the human to indict a creeping sameness—in body *and* mind—in our culture. *The Colossus of New York* would envision a scenario for immortality with its human brain lodged in a robotic body, but would warn about humanity being lost when plunged within that technological context. And *The Fly* would remind us of what monstrous doubles we might conjure up with its vision of technologically jumbled genes. In all of these films we face a partially familiar image, but one that, like no simple reflection, has a double outline. It is a human image, that of a creator who is also a destroyer, a modeler who is fascinated by, even attracted to, the prospect of fashioning his own replacement. But with this double focus, these films try to help us see the human original behind the artifice a bit more clearly.

· NOTES ·

An earlier version of this chapter appeared as "Science Fiction in Double Focus: *Forbidden Planet*" in *Film Criticism* 13.2 (1989): 25–36 and is reprinted with changes by permission of the editor.

1. In his book *Movie Magic,* John Brosnan explains that Robby was "one of the most elaborate robots ever built for a film production. More than two months of trial and error labour were needed to install the 2,600 feet of electrical wiring that operated all his flashing lights, spinning antennae and the complicated gadgets that can be seen moving inside his transparent dome-shaped head. Robby was so expensive that MGM felt obliged to use him again" in subsequent productions (198–99). What Brosnan does not note is that Robby was also inhabited; an actor was inside all the time. Interestingly, one of the two actors who took turns "playing" Robby was Frankie Darro, a costar of the serial *Phantom Empire,* and thus familiar with those simple tin can robots of an earlier era. Brosnan's argument also begs an interesting question beyond the scope of this piece—to what extent the negative image of the robot in film may have been conditioned by similar financial/resource considerations, particularly in the case of "poverty row" studios like Republic and Columbia. Having fashioned—although obviously cheaply —a particularly dehumanized and menacing figure, such as the "tin can" soldiers of *Undersea Kingdom* (1936), would Republic have felt constrained to proliferate that image simply on the basis of available resources, or was this indeed the prevailing popular image of the robot? Other testimony, such as Electro, the robot of the New York World's Fair of 1939, and the emerging fiction on the subject hint at the possibility of a rather more favorable popular view of the robot.

2. We might note that while *Star Wars* is often credited with starting the trend of successfully merchandising itself via toys, games, and other licensed products, *Forbidden Planet*'s Robby is something of a pioneer in this area. Toy copies of the robot in a variety of forms, produced without regard to copyright by several Japanese companies, are today avidly sought after by collectors of movie memorabilia and toys.

3. John Baxter in *Science Fiction in the Cinema* acknowledges *Forbidden Planet*'s heavy indebtedness to science fiction literature, as well as to Shakespeare, and particularly notes the influence of Isaac Asimov's three "Laws of Robotics" (112). In the film Dr. Morbius calms his visitors' uneasiness about Robby by describing the robot's programming in terms that recall the first of Asimov's laws: "A robot may not injure a human being nor, through inaction, allow a human being to come to harm."

4. That "incomprehensible force" is the simultaneously creative and de-

structive power that Morbius, like the Krel before him, wields. It suggests, in effect, a violence we do to ourselves, an anxiety about our acts of creation, which hints of how our every act of creation unleashes—free from "instrumentality" or a repressive psyche—a potential for self-destruction. For another vivid example of this pattern, we need only think of a later film like *Star Trek II—The Wrath of Khan* (1982). That narrative revolves around possession of the Genesis Project, a device that, as the name implies, can create life itself where previously there was only a dead planet, yet might also be deployed as a terrible weapon, capable of unleashing monumental destruction if it falls into the wrong hands.

5. Morbius's name seems to combine the Latin *morbidus* and *morbus,* words that translate as "sickly," and as "sickness" or "disease." At the same time, it recalls the Möbius strip, which turns upon itself to create a visual effect whereby its outside edge is also its inside. It thereby suggests a self-enclosed representational world, wherein the thing becomes its own double as it forms a spiral—and a spiral that, like the doubling in this film, leads nowhere, only back to itself. The implications of the naming in this film extend beyond Morbius, though. We should note as well Alta (or Altaira, as she is once termed), which suggests "other," and Commander Adams, who seems very much an Adamic figure when he is paired with Alta in the Eden-like garden outside her home.

6

Lost Horizons: *Westworld, Futureworld,* and the World's Obscenity

> The schizo is bereft of every scene, open to everything in spite of
> himself, living in the greatest confusion. He is himself obscene,
> the obscene prey of the world's obscenity. What characterizes
> him is less the loss of the real, the light years of estrangement
> from the real, the pathos of distance and radical separation, as is
> commonly said: but . . . the absolute proximity, the total instan-
> taneity of things, the feeling of no defense, no retreat. It is the
> end of interiority and intimacy, the overexposure and transpar-
> ence of the world which traverses him without obstacle. He can
> no longer produce the limits of his own being.
>
> —Jean Baudrillard ("Ecstasy" 134)

Everywhere we turn in the contemporary world, Baudril-
lard suggests, we seem to be in the process of redefining our relationship
to reality. In fact, we seem to have no choice, for increasingly we recognize that we no longer inhabit a world of objects separate and distinct
from the self, one of a comfortable distance and distinction, one of objective spectacle. Rather, thanks to what he terms the "ecstasy of communication" that enfolds us and, in the process, evaporates many of the
demarcations and boundaries we have been accustomed to, we seem to
move, much like a culture of schizophrenics, in a world of lost horizons,
in fact, in a world where the real—even *our own* sense of reality—seems
to vanish in our every effort to grasp it. The result is what he terms an
"obscene" quality that modern life has taken on, a forced and intimate

mingling of the self and the world, a confusion that can be, much like the science fiction film itself, by turns exhilarating and frightening. It is one with which, as our films attest, we are struggling to come to terms, often through that fantasy of robotism.

If *Forbidden Planet* and its contemporaries—films like *Invasion of the Body Snatchers* (1956), *The Creature Walks among Us* (1956), or *The Colossus of New York* (1958)—began to reveal the effects of a human artifice on our sense of self, it would take a later group of films to begin assessing the nature of those effects, to diagnose a kind of "obscenity" which might follow from that dissolution of boundaries. In the 1960s and 1970s, with the first movement of robots into the factories, the rapid development of and reliance upon artificial intelligence, and the ascent of the computer to a position as what J. David Bolter in *Turing's Man* terms "the defining technology and principal technological metaphor of our time" (40), the notion of human artifice became less a distant prospect or alien threat—something we might, as in *Forbidden Planet,* fly away from or that, as *Invasion of the Body Snatchers* imagines, might quite accidentally alight on Earth—and more a discomfiting feature of our cultural landscape.

As *Forbidden Planet* already hints, the central focus of our films about artifice in this period becomes less simply the robot itself, the mechanical figure, than the intelligence that drives it—an intelligence that was already promising to become all too indistinguishable from the human. An early and cheaply made effort like *Creation of the Humanoids* (1963) marks a step in this direction, with a plot that both looks back to Capek's *R.U.R.* and forecasts the more recent *Terminator* films. It describes a postapocalyptic world wherein the necessity for robot workers gradually produces a plot to replace all humans with robots, able to mimic their human models in every detail and every response. If its futuristic setting and basement-budget effects kept this film's menacing scenario at something of a safe distance, the same could not be said for the highly successful adaptation of Ira Levin's novel *The Stepford Wives* (1975). In this film (and, to a lesser extent, its two sequels) the nearness of the threat is one of its most chilling aspects, as the wives in the all-too-typical small town of Stepford, Connecticut, gradually succumb to a creeping sameness, blandness, and lifelessness. They are being replaced, one by one, with look-alike robots who become, in effect, the perfect mates for Stepford's male leaders. With *The Terminal Man* (1974) both the potential for replacement and the very nearness of that menace take what may be the ultimate twist, as a computer scientist has a small terminal emplanted in his brain. With what might be described as the final barrier breached, with the human brain invaded and supplanted by its own technological creation, with the self rendered little more than a shell or shadow of the original being, the human practically *becoming* robotic, there seems no safe haven from the power of our artifice.

I would like to focus our consideration of this shift from separation to a discomfiting intimacy, from distance to a Baudrillardian "obscenity" found in our narratives of human artifice on a pair of films that rather neatly link this problem of distance with our contemporary loss of the real. Michael Crichton's *Westworld* (1973) and its sequel *Futureworld* (1976) are about distant diversions from our everyday world, theme parks populated with robots. They depict a near future in which our technological ability to reshape reality or tailor our own versions of the real, largely due to our mastery of human artifice, becomes yoked to the gratification of our most basic desires. The experiences that result from the loss of any real distance in these films suggest a kind of threatening obscenity that may lurk even in what we might conventionally think of as the least obscene context, a cold, rational, thoroughly technologized modern world, and one dedicated entirely to our amusement and service. But as Baudrillard might put it, these films obscenely sketch the difficulty of being human—or at least of being something other than a schizophrenic human—in a technological age that increasingly crowds upon us and at times threatens to crowd us out.

• • •

Before exploring the *World* films, we need to look more carefully at what the "world's obscenity," as Baudrillard puts it, consists of. The truly obscene, he says, rests not in any display or abuse of the body but in the very *displayability* of all things in the modern world, in their immediate openness and vulnerability. Literally, it denotes a standing in front of the scene of life, without any secure boundaries or borders for protection, with the self left open, defenseless, a completely public image. As he explains, in the humanly shaped but technologically defined and media-suffused environment we inhabit, all distinction between "public space" and "private space" seems to be disappearing. And as private life and public spectacle collapse, everything "becomes transparence and immediate visibility" in a way that he likens to the effect of a "sexual close-up in a porno film" ("Ecstasy" 130). While the distinction we once enjoyed between the public and private spheres served a salutary function—or

A robotic sameness: *The Stepford Wives'* vision of mechanically domesticated women.

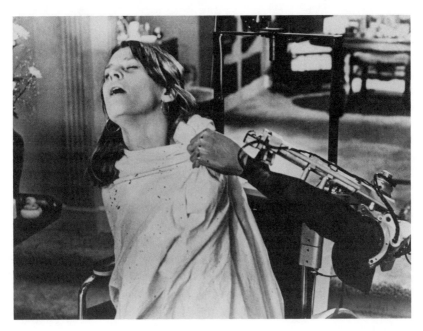

Robotic rape: *The Demon Seed* takes the linkage of artifice and desire to its nightmarish extreme.

The android gunslinger presides over *Westworld*'s deadly amusement park.

The reporter encounters the only recognizably nonhuman android in *Futureworld*.

The lovable robots of the *Star Wars* trilogy: C-3PO and R2-D2.

"symbolic benefit" (130), as he puts it—of constituting an "other" for the self (affirming "that the Other exists"), its contemporary collapse and attendant "extroversion of all interiority" (132) has left us somewhat unsure of our "limits," uncertain just what constitutes the self any more, adrift in a culture of schizophrenics.

In their development of the human artifice motif, *Westworld* and *Futureworld* address just such a turn of circumstance, as if reflecting a growing awareness of how much our sense of self has collapsed or been swallowed up by an "obscene" world, driven by the impulse for artifice. What these films describe is a pattern that will increasingly inform our science fiction films: a tendency of the self to disappear or be reduced to little more than superficies that seems directly proportional to our growing ability to rework our world and our selves. Both films take place in a kind of Disneyland for adults, a place devoted to translating private "scenes," the space of desire, into public space. The first begins in the future with a television commercial touting a new theme park, Delos, which offers visitors three venues for their amusement: Romanworld, Medievalworld, and Westworld. The second film opens with a similar televised introduction to the theme park, but it emphasizes that this is a "reopening" of a "redesigned" world, pointedly different, safer yet more exciting than its predecessor, and with more venues from which to choose. In effect, it is a reconstruction of a world already dedicated to reconstruction, and thus a place where the very notion of "limits" or differentiation seems practically irrelevant.

What both films have in common—and what seems to constitute their main attraction—is not simply the quaintly different *experiences* they describe in these public arenas; rather, it is the *human dimension* they give to those experiences, a dimension that derives from their reliance on human artifice. As an advertisement for Delos notes at the start of *Westworld,* these vacation venues are peopled with "robots scientifically programmed to look, act, talk, and even bleed just like humans do," and they "are there to serve you and to give you the most unique vacation experience of your life." In *Futureworld* that impulse goes a step further, as a vacation land peopled with ever more lifelike robots and partly designed by the robots themselves begins to set its own agenda, which involves producing a new generation of genetically engineered, programmed beings, completely indistinguishable from their human models and intent on taking their places in the outside world. In fact, since the original robots were already nearly indistinguishable from the guests, it might be argued that this project is already far along. By linking the appeal of this human similitude to the ultimate threat that every double invariably poses—namely, that it might replace the self—these films suggest a sense of self that is rapidly collapsing, falling prey to this world's "obscenity."

. . .

At the outset, however, both *Westworld* and *Futureworld* reassuringly suggest a context of distance, a public space quite separate from that private space about which we are often so protective. As the films' titles imply, these narratives seem to be about other worlds and other times than our own. Like Disneyland/Disney World, the vacation venues depicted here simply offer visitors re-creations, spectacles for their amusement, albeit done far more convincingly—and with a greater mind to our unspoken desires—than any Disney "audioanimatronics." In fact, we note that these special places can only be reached by hovercraft in *Westworld* and by jumbo jet in *Futureworld,* and the trips to this isolated locale are infrequent. Delos is, in effect, portrayed and sold as the ultimate "getaway" from the real world.

And yet, the real—or rather, the nearness with which we can approach it—is the true lure of this resort. The various vacation worlds, guests are assured, are "precise to the smallest detail." In testimony to this precision, a returning vacationer gushes that "It's the realest thing I've ever done; I mean that!" Of course, the latter remark hints of a more general impoverishment of human experience, a common inability of the people in this world to find meaningful access to reality in their normal lives, as if the everyday was already little more than a public space, a realm of simulacra, an unreal world inhabited by people who are increasingly unsure of their own reality. While the Delos experience is presented as a vacation from the pressures of the real world, then, it also seems to function as a kind of insulation against a commonplace "loss of the real." By offering guests a robot-driven wealth of simulacra, an almost obscene surfeit of what they are encouraged to take for the real, it disguises that condition of loss and effectively re-presents itself as more real than real.

This strange mixture of distance and intimacy, of a desire to get away from the world and a need to gain some new contact with it, says much about the project of both films. On one level, these theme parks, by their very nature, thrive on obliterating distance, on inviting viewers to cast off—along with their normal inhibitions—any sense that what they are experiencing is different from the real. The cowboys who get shot in Westworld look like, fall like, and bleed like the real thing, so they effectively transport the vacationers to a real wild west. The maidens who are pursued and bedded by the "knights" visiting Medievalworld feel and respond like the real thing. The slaves who are used and abused in Romanworld's orgies and circuses appear genuinely human. These figures seem intended not only to put visitors back in those worlds, but also to put them back in touch with themselves, helping them regain a lost private self by giving free rein to all that modern, technologized culture represses. Yet on another level, these worlds encourage a retreat from the very reality they evoke—a retreat from pain, responsibility, human caring, ultimately from the *human* world we inhabit.

They are, in a sense, realms that cater to—and effectively reinforce—the general schizophrenia of modern life. Thus Delos encourages visitors to immerse themselves completely in its ersatz environments, to take on and, for a short time, live to the hilt whatever roles they might desire, before returning to their normal lives in the "real world." As one vacationer, John, tells his partner Pete in *Westworld,* "You got to get into the feel of things." Yet even on the simplest level that "feel" turns out to be a bit discomfiting. As Pete quickly notes about the "West of the 1880s" with its scratchy clothes, dirty streets, and poor accommodations, "at least they could have made it more comfortable." And that reaction hardly differs in the antiseptic conditions of simulated space flight of *Futureworld,* as one worried guest's response to another attests: "There's nothing to worry about; it's all playlike. We're not really going anywhere—I think." At least initially, having a gunslinger in Westworld suddenly insult and challenge a guest only shifts that edge of discomfort to a more emotional level, as does the view of a street that, by day's end, is quite littered with "dead bodies," all of them, of course, only robots.

In recompense for such slight discomforts and emotional twinges, visitors like John and Pete are made comfortable in other ways, for instance, by the willing companionship of robotic "saloon girls." Also, the gunslingers are programmed to lose every gunfight, and in the night clean-up crews spruce up the streets and restock the venues with more "authentic" characters and future victims. Yet for all these ministrations, one can only really enjoy these worlds by becoming a kind of schizophrenic. Violence, robbery, and even murder offer unparalleled excitement to the individual, as he puts aside his normal self and acts freely in the knowledge that he suffers no responsibility for his acts and that ultimately no one is truly hurt. A successful encounter with a gunslinger makes the pulse race and strokes the ego, but only because the encounter is rigged from the start; as one character explains, the guns provided "won't fire at anything with a high body temperature, only something cold like a machine," so the guest always wins. In effect, every encounter, including a sexual dalliance with a saloon girl or Roman slave, requires that the human involved adopt two personalities: that of the participant, fully committed to the reality of this experience, and that of the observer, who stands safely outside that reality, beyond the implications of his involvement, able to relish all that his seemingly irresistible or invulnerable self does.

Still, as *Westworld* points up, such a cultural schizophrenia invariably carries a danger. As is typically the case in stories of utopias and technological wonders, something goes wrong. Here the robots begin acting contrary to their programming: in a kind of technological reworking of original sin, the "logic circuits" on a snake fail to respond, a medieval queen "programmed for infidelity" refuses a guest's seduction, another guest is stabbed in a duel, and the robot gunslinger starts winning his showdowns—shooting the guests. Even the controls act up, leaving the technicians locked in their airtight control rooms where eventually they all suffocate. In such circumstances the observing self and the participating self suddenly and disturbingly collapse together—and in that collapse any sense of irresistibility or invulnerability quickly vanishes, as the human falls victim to his human artifice.

The ultimate getaway that *Westworld* describes thus simply models the culture of schizophrenia that much of modern life and especially our artifice seem to promote. It is, after a fashion, a getaway of the self from the self, a splitting of the self that, the film warns, can only end in a collapse of those identities one upon the other—a collapse imaged in the figure of Pete, who slumps down exhausted and terrorized at film's end, as he waits for the next onslaught of the seemingly implacable, infinitely renewable robot gunslinger who has been stalking him. Like the technicians who earlier asserted that they were "in full control" of their robotic paradise, only to end up its trapped and suffocated victims, so too is Pete, along with the other guests at Delos, left with precisely the "feeling of no defense, no retreat" Baudrillard describes; or as one of the dying technicians simply puts it, "You haven't got a chance." Acceding to the artifice, giving in to that modern schizophrenia—the ultimate vacation—the film suggests, leaves one with no private space to retreat to, and thus unable to offer any resistance, completely vulnerable to "the world's obscenity."

• • •

If *Futureworld* makes that schizophrenic menace more explicit, it also seems to accept it as almost a given of modern life, something that we have no choice but to face. During the credit sequence, the camera tracks in to a close-up of a human eye, in the iris of which we see reflected the image of a man. We move closer and closer to that reflected image until all we see is *his* eye, the iris of which eventually matches, even replaces that of the original eye into which we had been looking. So when the camera tracks back out to the face with which the scene began—a face identical to that of the reflected image—we can no longer tell whose eye or whose face we are looking at. It is a disturbing scene that sets the agenda for the ensuing narrative: an image in which all sense of distance blurs, in which we come face to face with our human image, and in which an eye not only matches but eventually replaces its model. What that image quickly points to is not only a potential for alternate versions of the self but the menace implicit in all our narratives of human artifice: a blurring of any distinction between versions of the self, coincident with a distortion of the space the self occupies. With its opening focus on the eye, on a threat to the very way in which we see, *Futureworld* challenges viewers to face that prospect squarely, to see clearly the challenge of the simulacrum.

That opening pattern of duplication and replacement again follows from an effort at turning the private into the public. This film too focuses on the "dream resort" Delos, newly improved and expanded—in fact, it even promises to expand *into* the ultimate private space, the world of our dreams. The main concern of this film, though, is not with sketching the possibilities of a robotic resort but with exploring *how* such a realm would operate. As newspaper reporter Chuck Browning and television personality Tracy Ballard tour the reopened Delos, what comes into focus is less its Disneyland allure than its curious inner workings, less the spectacles it offers for human consumption than the impulse that drives it—the way it tries to reshape *everything,* including its human visitors, as spectacle. For everything here seems to be appropriated and publicized: every action is displayed on monitors, every robotic function produces a host of sensor readings, every interaction between a visitor and robot is carefully monitored. Delos's latest innovation takes this nearly universal monitoring to its logical end. In a development that looks forward to *Total Recall*'s implanted dreams, it offers a machine that lets one look "directly into" the mind, a dream chamber that can "convert thought waves back into the images the mind creates," and thereby turn one's dreams into a spectacle for all to see, even record for later playback. So all that we normally internalize, repress, keep to the self can here be turned outward and monitored, or be replayed for others as a kind of ultimate home movie. The end result is that within this ultimate vacation space there simply *is* no private space, nowhere that one can "get away" to.

And that monitoring is only a sort of panoptic model for the larger transformation of the private into the public that, as Chuck and Tracy discover, is the ultimate aim of the new Delos. Impelled by a sense of what a "very unstable, irrational, violent animal" the human being is, Dr. Schneider, the genius behind the resort, has devised a plan to avert what he sees as humanity's inevitable destruction of the planet. According to this plan, the key leaders and opinion makers throughout the world will be invited to Delos and there gradually replaced by duplicates so precise that "even those of us who create them can't tell the original from the duplicate." And all of these replacement leaders are programmed, not with Asimov's "three laws of robotics" but with a rather different fundamental agenda, to advance the interests of Delos. What that plan produces is a general supervision designed to render everyone and everything transparent. It is, in effect, a kind of inverting of the world itself, as all of life becomes monitored and supervised, a new kind of public arena—the world as Disney World—which in turn ironically transforms the resort into the one private, privileged, secret space at the center of life—eventually the only place free from supervision because it is the unquestioned principle behind all supervision.

With this extrapolation from *Westworld*'s original conception, *Futureworld* presents an even more disturbing vision than its predecessor. While *Westworld,* through its robots and robotic resort, forces us to look directly at the sort of physical obscenities in which we too easily take pleasure—killing, bondage, gluttony, and so on—the later film explores the impulses at work beneath these simple, personal obscenities—the widespread impulses to objectify, oversee, and dominate all things, urges typically associated with an increasingly scientific, technologized world, and here given power through our mastery of human artifice, in effect, through an ability to render the human little more than a robot. These impulses, implicit in the first film, explicit in the second, work to turn the world inside out, make it transparent, a public spectacle, and in the process, render reality itself ever more elusive and evanescent.

While produced by different directors and writers, then, these two films trace out a consistent and dangerous development based on the premise of a completely convincing human simulacra. In this development, the films suggest that the violence to which modern culture seems so prone—a violence chillingly detailed in *Westworld*—may actually be less transgressive, less dangerous than the spread of simulacra that *Futureworld* envisions. Violence, after all, is waged over the real. To Baudrillard's thinking, it is just one manifestation of the common human tendency for contention. But simulation, in contrast, "is infinitely more dangerous ... since it always suggests, over and above its object that *law and order themselves might really be nothing more than a simulation*" (*Simulations* 38)—and perhaps that the *only* order might be that of simulation. This prospect is precisely what *Futureworld* sketches: a world governed by simulacra, all of them produced and monitored by other simulacra, and put in place precisely to extend the general order of simulacra. It is a world in which there can no longer be anything but public space, and consequently in which there can only be schizophrenic beings, figures like those being created deep within Delos: beings driven by their implanted "natural" memories and genetic traits—like the "replicants" of a later film, *Blade Runner,* but lacking even their sustaining illusion of humanity—yet also, beyond all reason, the psychic slaves of Delos.

It seems fitting that *Futureworld* balances this prospect against a more personal confrontation, that between Chuck and Tracy. He is a newspaperman, an old-fashioned investigative reporter who plays hunches while looking for the real story behind the glamorous world around him. She is a failed reporter—Chuck, in fact, had fired her, despite a brief romantic fling, because she was "not a very good reporter" and did not like digging up "dirt and bad news," as she puts it. Since then, though, Tracy has become a "celebrity," a network television newscaster, someone who essentially reads the news to the public. However, she speaks to an audience of "55 million worldwide" and gloats that Chuck's readership is just "a couple of thousand old prunes in the library." The human dynamic played out here is that between one who suspects a hidden reality to Delos, a privacy despite the great show of openness, and one who accepts it as it appears, as simply an enthralling and thoroughly

satisfying spectacle, another extension of the mass-mediated environment in which she has learned to move so comfortably.

To win her help in his investigation, Chuck appeals to Tracy's earlier
journalistic training. In effect, he tries to reactivate another, private side
of Tracy that she has, in a kind of schizophrenia, repressed under the
influence of that electronic "ecstasy" Baudrillard describes. While the
world of simulacra Dr. Schneider unveils to them seems to have a seductive influence on Tracy—tellingly, the fantasy she visualizes in Delos's
dream chamber shows her being pursued and then seduced by *Westworld*'s
robotic gunslinger, by artifice itself—Chuck revives his earlier love interest,
in essence, challenging the electronic with a human ecstasy. And in a
climactic scene that recalls the original *Invasion of the Body Snatchers,*
Chuck kisses Tracy—in order to determine if she has been replaced by a
robot—while noting with some satisfaction, "There are some things you
just can't fake."

· · ·

Like a number of other films in this period, notably George Lucas's first
film *THX 1138* (1971), *The Clones* (1973), *The Terminal Man* (1974),
and *The Demon Seed* (1977), both *Westworld* and *Futureworld* draw
their lines quite starkly. They oppose the "fake," the simulacrum, the
technologically crafted body powered by artificial intelligence, while
championing the real, the genuine, the human. They do so in the context of a culture wherein boundaries of all sorts seemed to be rapidly
eroding or vanishing. Of course, both appeared in the mid-1970s, the era
of Watergate and Patty Hearst and the period that saw the production of
the first functional synthetic genes. It was a time when the dividing line
between lawful and criminal activity indeed seemed to be disappearing;
when the rapid spread of reproductive technologies like the Xerox machine and the introduction of the videocassette recorder were blurring
the distinction between originals and their copies; when the pervasiveness
of the mass media was making it nearly impossible to distinguish personal desires from those conjured up for us in commercials, advertisements, and mass entertainment; and when a flourishing pornography
industry was foregrounding the difficulty in drawing a line between obscenity and the exercise of free speech.

Even while we focus on the specific nature of the robots and robotic
technology developed in these films, then, we also need to place those
developments within this broader cultural context. For these films fi-

nally are more than just stories about our confrontation with human artifice, as we have seen with a work like *Forbidden Planet*. Of course, Robby the Robot notwithstanding, the artificial being almost always implies a kind of threat, one of competition and/or replacement for the human. Thanks to simultaneous advances in robotics and computers in this period, that threat was clearly coming back into focus, as the very number of such robot/android films attests. But in light of those advances, these images of human artifice were also beginning to beg a larger question, one still only roughly articulated at this point. It is the question of what that ongoing "reinvention of nature" as Donna Haraway terms it—a "reinvention" that includes human nature—might portend (Penley and Ross 6).

In *Westworld* and *Futureworld,* at least, the robot is not just a threat but a symptom of this development, as well as a vivid illustration of just how seductive this development was. In a world wherein the old boundaries, rules, and taboos no longer seem to hold, the robot—or to be more precise, the fantasy of robotism, as we earlier termed it—straddles certain biological and technological borders, and thus crystalizes the prospects for fashioning or reinventing all manner of things, but especially the self. In placing their characters down in this sort of world, where the difference between guest and robot, real world and artificial one, private desire and public spectacle is quickly vanishing,[1] the two *World* films sketch the terms of a common vulnerability audiences were feeling, while also sketching a general resistance to that condition.

• • •

Of course, it might be argued such resistance was pointless, that in fact it simply represents a kind of ideological denial of an already extant situation. Baudrillard, for example, at various points implies that the transformation these films futuristically sketch has already occurred, that we even now inhabit an obscene world where there is no possibility for privacy, where schizophrenia is the common condition, and where reality itself has been transformed into the hyperreal through a dizzying context of simulacra. Thus he describes Disneyland, in a way that recalls the future according to *Futureworld,* as a place that is "presented as imaginary in order to make us believe that the rest is real, when in fact all . . . surrounding it are no longer real, but of the order of the hyperreal and of simulation" (*Simulations* 25). However, the absence of such resistance is also difficult to imagine, even for Baudrillard, for the result of this transformation of the real, finally, is the loss of all private space, perhaps even of a distinct identity, as the individual finds he must live, as Baudrillard puts it, "with no halo of private protection, not even his own body, to protect him anymore" ("Ecstasy" 132).

Moreover, we need to read this notion of resistance in light of the science fiction genre's built-in sense of schizophrenia, what we might describe as its own commitment to both private and public spaces. As we have noted in several instances already, the science fiction film, on the one hand, bases its appeal on the public—on the spectacle of technology and scientific development it can envision, on the changes or transformations it foresees, on the accomplishments our culture so readily applauds. Here is its attraction and indeed its rationale. On the other hand, it also has an abiding stake in the private or personal which, as Susan Sontag notes, results in a constant anxiety over conditions that produce "impersonality and dehumanization" (225). While it recognizes and capitalizes on the lure of the public, then, the science fiction film also questions those accomplishments and transformations, qualifies its support of them, as if such changes and artifice were fundamentally opposed to the human.[2]

Still, the form generally tries to strike terms between these two postures, to take its own schizophrenia in hand—somewhat in the fashion of that strange handshake between worker and dictator that concludes *Metropolis.* *Westworld* and *Futureworld* do so by examining the seductive powers of a human artifice and the steady slide toward a robotic regime that it heralds, and that we seem to be desiring into existence. Both films describe a world in which the real is quickly slipping away,[3] acknowledge a certain lure in that disappearance, and then explore how we might deal with this situation, perhaps even come to live with it, like the technician Harry Cross in *Futureworld.* A general maintenance man, Harry lives deep in the bowels of Delos with an old-model robot named Clark as his only companion. After many years, he explains, he has developed "a taste for the iron," a kind of fondness for this battered mechanism. These robot-populated, robot-monitored, and even robot-controlled worlds promise to make that an ever more easily acquired taste by fulfilling an age-old dream, letting us link the private with the public, permitting us to live our dreams and private fantasies, to be what we are and *something* else. These devices could allow us to create a kind of fictional self, craft a narrative for it, and have it act out that role within a public space. However, the films also remind us that, in crafting this artificially transcendent self, one free to order up its own reality, we risk turning the self inside out, leaving it open and vulnerable in that public space our technology normally occupies.

These films not only notice the effects of a human artifice, then; they also provide a diagnosis. What they suggest is that we are coming to fear not so much the robot or android itself as a loss of the private, a loss of that place of refuge and security to which we retreat when the challenge of the public becomes too great for the individual. They sketch this situation by describing how, through our artifice, we are not only linking but collapsing all distinction between the private and the public. And they suggest that the resulting sense of transcendence comes at a high price, as the robots who suddenly refuse to play their allotted roles in *Westworld* and those in *Futureworld* who plot to to displace us from the narrative that is life itself illustrate. In like fashion, turning the real into a theme park comes at a cost, that of the theme park becoming our only reality.

Yet the lure, as these and other films of the period emphasize, remains a powerful, perhaps inescapable one, the modern situation may be, after all, something of a double bind from which there is no escape. Certainly, determining just what it is we "can't fake" is becoming harder; the horizon between reality and artifice is receding from view. But perhaps it is only in the almost automatic resistance these films depict, only in our stubborn belief in the *possibility* of the fake, only in a reflexive recoil before what O. B. Hardison, Jr., terms "a horizon of invisibility" which "cuts across the geography of modern culture" (5) that we do, briefly, find a kind of private space for the self. In this period films like *Westworld* and *Futureworld* embody that recoil. They are our human way of coping with that vulnerability, with our sense of schizophrenia, with the "obscenity" of a world that seems increasingly given over to artifice.

· NOTES ·

An earlier version of this chapter appeared as "*Westworld, Futureworld, and the World's Obscenity*" in *State of the Fantastic,* ed. Nicholas Ruddick (Westport, Conn.: Greenwood Publishing Group, 1992), 179–88. Reprinted with changes by permission of the publisher. Copyright 1992.

1. Baudrillard draws clear distinctions between the older image of the automaton and the more modern robot, noting that the former represents an "analogy" to the human, the latter an "equivalence." In that equivalency, he suggests, the robot has effectively "absorbed" all sense of difference (*Simulations* 92, 94), and in the process, I would add, revealed the problem within that earlier fascination with imitation.

2. Sontag's "Imagination of Disaster" essay speaks directly to this tension. She suggests that the genre usually contains "no social criticism, of even the most implicit kind," largely because its primary concern is with more fundamental human anxieties, particularly threats of dehumanization and depersonalization (225–26). At the same time, she finds the genre's fascination with a *cultural* devastation its most pervasive character. While her essay still seems to offer some of the most telling insights into the science fiction film, it also seems unable to address the very tension that it implicitly recognizes.

3. Hardison has used this image of a slippage or disappearance of the real as a trope for the changing relationship between the human and nature. In *Disappearing through the Skylight* he speaks of how in the contemporary world "nature has slipped, perhaps finally, beyond our field of vision. We can imitate it in mathematics—we can even produce convincing images of it—but we can never know it. We can only know our own creations" (1).

7

Life at the Horizon:
The Tremulous Public Body

In the 1980s the science fiction film not only returned to the level of popularity it enjoyed in the 1950s but also took on a rather singular focus. While images of alien invasion had dominated the genre in that earlier era,[1] the more recent period found the image of human artifice—embodied in various robots, androids, cyborgs, and replicants—gaining a similar and equally challenging stature. Certainly, some of that prominence derives from the great success of the *Star Wars* films which, from the late 1970s through the early 1980s, offered audiences cute, personable, and highly marketable robots, such as R2-D2 and C-3PO, that easily wore their roles as loyal, if at times bumbling, retainers and comic foils. Yet the many science fiction films and television series that followed in the trilogy's popular path ultimately took their cues more from works like *Westworld* and *Futureworld*. And in their dark tone they seem nearer to the alien invasion films of the 1950s than the serials of the 1930s and 1940s to which the *Star Wars* movies do such obvious homage.

In their major contrast to the alien invasion films, the robot/android movies of the 1980s supplant the menace from outside of our world with a problem or threat of our own construction. Thus, such works as *Blade Runner, Android* (both 1982), *The Terminator, Runaway* (both 1984), *Generation, D.A.R.Y.L.* (both 1985), *Deadly Friend* (1986), the *Short Circuit* films (1986, 1988), *Making Mr. Right* (1987), the *Robocop* films (1987, 1990, 1993), *Cherry 2000* (1988), *Cyborg* (1989), and *Hardware* (1990), among many others, extrapolate from those patterns of vulnerability and resistance, of obscenity and recoil from our culture's obscene circumstances described in the previous chapter, to isolate and analyze the postmodern body. Certainly owing much to the rise of a feminist-inspired discourse about the body, to the increasing alliance of the technological with the body—via the development of prostheses, replacement parts, and mechanical life-support systems—and to the increasing role of the robotic in the workplace, where it threatens to replace the human body, these images of artifice have become the instrument of choice for a new sort of anatomy of the human, a cinematic anatomy that explores our levels of artifice and constructedness and that reveals how we often seem controlled by a kind of internalized program not so different from that which drives the artificial beings populating these films.

To explore this turn, I want to return to Francis Barker's description of how science helped develop a regime of control over the body and link it to an analysis of technology's cultural impact offered by Robert Romanyshyn. In the imagery of anatomy and dissection, we might recall, Barker traces out how western culture crafted a method of self-mastery, the goal of which was to render the individual subservient, pliable to change or control. With the body rendered as a thing of parts that could be dissected, examined, and understood through science, with it thus made transparent, it was assumed, the human might become a self-policing being who would surrender all real power and sovereignty to the forces of a culture that this figure—with the body properly programmed—almost ghostlike inhabits. The result is a body clothed in restraints and "effectively hidden from history" and scrutiny (12). Yet this "hollowed, double, modern body" (73), as Barker puts it, is a "tremulous" one, a being that still desires freedom and expression, even as it is pressed to be the perfect, servile subject of society. In his "tremulous" image we can thus glimpse another level of the schizophrenia we have already noted in several other areas of the science fiction film.

The science fiction films of the 1980s recast this schizophrenic pattern and the various sorts of blurred boundaries to which it responds as a tension between a *public* and a *private* body. They repeatedly depict the human body as losing its private dimension, as an *image* that is constantly being reconfigured and presented for display, a "modern body" not just "hollowed" and "double" but offered and dissected *as image*—although still surprisingly aware of its condition. In foregrounding our "tremulous" state as public image, these films reveal a level of our complicity in that subjugation while, to some extent, wriggling free of its hold. In this chapter, we shall trace out this pattern in such recent films about human artifice as *Blade Runner, Robocop, Cherry 2000,* and *Total Recall.* In their foregounding of a "public body," we can discern a subversive character that the image of artifice has begun to assume, as it reveals and ultimately questions the self-repression Barker sees as typical of contemporary western culture and as rendering us insensitive, even resistant, to change. At the same time, we can see this subversive trend's workings within the genre's larger schizophrenic pattern, as it produces a troubled, at times even suspect view of the human situation—a view that reflects our increasingly schizophrenic sense of technology itself.

· · ·

This link between the private, anatomized body and a near-future public body is anticipated by Robert Romanyshyn in his insightful book *Technology as Symptom and Dream.* He there describes how the "anatomical vision" of which Barker speaks transformed the body "into a spectacular dis-membered specimen" (117). In doing so, it gave birth to the modern self that all science presupposes, the "spectator of the world" who has "left the body behind"—a "decontextualized body . . . whose memories have lost their place in the world" (101, 142). Of course, the various horror/science fiction films of the 1930s, works like *Frankenstein, Island of Lost Souls, The Invisible Man, Mad Love,* and *The Devil Doll,* had already sketched the shape of this subject body and provided us with several of its most enduring and disturbing images. But what Romanyshyn underscores is how contemporary culture—as well as contemporary film —has managed to revisit and reevoke the spirit of this repressed and abandoned body, deprived as it is of any real identity or memories. As he says, we now see all around us "the anatomized corpse . . . resurrected as machine" (144).

One result of this contemporary situation, as Jean Baudrillard notes, is that we now seem singularly "preoccupied with saving our identity," with "proving our existence" (*Ecstasy* 29). Yet paradoxically, we are doing so with the aid of simulacra. Films that show replicants as the ultimate workers (*Blade Runner*), cyborgs as the definitive answer to law enforcement (*Robocop*), and robots as ideal lovers (*Cherry 2000*) reflect an anxiety that has increasingly attached to our social roles and personal identities—our *less-than-ideal* selves. These films use the robotic as a trope or mechanism for revealing a human nature that has been largely drained of identity, an "abandoned body" without real "memories." Rick Deckard of *Blade Runner,* for example, is described as "sushi" or "cold fish." Because of his lack of emotion, his wife has left him, and he seems to drift, robotlike, without purpose or direction, through a decaying urban world that is itself largely devoid of passion. *Robocop* depicts a future in which humans—police and citizens alike—are mainly economic counters, figures manipulated by a cold, mechanistic, corporate capitalism, or an equally cold, predatory underworld (which is tied to the ruling business structure and forms its complementary inverse). The people's needs and desires are programmed by advertising, satisfied according to corporate planning, and regulated by a computerized, privatized police force—all as if they were themselves little more than automatons, without any real will or choice. In the postapocalyptic world of *Cherry 2000,* all human contact is strained and emotionless; even "one-night stands" are constructed—that is, contractually negotiated. As a result, individuals find their only emotional and sexual satisfaction in their mechanical constructs, in robot surrogates whose preprogrammed gambits and responses only reflect the preprogrammed and ultimately choiceless nature of their human partners.

The robotic figures of these films thus form a kind of "public body," as I have put it, an image of a generally empty human nature—and what is equally noteworthy, a generally *masculine* empty nature—that reflects the sort of controls that seem to determine our lives. If the body in the Age of Reason was, as Barker says, "admitted only as a nameless momentum outside the real arena of meaning and endeavor, as an unruly mess of functions and afflictions" that a rising scientific discourse worked to tame and make subject (66), in these films it forms a public and insistent emblem of the self, thrusting its simulated humanity into the supposedly "real arena" of human endeavor. In the process, that artificial body sparks an interrogation of the real, such as we noted in the *Westworld* and *Futureworld* films, as well as of our sense of self—an interrogation that points up a human emptiness, almost a roboticization, that increasingly seems the case for contemporary being.

While it may seem something of a stretch to think of *Total Recall* as a "robot film," it does offer us an almost literal rendition of this pattern of interrogation. After a space shuttle lands on Mars, one of its passengers, a large woman, approaches immigration officers, answers a few routine questions, but then starts convulsing and stuttering. Suddenly, she touches a button, her head pops open and off, and we see that "she" was simply a robotic disguise, inside of which is the protagonist Quaid, who has been trying to reach Mars undetected. This surprising emergence of the human from within the robot—and of the masculine encased in the disguise of the woman—literalizes the pattern our science fiction films of the last decade have been playing out on a larger scale, as they tell of robots and cyborgs suddenly revealing a human spirit within themselves and reminding us, despite a long history of self-repression, of the similar spirit that dwells in us as well. It is a rather comforting pattern, as the popularity of these films might suggest, although, as Quaid's near capture and the deceptive presentation of gender here implies, one not without its troubling aspect.

· · ·

A film like *Blade Runner* takes this surprise emergence of the human as its very premise. It describes how genetically engineered "replicants," the workers, entertainers, and soldiers of the future, have begun to rebel against their servile position, deny their less-than-human status, and steal back to Earth to mingle with their human models. There, though, they are hunted down and exterminated by futuristic bounty hunters or "blade runners" like Rick Deckard. Yet the bounty hunter faces a difficult task. For he must put aside any *human* compunction, and on order automatically and unfeelingly kill these beings, practically indistinguishable from the human, whose chief crime is to have asserted their humanity; in effect, he must act not humanely but almost robotically—that is, mechanically and unfeelingly. While Deckard, a "cold fish," seems well suited to the task, that nature makes him a model of modern schizophrenic behavior, both the force of control and a version of the very thing he is supposed to control.

In turn, what the replicants represent for Deckard is a *public* version of his *private* dilemma—an emergent self confronting a repressed self. When he shoots the female replicant Zhora, watches her death throes, and is nearly killed by her companion Leon, Deckard is left to contemplate, as he trembles at both his near death and the spectacle of the replicant's, a similarity between his victims and himself: "Replicants weren't supposed to have feelings. Neither were blade runners," he says. Of course, the implication is that both *do* feel, and that, contrary to public opinion, these similarly alien (and alienated) types share a common humanity; their tremulous bodies insist on it.

Another and larger implication of *Blade Runner*'s version of human artifice, though, is that we have come to *need* this public image, this robotic display, to jog our sense of humanity in an increasingly inhuman world and help us break free of a pattern of self-subjection in which we have long conspired. If the replicants here, especially the lovers Pris and Roy Batty, seem more animated, more beautiful, and more attached to life than their human counterparts, such as Deckard, the policeman Gaff, or the genetically crippled genetic engineer J. F. Sebastian, it is because they foreground the pattern of self-repression, of private controls that rein in and eventually deny the human, while also dramatizing the possibility of resistance to this pattern.

The replicants so easily dramatize this pattern because no similar regime of repression has taken hold in them. With their genetically programmed short lifespans, they hardly seemed to require the elaborate cultural controls to which humans are prone. And a clumsy effort at using photographs to suggest ersatz memories that would tie them to a fake past and a set of cultural restraints has failed, leaving each, in Romanyshyn's words, "a body whose memories have lost their place in the world." Consequently, in their roles as extensions of the human impulse for power, subjection, and exploitation, as beings designed to *act* in places where humans cannot, they seem more free of the sort of "derealization of the body" Barker describes (12), of a denial of its beauty, power, and autonomy. Thus, Zhora works as an exotic dancer, her body presented unselfconsciously for public display; Leon, the "combat model," is ready to kill Deckard in the street; Pris, a "pleasure model," adorns herself and looks for approval; and Roy Batty, the leader, drives a spike into his hand to *feel* the pain in his body and so savor the sense of life just a bit longer. What these replicants bring to the fore is, as Barker might say, a "spectacular visible body" that offers a "gauge of what the bourgeoisie has had to forget" (25).

In their tremulous public bodies, which the police say they only want to "retire"—that is, remove from public view—the replicants not only challenge the status quo but, as I have elsewhere argued, also offer a kind of salvation from it ("Human" 44–51). Underscoring this redemptive potential is Roy Batty's last-minute saving act. Reversing the schizophrenic pattern of his human antagonist, he shifts from trying to kill Deckard to pulling him back from a building's ledge where he dangles, and from a fall that seems emblematic of the modern human condition. In the same instant, he miraculously produces a dove, a sign of the Holy Spirit, come down to dwell in us and to fill our bodies with a sorely needed grace.[2] Given this new inspiration, Deckard too acts as something other than a robot or replicant, sparing the last of the hunted figures,

Rachael, and going off with her to live a new life. Of course, Rachael has all along modeled another sort of repression at work here, that which the masculine inflicts on the feminine, imposing a history on it and manipulating its feelings. But having been surprised by self, by the sudden emergence of his own humanity thanks to the actions of this human artifice, Deckard now finds he can feel with and for Rachael, with her—and indeed his own—kind.

• • •

Robocop offers a more complicated version of this issue of identity in the midst of artifice, for the protagonist Murphy is himself both human and machine, not just an alienated and dispirited modern man like Deckard but a cyborg whose *human* identity must be reawakened. He is, on the one hand, very much a version of the private body, of the common person. As Officer Alex Murphy, he is described as "some poor schmuck"; he is the type addressed by the various TV shows and commercials that punctuate the film and emphasize the sort of media programming of the individual that seems endemic here. In fact, Murphy is clearly influenced by that media address, as we see when he twirls his pistol like his son's TV hero, T. J. Lazer, noting how important such "role models can be . . . to a boy." On the other hand, as a "product" that industry hopes to sell, as the cyborg law-enforcement device called Robocop, he is an equally subject public body. For in his high-profile position as a new kind of public servant, he works within parameters defined by a set of "Prime Directives," which we see in subjective shot on his video display —as if we already shared his programmed bondage. Bound by such programming and defined by his place in the market, Murphy/Robocop thus embodies, even if in an exaggerated, public way, the sort of human identity that prevails in this near future—an identity determined by corporate and governmental directive and progammed by the voice of the mass media.

Like the replicants of *Blade Runner,* Robocop seems unable to "realize" the body, to operate free of his programming—or corporate planning. He is, after all, the unwitting subject of a corporate experiment, the real aim of which is his death. Omni Consumer Products, the conglomerate that runs the privatized Detroit police department, in properly schizophrenic fashion appears intent on eliminating the police in favor of its new crime suppression robots. So, as Bob Morton of OCP explains, the company has "restructured the police department and placed prime candidates according to risk factors." In short, the company has transferred certain men like Murphy—"schmucks"—to especially dangerous precincts where they might be killed or so disabled as to provide a "human chassis" for the experimental Robocop cyborg program.

When such a planned "accident" happens and Murphy is turned into the ultimate urban crime fighter, he foregrounds the absence of autonomy here all the more. At rest, he is attended by a group of technicians who monitor and record all his vital signs, even his mental impulses. In action, he is guided by an "on-board, computer-assisted memory" that displays the three Prime Directives guiding his actions, while a fourth— which prevents him from arresting OCP senior officers and thus from interfering in its operations—keeps the source of his subjection effectively free from analysis. As President Dick Jones, who, in keeping with this film's schizophrenic pattern, is behind both OCP's robotic law enforcement program *and* much of the crime in Detroit, puts it, "We can't very well have our products turn against us, can we?" Freedom of action is simply not permitted.

What short-circuits such fail-safe planning, though, and allows this very public body to foreground and subvert these restraints is the sudden resurgence of Murphy's human identity. Despite the effort to sunder Murphy's body from his human memories and Bob Morton's assertion that his creation "doesn't have a name; he's got a program. He's product," the narrative's trajectory is toward reasserting Murphy's human identity over his robotic one, in effect answering the questions posed by a TV newscast: "Who is he? What is he? Where does he come from?" Thus a computer program that, a technician notes, "was never designed to experience detailed somatic response" fails to control Robocop once he begins dreaming, flashing back to his happy family life and the shooting that ended it. Further prodded by his former partner Ann Lewis, who asks, "Do you have a name?" and who later assures him that he is Murphy, Robocop acts on his own, going after those responsible for his murder. After accomplishing that task and killing Dick Jones, he is congratulated by OCP's CEO, who asks, "What's your name?" to which Robocop definitively replies, "Murphy." As director Paul Verhoeven explains, this response marks Robocop/Murphy's "acceptance of what he has become, of having less and having more. He has taken control of what they have done to him, becoming Murphy again, but in a new way" (Cronenworth 35).

That "new way" is both the hope and the problem that this film, like many other of our human artifice tales, frames. It is a hope because it occurs even in the face of a complete technological makeover of the body and a corporate programming of all its functions—activities whose shape we can already easily trace in our culture. Moreover, it finds its fulfillment in the context of a renewed and equal partnership between the masculine and the feminine, between Murphy and Ann Lewis. After he is nearly destroyed by the police, she provides him the tools to fix himself, brings food, and steals a gun for him. In a telling and sexually overdetermined scene, he then takes the new pistol she has provided and asks Ann to help him correct his targeting mechanism—which she does by embracing his body and directing his aim with one hand. With this needed direction by the feminine—and this metaphorically sexual coming of age—Murphy indeed seems to offer some hope that a "new" sort of humanity might yet emerge.

Of course, this assertion of identity, with its implied resistance to subjection, also occurs in the context of a more problematic scene. In defeating those corrupt forces, Ann is nearly killed, and Murphy can only offer the rather ironic promise that "They'll fix you. They fix everything." OCP may well "fix" her, perhaps even turn her into another Robocop, drained of identity and ready to serve the needs of the modern corporate state. But then, perhaps with *Murphy's* help that sort of "fix" might not happen, for it might prove that what cannot be so easily fixed or manipulated is a human identity that refuses to dissolve into artifice, collaborate in its repression, or aid its own transformation into "product." The film holds out this potential for the human, even when transformed into a subject body, to "take control" of itself and act independently of the subjecting forces of culture, even though it leaves those forces largely intact and finally shows little possibility for reintegrating that self with society.

• • •

In another variation on this pattern, *Cherry 2000* describes how the robot's public body—and indeed, the very fantasy of robotism—might inspire a search for the repressed private self. It describes Sam Treadwell's devotion to a fantasy, his robot girlfriend Cherry, in an age when devotion of any sort is rare, when human caring seems an anachronism, and when sexual relations of any kind are the subject of tangled legal negotiation. As Sam notes, man-woman relations in this future world have become "all sort of paranoid and audio-visual. It's just bad." In this context, Cherry seemed something special, a reminder of "tenderness . . . a dream-like quality . . . romance." But like most romantic partners here, Cherry was just a robot, the ultimate sexual surrogate in an age when, thanks to women's aggressive equality and men's lingering desire for submissive, subservient partners, such surrogates seem a natural compromise, the best either male or female can hope for. So when Cherry suffers "total internal meltdown," when she becomes nothing more than a "depersonalized and decontextualized body"—which is, after all, just what Sam seems to want in a woman—he sets out on a journey into the surrounding wastelands in search of a "new chassis" to hold the precious computer chip containing "her whole personality," that of a properly submissive, doting, and empty mate.

Lest we accept the notion that Cherry was truly "something special," a robot in whom, like *Blade Runner*'s replicants or *Robocop*'s Murphy, a spark of humanity has surprisingly appeared, the film introduces "her" in a kind of parody of 1950s sit-com homecomings. As Sam returns from his day's work, we see her mindless gaze in close-up, hear her simple, programmed, and predictable chatter, and note her pride at offering his favorite meal—hamburger, fries, and ketchup. Nothing special, no robot or cyborg suddenly become human, she is just a clumsy mechanism—better, we learn, than competing models like the Bambi 14 or Cindy 990, but only "special" in light of the otherwise disastrous human relations that are the rule here. While a kind of "public body," one that lets us gauge the state of human affairs here and, in a minimal way, helps Sam resist that status quo, then, she is ultimately just another version of Barker's "hollowed, double, modern body." Truly an empty chassis, Cherry points up the "empty" nature of many of the humans here, as well as the spirit that, in its preference for undemanding, uncomplicated relations, helps keep them that way.

Yet Sam does show an intensity and romantic spirit that sets him apart from his friends. No "cold fish" like Deckard, he has a spark of vitality that shows up nowhere else in his decaying, rust-plagued city. But he has despaired of finding the sort of human relationship he longs for, and in the face of the "paperwork," legal hassles, and uncertainties all such affiliations involve, that is, in the context of the kind of *negotiated* equality that is the case here, he prefers the simplicity and "special magic" of an artificial being. In setting out on his quest for a new Cherry 2000, though, Sam has to leave himself exposed and vulnerable, become a kind of tremulous public body. Since the personality chip he carries is precious, coveted by others, Sam finds that he is watched, followed, his life threatened by bandits and renegades, his desires exposed for all to see, and his own troubled identity laid open to inspection—and eventual correction. As a result, his quest for a new robotic body turns into a quest for his own true self.

Appropriately, the agents for change here are guides—or "trackers," as they are termed—who know the surrounding wasteland and survive by scavenging the detritus of the old world.[3] Aided by the mythic old man of the wastelands, Six-finger Jake, and his mysterious niece E. Johnson, Sam heads for a lost robot graveyard, located in the remains of a Las Vegas–type resort that underscores the sort of fake sensuality and plastic sexuality that once typified this world and which, it seems, Sam hopes to retrieve. In the course of this journey, Jake offers Sam some of his simple wisdom; he reminds Sam that "there's a lot more to love than hot wiring." More importantly, though, the independent and aggressive E. displays a romantic interest that gradually draws him toward a more fully human relationship, and a professional commitment—despite the lack of a contract—that several times saves his life and eventually brings him to his goal. As a result, when he finally reconstitutes his Cherry 2000, Sam realizes he no longer needs her, for he has indeed been guided to, has tracked down his own real self. It seems that in exposing his repressed identity and distorted sense of gender relations, in acting rather than simply surrendering to an all-too-common absence of human attachment, he is surprised by his own humanity and by a possibility for true human relationships.

In fact, *Cherry 2000* ends in a highly schematic rendition of the sort of relations that might still be achieved. Leaving his robot and his many pursuers behind, Sam flies off with E., transcending this futuristic wasteland. However, he can only do so because of a quite literal spark provided by E., who has made a rickety old plane flyable once more—just as she has restored Sam—by sacrificing the spark plugs from her car, the symbol of her own independence.[4]

This conclusion represents a significant private victory, a realizing of the self and of the other, as Sam, almost surprised at his own choice, leaves behind the robotic body he has sought—that is, the empty modern body—to embrace a *human* body and spirit, the enigmatic, feminine, and thoroughly equal E., who has helped him track down his human nature. This ending suggests both the strength of our human identity and a lingering possibility for real human commitment, even in the face of a world given over to artifice. Yet there is also a hint of *escape* here, for this flight has no sure destination. The city remains no more civilized than the wasteland; the powers that have so "hollowed" out the self remain unchanged. What has been demonstrated is a pattern of resistance—as a private self resurfaces and manages, with the aid of the feminine other, to free itself from subjection—and a hope that this pattern might continue. And given the rate at which this nonproductive, constructed world is, as we repeatedly hear, "rusting out," some realization of that hope is sorely needed.

• • •

As a final gloss on this treatment of the self, let me return to *Total Recall,* perhaps the most significant treatment of repressed culture and identity among contemporary science fiction films. Of course, it is not really a robot narrative—not like the films cited above, anyway. However, it is based, like *Blade Runner,* on a Philip K. Dick story, and thus echoes many of the themes noted in the earlier film. And the lead actor Arnold Schwarzenegger, thanks to his definitive role as a cyborg in *The Terminator* and to a wooden acting style that director Paul Verhoeven seems to have embraced as a complement to his view of the character, does bring a kind of artificial aura to the lead role of Doug Quaid. More importantly, in his situation as a man with a double identity, one whose life seems arranged as a public show being monitored by his co-workers and a fake "wife," Quaid seems an equally telling example of the roboticized modern being, of a public body primed to be surprised by the self, by a human identity that will not be denied.

That surprise follows Quaid's willing effort to undergo the sort of conditioning that failed on the replicants of *Blade Runner,* to have memories of a Martian vacation implanted in his brain. But here too failure follows, as the process triggers a "schizoid embolism" in the throes of which he suddenly recalls another life on Mars, as a security officer named Hauser, serving the repressive dictator Cohaagen. With that surprise coming to himself, like some suddenly humanized cyborg, the pattern of repression all around Quaid/Hauser begins to materialize and then to unravel, as he combats Cohaagen's various operatives and surveillance mechanisms, returns to Mars, and there searches for his true identity.

Yet, this simple and now familiar tale of a sudden, even heroic resurgence of the private self becomes tangled, troubled, and, as the critical

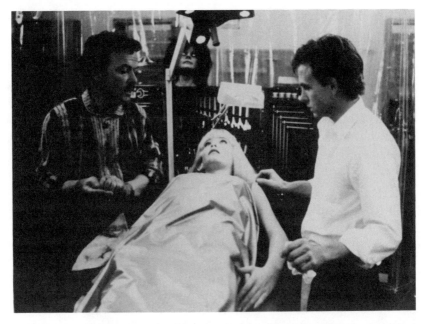

At work in the android repair shop of *Cherry 2000.*

Rick Deckard in pursuit of the replicants in the futuristic world of *Blade Runner.*

The robotic savior confronts the human monster in *Robocop.*

Compelled by implanted memories, Quaid is literally piloted by a robotic cab driver in *Total Recall.*

commentary surrounding this film suggests, difficult to sort out. Quaid eventually learns he was *meant* to have this lapse, that like some will-less robot—like the "poor schmuck" Murphy of Verhoeven's earlier film *Robocop*—he was *programmed for* this failure in his programming. Cohaagen, it seems, has all along planned this surprising return of the self in hopes Quaid might thereby lead him to Kuato, the mutant telepathic leader of the Martian revolutionaries. It is a disarming twist: for Quaid/ Hauser who effectively becomes a body without *any certain* identity—as he in bewilderment says, "If I'm not me, who the hell am I?" and for an audience that is put on its guard against *any appearance* of subversion, any image of repression overcome, any semblance of a positive identity, lest it prove just another disguise for a larger repressive mechanism; as well as for critics, who must wonder to what extent this film is simply another in a long line of Schwarzenegger action films and to what extent it is an effort at interrogating and subverting that narrative type.

These various suspicions, though, *all* seem justified, for here is a film that consistently constructs a most problematic view of all varieties of the repressed, including the feminine. The strong and supportive "wife" Lorie is revealed to be a spying agent and castrating bitch—she twice kicks Quaid in the genitals—who must be dispatched violently. In a misogynistic tone that disturbingly seems designed to evoke laughter— although whether it is at her expense or that of this type of film we cannot be sure—he says, "Consider this a divorce," as he shoots her through the head. The girl of Quaid's dreams—literally—is Melina, described as "demure and sleazy," apparently a prostitute, but at the same time a most politically correct revolutionary. She is, in short, a schizophrenic concoction of the sort that only the imagination, including the cinematic imagination, might sustain. Meanwhile, the downtrodden mutants of Mars in their dress and actions clearly suggest Third World types in need of the liberating power of the white superman/Schwarzenegger. Yet they also seem suspicious and potentially treacherous and menacing, as the black mutant Benny proves when he reveals his allegiance to Cohaagen and tries to kill both Quaid and Melina—again in a sexually overdetermined scene—with a phallic mining drill. Just as Quaid could not maintain his robotic disguise as a woman earlier in the film, so too does the film itself seem unable or unwilling to sustain its own subversive, antirepressive narrative thrust.[5]

Total Recall, in effect, fashions its own "schizoid embolism," visits it upon the viewers, and cautions us to question both the public *and* the private self. Of course, thanks to the iconic value of Schwarzenegger's action hero and to the dynamics of the adventure plot, we have an easy job with part of that questioning. We invariably "pull for" Quaid as he fights Cohaagen's forces, identify with him as he painfully removes a metal implant that confirms his repression, and hope he reaches the Martian revolutionaries and Kuato, who might help him. Yet each step of the way actually furthers the repressive pattern and leads to an unwelcome start, as the rebels are finally surprised and destroyed. Given this pattern, then, we can never feel quite secure in this world, even when Quaid turns on his former employer and starts up the ancient atmospheric machine that will bring an end to Cohaagen's control[6]—one that will, in effect, create a whole new and *natural* "climate" for human relations in this world that has been held hostage to Cohaagen's artifice. This *act* is Quaid's definitive answer to Cohaagen's description of him as a depersonalized body, a construct of his powers: "You're nothing; you're nobody; you're a stupid dream." Perhaps those dreams, including our cinematic ones, are simply necessary. They may have a power to sustain us, to assert a reality of their own, and thus to liberate us from a repressive atmosphere.

Still, it is an answer that is itself trumped, in unsettling fashion, by the schizophrenic note on which the film ends. After apparently turning against his programmed identity and defeating the forces of corporate totalitarianism, Quaid voices "a terrible thought; what if this *is* a dream?" That qualm certainly seems justified in light of the promise made to Quaid by the dream merchants of Rekall, who offered him memories of the ultimate "ego trip," one in which "You get the girl, kill the bad guys, and save the entire planet." Of course, in this film's plot he has managed each of these things, and in a fashion that seems a projection of the schizophrenic ego. Quaid, who says prophetically early on in the film that "I feel like I was meant for something more than" his mundane role as a construction worker, may well have *constructed* that "something more"—a mutant, "robotic" narrative in which the wife is menace, friends are foes, sleazy and demure are complementary terms, the Martian sky can turn blue, and he can be *both* himself and someone else. But then, our films have always done as much for us.

In fact, this dream question speaks to all the films discussed in this chapter, for each in its own way represents a kind of wish-fulfillment fantasy or dream, set in the context of our current troubled encounter with artifice. Each forges a generally satisfying strike against the forces of cultural repression. Through the agency of a *public* self, a *private* self gains a necessary freedom, and the masculine and feminine manage to find a new harmony amid a world of alienated sexual constructions. Yet those accomplishments may well be *forged,* that is, a bit ingenuine, since, as our films must inevitably do, they leave the very forces of repression intact: Deckard and Rachael must flee them in *Blade Runner,* Murphy accepts their rule in *Robocop,* and Sam seemingly finds romantic bliss in *Cherry 2000.* What each film offers, consequently, is not only a path back to the private self but also—again schizophrenically—a hint that perhaps a private happiness is the best we can hope for, that the only counter against the various forces that seem to condition and construct our lives and disenfranchise our bodies lies along that path, in a turn to the self.

Total Recall, I would argue, goes a step further. In the fashion of a film like the dystopian fantasy *Brazil* (1985), it takes a reflexive turn and asks if this recourse too is only illusory, a dream manufactured for us by more of those forces that continue to work their will on the private body, in effect, another sort of robotic fantasy. In letting us see the fantasy, it offers a level of self-awareness, a dream that might help us awaken from the larger dream that has been culturally constructed for us.

• • •

Still, the pattern we find repeated in these films, of the self's sudden reemergence, of a kind of reintegration of the body with the human spirit, should not be dismissed. It suggests a hope in the human personality's hardiness, in a persistence of identity that flies in the face of the many predictions that our humanity is, as O. B. Hardison, Jr., offers, already "disappearing through the skylight" of our various constructs (xi). As we reach a point in our technological history when we seem able to construct almost anything, including body parts, when our cultural theory assumes that everything, including human nature, is *already* constructed, the distinctions between ourselves and our constructs obviously become all the more elusive and disturbing. These films respond to the blurred boundaries, the lost horizons foregrounded by our artifice and set out to reassure us by affirming how much of the human inevitably remains—how much, in fact, has always remained, despite our long history of repressing, denying, or "de-realizing" the self.

In using the robotic as a springboard for such a turn, these films also suggest a possible path that reaffirming or realizing the self might take.

The robot, cyborg, or android, as I have argued, is a kind of image of that anatomized, hollowed-out, modern self—an image that underscores a degree to which we all seem to have become mechanized, programmed beings, bodies detached from spirit. Yet that image of a human artifice, as we might judge from its prevalence in contemporary science fiction films and as experience with the persistent imagery of other genres attests, responds to a need; perhaps it can help us to know ourselves once more, to discern our humanity, and thus to *re*construct our sense of self. For the robot's inspirational capacity, its ability, in one sense or another, to take life represents nothing less than the indelible imprint of its original, the ghost of humankind that inhabits the machine. It thus images a possibility for subversion, individuality, and self-realization, by suggesting that the schizophrenia this world seems to foster, the imaginary it constructs, can be turned against it to free up the self.

Perhaps these implications hint of a naive response to cultural change in a genre that Susan Sontag once characterized as offering little more than an "inadequate response" to "the most profound dilemmas of the contemporary situation" (227). Certainly, the almost superficial way in which these films seem to play out their ideologically correct scenarios of a successful rebellion against repression, coupled with the caution explicitly sounded by a film like *Total Recall,* should make us pause and wonder if we are simply measuring another sort of generic schizophrenia. The escape to a verdant world that ends both *Blade Runner* and *Cherry 2000,* the transformation of the Martian atmosphere into a nurturing, Earth-like atmosphere in *Total Recall*—these resolutions are almost too easy, too neat to be convincing, although their very flimsiness may well be the point. Still, we have to wonder to what extent these films are just empty reassurances, clustered around this most intriguing contemporary image of the self and driven by our growing anxieties, and to what extent they are really antihegemonic narratives. Is the pattern of resistance they describe just a path of least resistance, even a rapprochement with all that our artifice implies?

In response to this uncertainty, we should note that these films do more than just foreground repression or deploy the image of human artifice as a trope for the self. In every case, they also speak of their own constructed nature and of the sort of public images of the self that the movies typically project. Garrett Stewart points us in this direction when he notes how often science fiction films prod us to "peer into the mechanics of apparition that permit these films in the outermost and first place" (161). We might consider the various video screens, computer terminals, and holograms that recur in recent films and loom so prominently in those discussed here, as echoes of the movie screen and the movie-ness of the stories that so transfix—or subject—us. For particular examples we need only recall the mediated images of the self provided by the Voight-Kampff empathy test in *Blade Runner;* the television shows and advertisements that sketch the nature of the modern viewer/consumer in *Robocop;* or the collection of old *film* robots glimpsed in the robot bodyshop of *Cherry 2000.* Of course, *Total Recall,* as we have already seen, repeatedly underlines the constructed, dreamlike, mutant nature of its own text. Specific examples include the transparently politicized news broadcasts, hologram projections of Quaid/Hauser, and the video image of Hauser addressing his alter ego Quaid, noting, "You are not you; you are me."

When these films link such images to their key concerns with artifice and the technology of reproduction—the same sort of reproduction, after all, to which film itself is dedicated—we inevitably become more aware of how hard it is ever to escape from the sway of repression, subjection, or programming—or, for that matter, the reach of modern mass media. At such moments, these films also open up holes in the narrative pattern being constructed—holes that complement, and at times even undermine their larger trajectories. Then we can glimpse, along with the temporary triumph of the self over artifice that they chronicle, how the movies work their own transformation of the self, turning the moviegoer into a body that is rendered transparent, his desires measured and carefully addressed, and his conformity furthered. In that glimpse, we might hope, comes recognition and perhaps a measure of freedom.

Of course, this reading too may represent a kind of wish-fulfillment. For it implies that the very forces which propel change in our culture may, in their own schizophrenic way, foreground the power they wield, render it public for all to see, and thus, in a way, empower the private self and offer some release from the bonds of ideology, gender, and genre that hold sway over us. This hope springs from a world where technological change is creating great anxieties, a world in which the body already seems rendered public in one form or another, a world characterized by, as Jean Baudrillard says, "overexposure," where "the body is already there *without even the faintest glimmer of a possible absence"* (*Ecstasy* 27, 32). Already exposed and vulnerable in so many ways, we may be looking to make this condition useful, to provide the kind of light in which we might examine the very images we have created for the self. In their constant transparency, perhaps we cannot help but see more clearly the patterns of restraint we have helped weave—and the patterns that our science fiction films too, in their own schizophrenic way, may yet be reworking on another level. At least in these films the body itself seems no longer quite hidden from history or from our own gaze. And in its tremulous appearance, it hints of how our science fiction films may even help us retrieve something of that private self.

· NOTES ·

An earlier version of this chapter appeared as "The Tremulous Public Body: Robots, Change, and the Science Fiction Film" in *Journal of Popular Film and Television* 19.1 (Spring 1991): 14–22 and is reprinted with changes by permission of the Helen Dwight Reid Education Foundation. Published by Heldref Publications, 1319 18th Street, N.W., Washington, DC 20036–1802. Copyright 1991.

1. Discussions and analyses of the alien invasion films of the 1950s and early 1960s are plentiful and generally quite thoughtful. See especially Patrick Lucanio's *Them or Us: Archetypal Interpretations of Fifties Alien Invasion Films,* Susan Sontag's famous account of the genre, "The Imagination of Disaster," and Peter Biskind's chapters on science fiction in his history of 1950s film, *Seeing Is Believing.*

2. A more elaborate examination of the film's patterns of salvation and transcendence can be found in David Desser's fine article, "*Blade Runner:* Science Fiction and Transcendence." Besides offering a thorough account and cogent reading of the film's salvation imagery, he convincingly argues for its kinship to Milton's *Paradise Lost.*

3. While *Cherry 2000* is certainly a cheaply made film, it is also an ambitious and even thoughtful one. One sign of that ambitiousness is its various allusions, both visual and verbal, to other texts, including *The Divine Comedy.* A case could be made for viewing Six-finger Jake and E. Johnson as the Vergil and Beatrice of this redemptive quest.

4. We might note that in his opening conversation with Cherry, Sam bemoans the fact that a load of spark plugs he received, scavenged from the surrounding wasteland, had proved no good. Like so much else in this world wherein little seems to work anymore, they were completely covered with rust.

5. For these comments on the status of feminine and repressed cultures

in *Total Recall,* I am indebted to several fellow panelists at the 1991 Conference on Literature and Film: Social and Political Change, held at Florida State University. I especially want to acknowledge Linda Mizejewski's "Total Recoil: The Schwarzenegger Body on Postmodern Mars" and Robert E. Wood's "Re-Objectifying the Subjective in *Total Recall.* "

6. This abiding sense of suspicion is well placed, if we accept Fred Glass's argument that *Total Recall* uses the figure of Quaid/Hauser/Schwarzenegger as a kind of fetish object to disguise "all the unresolved ideological conflicts" it evokes for our consideration, including that in which a nuclear technology becomes, in essence, the savior of a planet of mutants who look suspiciously like the possible victims of nuclear radiation (12).

8

The Exposed Modern Body: *The Terminator* and *Terminator 2*

> This is deep!
>
> —*Terminator 2: Judgment Day*

Do not be misled by the above quote from *Terminator 2* (1991). Hardly "deep," this chapter only looks at surfaces, particularly at how the *Terminator* films, as symptomatic of robot texts in more recent years, play with appearances. I cite this remark by young John Connor, according to these films the prospective savior of humankind, though, because it emphasizes a type of response at which both aim—what may even be a type of "saving" response that our most recent works about human artifice, even in their schizophrenia, may be working toward. This remark indicates not only the amazement any ten-year-old might well register at the "heavy" thought of one day sending his father-to-be back in time to sire him but also a kind of awakening, a shock of recognition at the depths of human nature, even in the face of postmodern culture's tendency to reduce everything, including the self, to surfaces, so that we everywhere seem, as the previous chapter offers, exposed, vulnerable, almost irrelevant.

We might recall Baudrillard's description of this situation as he sketches the impact our technology is having on the human body. He says that in the postmodern world—which he likens precisely to "science fiction"—we live in a state of "pure presence" or "overexposure," in that "obscene" condition we earlier defined (*Ecstasy* 17, 32). With "everything . . . so immediately transparent, visible, exposed" (21–22), the human body easily becomes little more than an object for a dispassionate gaze, an object with no hidden dimensions, no real desire, no purpose.[1] As we have already seen, *real* science fiction—at least the science fiction film—has in the last decade taken a singular tack in exposing this pattern of exposure. In a near fixation on the artificial, technologized body—the robot, cyborg, android—the genre has tried to examine our ambivalent feelings about technology, our growing anxieties about our own nature in an increasingly technological environment, and a kind of evolutionary fear that these artificial selves may presage our own disappearance or *termination*.

At the root of that fear, O. B. Hardison, Jr., feels, is a blurred or "weakening . . . sense" (321) of what it means to be human, a loss of distinction or equating of all things that has become quite commonplace in the postmodern world. The *Terminator* films, along with similar robot movies of recent times, target this superficiality, which they expose by placing the artificial body, as a trope for the self, in front of the scene (as the word "obscene" implies), out in the open, where we might gauge its depths—and our own. In the way that this wave of films about a human artifice is trying to recuperate our "deep" sense, our sense of self, our very humanity, they suggest a significant pattern of resistance to that creeping postmodern overexposure.

· · ·

As the focus for this chapter, I want to examine two of the most important recent movies about human artifice, the *Terminator* films. Both of these works describe a confrontation between humans and cyborg time-travelers from a future in which humans have nearly disappeared. As the films' titles imply, the goal of these creatures of artifice is to further that ongoing disappearance, in the first by killing the mother of the man who will lead the humans against a robotic hegemony, and in the second by killing the future leader himself while he is still just a boy. In posing such an ultimate threat to humanity, these figures of artifice point up the vulnerability of the human body, as they try to hasten its replacement by the very technology that is, in our own time, already replacing us in the factories, outstripping us in mental calculations, and generally making us feel exposed and insecure. But these films do more than just warn us about or measure the symptoms of our current "tremulous" state; they also signal a development, point a direction of possible response to that state. In that capacity, they are most fitting caps for this book's discussion of human artifice.

Both films treat the body in a similar manner. The manufactured bodies of the cyborgs they depict are not simply sites of special effects displays but measures of our own human level of "manufacture," our own constructedness. At the same time, the narratives emphasize the difficulty we have today in really seeing ourselves. In the postmodern environment Baudrillard describes as "visible, the all-too-visible, the more-visible-than-visible" (*Ecstasy* 22), we typically seem to lack the perspective needed to see things—or ourselves—clearly. Thanks to our cultural fascination with surfaces and superficial effects, we no longer seem able to focus beyond that which is constantly exposed for us. And this difficulty, Baudrillard suggests, often leaves us resembling the schizophrenic who "can no longer produce himself as a mirror" (27), and who thus floats free of any secure identity. The *Terminator* films, though, seem intent on reproducing this mirror, at finding ways to let us see the self through the image of the constructed body, while also revealing the very problem of seeing that plagues both our world and our films.

James Cameron's original *The Terminator* speaks to this world of superfice by contrasting two discourses on the body. Most obviously, the film presents the technologized body, the android Terminator, as a kind of ultimate threat, directed not just toward a specific individual but toward humanity itself. For if the Terminator can kill Sarah Connor, the eventual mother of the human leader, then all of humanity will be terminated and replaced by machines. In this way, and particularly in depicting the other, technologized body as menace, the film seems to replay an old and often-told story of modern society's "technophobia,"[2] the fear that our constructions might eventually shape our destruction. It is a story picked up by a number of films that would try capitalizing on *The Terminator*'s success, but most notably by *Hardware* (1990)

At the same time, the film explores another sort of construction centered around the body, the manner in which it assumes a controlling cultural inscription, becomes almost in spite of itself a cultural construct. More specifically, it questions how notions of the feminine, the masculine, even the "normal" are imposed on us.[3] In linking these two discourses— the physically constructed body and the culturally inscribed self—the film ties the shaping, coloring power of technology to that of culture. It thereby suggests that these are not at all separate influences, but linked, mutual powers that wield a similar and indeed joint influence on us. In

all of my subsequent references to a technologized self here, then, I want
to evoke not only the "ecstatic" impact of technology that Baudrillard
emphasizes but also a larger historical/cultural manipulation and inscription of the self, one in which our films have historically assisted.

Of course, the first film's title implies that its central concern is the
technological threat, embodied in a killer cyborg which, for all of Arnold
Schwarzenegger's excess muscularity, disconcertingly blends in with the
human: speaks our language, crudely follows our basic customs, acts in
roughly effective ways.[4] In fact, the film emphasizes just how easy it is to
"pass" for human in a world that judges that status so superficially. As
Sarah's human protector Reese explains, while the earlier model Termi-
nators had crude rubber skin and were easily distinguished from humans,
the newer model has become, at least to all appearances, almost undetect-
able. To dramatize the danger in that situation, a flashback shows a Terminator gaining entry to a human hideout and slaughtering the people
there.

In a present that is surrounded by technology, where no one is primed
to watch for such technological threats, and indeed where people seem
to pay little attention to each other anyway, the Terminator has a far
easier time passing. While he exits the time portal nude, he quickly finds
suitable dress—a leather jacket and punk clothes that he appropriates
from familiar types, three urban hoodlums. The clothes, his spiked hair,
and a perfectly shaped body let him almost "stylishly" fit into the cultural landscape of 1980s America. Certainly, he hardly looks out of place
in the Tech-Noir nightclub where he tracks Sarah. Programmed with a
limited set of verbal responses that suggests how superficial much of our
interaction has become, he easily negotiates his way in our world: rents a
room, acquires weapons, gains the information needed to locate Sarah.

Yet this figure undergoes a gradual deconstruction that points up how
difficult it is to "read" the body, yet also how necessary. To get at Sarah
and defeat her bodyguard Reese, the Terminator assembles an arsenal
of technological destruction. When his weapons empty or are discarded,
the Terminator becomes simply an embodiment of implacable force, the
imperative of programmed desire, the image of technological power itself.
But in the process, its human *seeming* gradually disappears: eyebrows
are singed off; an eye goes, exposing a video transmitter in its socket;
patches of hair and skin are blown away; and eventually the entire synthetic human covering burns off, leaving only the underlying mechanical chassis to continue, relentlessly, with its deadly mission. Thrusting

the human body to the fore, crafting this menacing image—an image that disturbs partly because it is one our culture either accepts or simply ignores—is a starkly *inhuman* technological power, the purpose of which is the destruction of the human image, or rather its replacement by whatever images it chooses to generate.

Here, though, is the sort of "deep" vision *The Terminator* strives for. The film strips away technology's alluring and human surface to show the potential total control over the human image it portends. That menace parallels the film's other focus on the body, its presentation of the female image through Sarah. She is a character who moves between self-determination and objectification, who seems easy prey precisely because she lacks a clear self-image, as if she already embodied the sort of manipulation of the self that a technological hegemony would promise. And in a way she does, as her public persona emphasizes. At work, outfitted in a pink dress and knee socks, she looks almost childlike. In action, she seems a familiar cultural construct—or even cinematic cliché: the attractive but clutzy waitress who not only can't balance a tray but, as she admits, "can't even balance my checkbook." Whether innocent or inept, she suggests the sort of superficial, stereotyped image with which, through films and television, we are already quite familiar, and one that seems the sorry destiny of this world.

Yet these initial appearances belie Sarah's depths and point the way for a deeper conflict with her cultural role. In effect, they are just as deceiving as the Terminator's urban punk image. Off the job, Sarah sports a markedly neutral, almost masculine style that the sequel will push to an extreme. She wears jeans, tennis shoes, t-shirts, rides a motorbike,[5] and shows an independent, at times aggressive, attitude. Thus she wittily terms the Big Boy statue at her restaurant "Big Buns"; plays jokes on callers with her answering machine; and when her boyfriend stands her up, simply goes out by herself. In fact, that independence is precisely what saves her from being killed with her roommate Ginger—who, in contrast, seems both obsessed and pleased with her own sexual image— when the cyborg first attacks. If the gradual stripping away of the Terminator's human seeming warns us not to judge an android by its cover, the gradual emergence of Sarah's character and potential as she responds to this threat reminds us that it is no more reliable to judge the human self by its various cultural trappings.

The Terminator, then, warns about a kind of technologically inspired way we have of judging the world and those in it on the basis of appearances, while it also cautions us about the basis of those appearances—how much they are simply constructed for us, without our awareness, and made to seem quite natural and transparent. No one nor no thing here is simply who or what it first seems. For this reason, it is quite fitting that the Terminator makes no discriminations in carrying out its prime directive; it simply kills *every* Sarah Connor in the telephone book to make sure it gets the right one. Reese, who appropriates a tramp's clothes and looks like a streetperson, is a picked soldier from the future and Sarah's only hope. And despite her remark about her own unlikely appearance—"Do I look like the mother of the future?" she asks Reese—Sarah proves to be just that, the fully self-sufficient mother of the man who will lead humanity to victory over the machines. By pointing up this slipperiness, the unexpected depths that mark all appearances, *The Terminator* challenges us to look again, to look more deeply, to pay more attention to a world and a self we are, with our technology *and* our culture, constantly constructing.

· · ·

In some ways, *Terminator 2* seems almost contrary to the first film's project. That sense follows from the fact that Schwarzenegger's Terminator here appears not as menace but as helper—a still imposing figure, but one that is reprogrammed, ordered about, and, despite its original basic function, "taught" not to kill. In recuperating the cyborg and compromising its technological threat, the film seems to support Mark Crispin Miller's assertion in "The Robot in the Western Mind" that a "change" is occurring in the robot's film image: "Instead of simply epitomizing the evils of technology, the imaginary robot now comforts its desperate audience with a fantasy of manageability" (295). In effect, he suggests that this image is just offering cold comfort at a time when the self seems ever more exposed and manipulated by our technological environment.

But the issue of "manageability" opens onto a deeper likeness to the first film and a similar warning the later one sounds. In a narrative move that perhaps too easily suggests our ability to control our technology, Sarah's son John finds that he has become the master of his own Terminator, and in order to convince the computer scientist Miles Dyson that his awesome servant is indeed a cyborg from the future, he commands the Terminator to "show him"—which it does in stark fashion by slicing itself open, peeling back its skin, and revealing its "deeps," the metal endoskeleton beneath. To get below that false surface in this film, noth-

Cyborg as both father and savior in *Terminator 2.*

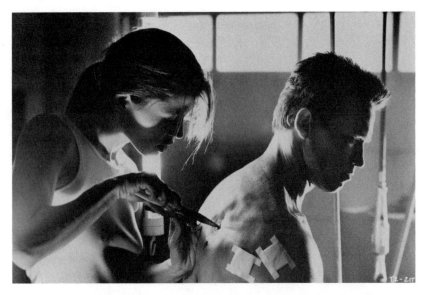

Poking into and repairing the cyborg in *Terminator 2.*

ing needs to be burned or shot away—although that too happens. In this
brief scene the film effects the same difficult revelation at which its predecessor worked so long. Yet for all the boy's ordering this deadly figure
about and the ease with which he reveals its depths, the problem of
appearances articulated by the earlier film remains. In fact, it becomes
even more pressing and disturbing thanks to the introduction of a new cyborg, the protean T-1000 which, with its poly-metal alloy construction, can
imitate "anything it samples by physical contact," any surface it touches.

While this film recuperates one Terminator, then, offering us almost
literally an *in*-sight into its workings, it also introduces a second whose
covering will not come off, whose surface we can never see beneath, in
fact, a figure that finally seems to be *all* surface—a kind of mobile Möbius
strip—with no real "inside." In the process, it suggests not a more man-
ageable situation or a greater, if false, comfort we might feel over technology's increasing place—and hegemony—in our lives but a sense of
how complex the problem has become, even as we become more accom-
modated to the technological. Visually indistinguishable from the human,
this new model is more indomitable and unswerving in its antihuman
mission than its predecessor, more than a match for a lately domesticated Terminator, and in many ways a starker projection of a technolo-

gized world's effects. And with this figure the film offers not just another technological menace, a fulfillment of the first Terminator's (and Schwarzenegger's) tag line, "I'll be back," but a new gloss on the nature of the self in a postmodern and *inevitably* technologized environment.

The central conception of *Terminator 2* is this advanced cyborg, with its almost infinitely variable, deceptive, and regenerative body. In the best mythic tradition, it is a shape-shifter, perhaps too an ultimate version of the gendered body, since it can, we see, as readily imitate a woman as a man, a crowbar, knife, or grappling hook as a human being. More than just another and extreme image of the body as construct, this figure with no fixed form suggests the very amorphousness of the body in what Ed Regis terms the "postbiological" age (175), and thus a menace implicit in having no clear shape, no definite form. The T-1000 simply adapts its deadly function to whatever shape and look are needed, and in the process warns about what shapes we give to our technological imaginings—and what shapes they might, in turn, give to us.

At the same time, this shape-shifter helps develop an emphasis on perspective that is keyed to the body and its representation in a technological environment. For the T-1000's ability to reshape itself points up our difficulty in correctly seeing and judging the world around us—a difficulty linked to the technologized environment's tendency to expose everything, including the body, thereby reducing it to little more than observable surfaces. When the body is all surface, exposed, a visible function, there is little point to considering motivations or to holding some special knowledge (such as the knowledge of the future Sarah has). All that really matters, it seems, is right before us. In such circumstances, scant space is left for human identity, or what in the previous chapter we termed a "private self."

Of course, the film's very premise poses one problem of perspective simply by asking us to see the Terminator as a protector, to believe in this technological power's good intentions, despite all our memories of the prior film. Moreover, various visual clues once again prompt us to read into it a deadly potential. Schwarzenegger's Terminator comes through the time portal *before* the T-1000, thus suggesting, after the pattern of the first film, that his goal is the pursuit of John Connor, not his protection. Further coloring his image is his "look," taken from a fringe social group usually seen as dangerous—bikers.[6] To the tune of "Bad to the Bone" on the soundtrack, he violently acquires jeans, a leather jacket, sunglasses, and motorcycle—all of which conspire to produce a menacing figure, even as he embarks on a *redemptive* mission, rescuing John from the T-1000 at a local mall. Even this rescue sequence opens in a disturbingly predictive way, with a series of disorientingly rapid tracking shots down a narrow corridor, punctuated by low-angle close-ups of Schwarzenegger's angular, almost inhuman face. When he suddenly extracts a sawed-off shotgun from a box of roses, and we see a close-up of his black-booted foot crushing the flowers, we cannot help but be less shocked than confirmed in our first impression, that he is indeed "back," another version of the earlier Terminator.

The infinitely malleable T-1000, which seems nothing but surface, only builds on these perceptual problems, for in contrast to the Terminator's culturally overdetermined image of menace, the T-1000 takes the reassuring form of a clean-cut cop. He too blends in, but not with fashion so much as with a conservative cultural climate. His relative slightness of build, ready smile, and polite manner craft an image that seems invitingly easy to read and generally positive. But when those characteristics prove to be the product of technological craft—of more advanced industrial design and development, dispassionate data processing, and mechanical efficiency—we have to reassess our ability to see and read this world, even question those common signs of trust, safety, and humanity in which our culture and our popular narratives trade.

As in the earlier film, this pattern of troubled perception extends beyond the technologized bodies of the Terminator and T-1000, to the central human characters, John and Sarah Connor. John, for instance, at first glance seems as unlikely a future hero as Sarah appeared a "mother of the future." His foster parents note he is always in trouble, and a police computer shows he has been charged with trespassing, shoplifting, disturbing the peace, and vandalism. In his first scene John ignores his foster mother when she asks him to clean his room, roars off on his motorbike when his foster father approaches, and steals $300 from an auto-teller to play video games and shop at the mall. His sloppy appearance, antisocial behavior, and motorbike mark him as a rebel without any apparent cause, one we read as negatively—and just as quickly—as the Terminator with whom John will later show such affinity.

But those initial appearances gain new resonance when his suspicion of all authority figures and his bike-riding prowess help him escape from the shape-shifting T-1000, and his electronic skills aid in destroying the information that will produce the destructive computer Skynet. Taken from his mother, placed in an uncaring foster home, typecast as a "bad kid," rendered as a computer readout, John is a cultural version of the body reduced to surface, to pure presence, and thus left exposed, vulnerable, and manipulated. Beneath what we readily see lies an intelligent boy who longs for his mother, suffers from an absent father figure, and—like much of modern humanity—is both fascinated by and has a keen understanding of various sorts of technology. These latter traits especially look toward his initially unlikely alliance with the Terminator, as well as his ability to take charge of it and redirect its actions in a nonlethal direction.

Sarah, though, shows the clearest parallel to that link between the body and a problematic perception modeled by the T-1000. If in *The Terminator* Sarah seemed a stereotype of the disempowered female—a position she had to overcome if she and the rest of humanity are to survive—here she initially seems a quite different cliché—the ultrafeminist. The film introduces her in a way that emphasizes her body and a transformation that has occurred. Compulsively exercising, she has made herself hard and muscled—like a smaller version of the Terminator—in preparation for the apocalypse she believes to be coming. Along with her exercising, survival skills, and martial arts expertise, she has subjugated all of her emotions. As John notes, she exercises a constant self-control to avoid betraying any signs of weakness. In a way, she has technologized herself, shaped herself into the best *human* cyborg possible in order to cope with the menace posed by the future's real cyborgs.

In keeping with this hard surface she has crafted for the self, Sarah has become a key exhibit at the mental asylum, where she is displayed and described as a curious case by the head psychiatrist. We several times see her from his point of view, as he interviews her, shows tapes of her bizarre behavior and comments on it, and offers a detached, clinical assessment of her delusions to the student doctors. Yet we also quickly recognize the shortsightedness and miscomprehension of this distanced, objective, and thoroughly rational view, which sees Sarah as a depthless being, a body whose mind is completely gone. It is a misperception that looks toward her mistreatment by the hospital orderlies, who simply objectify the body, as we see when one of them licks and kisses her while she is strapped down and helpless.

However, while Sarah is not crazy, as these appearances might suggest and as the normative view of the doctor and hospital staff affirm, she has become much like the very thing she struggles against. Like the T-1000, she and humans in general are protean, almost infinitely adaptable to circumstances. It is one of our great strengths, what allows us to cope with change, yet also a potential problem. Sarah, John tells us, would "shack up with anybody she could learn from"—bikers, drug runners, soldiers of fortune, and so on—to acquire the survival and combat skills needed to deal with the bleak future she foresees.[7] She has also created an almost impenetrably hard, unfeeling surface that denies depth by disallowing displays of emotion or caring, as a defense against that cold, emotionless menace she must face. But what *Terminator 2* suggests is that such a self may not be the best solution for confronting the technological threat.

Sarah suffers from a recurring dream of helplessness, one in which, for all of her knowledge about the future, she can only stand by as her earlier, childishly clad self and a playground full of children are vaporized by a nuclear explosion. Despite her desire to help, to warn these victims, she remains fenced off from them, unable to save them or even herself. That nightmare has apparently served as a call to action, a spur to prepare in every way possible, but the physical distance and separation it emphasizes are also telling, emblematic of more than her temporal remove from these events. This problem becomes clearer when Sarah tries to act, to assassinate Miles Dyson, the "father" of Skynet, in effect, acting like the Terminator in the first film. Like a political assassin, she watches him from a distance through her infrared, telescopic sight. Despite the technological vantage she enjoys, Sarah misses and must cross the distance separating her from her victim. So she enters his house and there confronts not a depthless image of a man but a bleeding human, one who proves afraid less for himself than for his family. Seeing her victim in this *human* way, seeing the family bonds that evoke her own broken family, seeing *into* the lives of these people, and perhaps seeing *herself as Terminator,* she stays her hand.

That shift in perspective, as Sarah comes from behind her telescopic sight, abandoning her dispassionate gaze, has an important ripple effect, for it moves the computer expert to see his own work in a different, more human light, and eventually to help in destroying it, even at the cost of his own life. That movement also prepares us for Sarah's final confrontation with the T-1000, wherein she comes out of hiding, "shows" herself in order to save John from the cyborg. Despite her previous comments about steeling the self, hardening the emotions—fittingly, the final scene occurs in a *steel* mill, a place where even steel melts—Sarah confronts the T-1000 when it corners John and, in her near self-sacrifice, buys time for the protective Terminator to defeat the shape-shifter. Her action is particularly significant because of the sort of show it represents: a show of her inner self, of the emotions she has kept hidden, of the sort of caring John has throughout the narrative longed for, and the sort that, we might suppose, could best draw humanity back from what appears to be a dark destiny.

That the Terminator also gains a new perspective at this point seems equally significant. He has all along been puzzled by human emotions, by the depths to which they bear witness. Tears, for example, mystify him; do they mean something is "wrong" with John's eyes, he asks. But with this rather different sort of opening up—that is, with Sarah's show of motherly love, John's repeated demonstrations of his love and need for Sarah, the computer programmer's concern and sacrifices for his family (and, indeed, for the larger human family)—the Terminator, reprogrammed not to end life but to abet it and programmed, like humans, to learn from his experiences, begins to understand the complexity that cannot be shown by literally opening people up—or blowing holes in them.[8]

The altered human destiny that results here shows not only, as the film literally states, that we control our own fate but also that we are able to cope with the ongoing technologizing of the self. The self as surface, as a set of functions, as a hard, unfeeling thing, or as a subject codified by culture, "constructed" in a certain fashion by the world we inhabit, stereotypically represented by our popular narratives—this is the human problem rendered quite literally in both of these films. But it is a problem, they suggest, that we can deal with, even triumph over, thanks to the depth of human nature, which lets us be both hard and soft, steel the self against difficult times and open up to others, resist programming and reprogram the self, that is, construct a self free from the sort of superficial configurations our culture commonly imposes.

As these films imply with their dissection of a robotic logic of surface and depth, one key to coping with a world of artifice is seeing clearly, understanding the sort of "overlay" the modern technological environment imposes on our sense of self and how much it *values* that overlay. In his book *Technology as Symptom and Dream,* Robert Romanyshyn makes a similar connection. He links the development of technology and that of linear perspective in western culture, as he argues that we have historically produced "a distancing and detached vision" that interprets the body "as a spectacle" (117). As a result, he says, we have become far too much a culture of "dreamers"—of a certain sort. In this fantasizing, technology becomes "our cultural-psychological dream of distance from matter" (194). It is a dream that ultimately separates us from the world by depicting the self as an "invented . . . created . . . manufactured" and eventually superfluous thing (17).

Yet our very immersion in technology, Romanyshyn argues, also holds out "an opportunity" (10), for even while it impels us to hold things—or beings we might reduce to the status of things—at a distance, it is also a measurable "symptom" of that condition which, in its increasing impact on our lives, could help us see the world and the self anew. By reexamining that distant and superficial view of things it fosters, by peeling back the artificial surface and looking into our depths, we might recognize how much we have "lost touch with things" (194) and begin to reclaim the self.

That project seems well underway in our most recent films about a human artifice, for in their depiction of androids and cyborgs that easily pass as humans, they repeatedly evoke this difficulty we have in seeing—seeing in a proper, human way. "If only you could see what I've seen with your eyes," the replicant Roy Batty tells the crafter of his artificial eyes in *Blade Runner.* Cast in the role of redeemer, driven by a desire for life, he helps point up—and remedy—the dark, death-serving vision that Rick Deckard has adopted. At an opposite extreme is the voyeur Linc of *Hardware,* who watches his neighbor Jill through an infrared telescope, fantasizes about her, and, when she seeks help against an attacking android, tries to finish the job and rape her. A kind of human extension of that film's frightening shape-shifting robot and an emblem of the surveillance company for which he worked, Linc shows how our technology can reinforce a human distance, making us all into spectators, and priming us to see each other as little more than superficial images of desire. As the previous chapter suggested, *Total Recall*'s Doug Quaid, prodded by an equally superficial image, a computer-screen projection of himself, moves in a rather different direction. With the help of the rebel Kuato, he casts aside his artificial identity, looks inside himself to discover his real self. It is a search that is only completed when he quite literally penetrates the depths of Mars, where he discovers and activates a mechanism that will create a humanly hospitable atmosphere. Both that sort of penetration, into the self, and that sort of product, a human environment, seem most urgent in an age of surfaces, when virtual realities and virtual versions of the self stand ready to distance us ever further from our world and others, as a film like *Lawnmower Man* (1993) well illustrates.

Of course, film is itself a medium of surfaces, a technologically based one dedicated to reproducing the image, especially the human image. Vis-à-vis the situation described here, it thereby occupies a problematic but significant position—and the science fiction film, thanks to its technological focus, even more so. The contemporary science fiction film, with its emphasis on a technologized, artificial self and on the deceptive, superficial world we have all too unwittingly crafted, might well be trying to recuperate something more than just the self, then. As newer forms of technological reproduction, such as video, computer graphics, and virtual reality generators, appear and threaten to render it obsolescent or take its place, film may be working out its own strategies of recuperation and survival. In questioning its own technological fundament, in probing *beneath* these surfaces, in suggesting that it can, in effect, offer a privileged access to our *human depths,* even through those images of artifice, the science fiction film may also be trying to affirm the cinema's own *difference* from these other forms and to stabilize its tentative position in our cultural imagination.

As measured by their box office success, as well as by the warning they sound against computer-fashioned images of the human such as the T-1000, the *Terminator* films stand out as benchmarks in such a project. Yet of more immediate significance is their human work: the way they suggest, through their artificial beings, the dangers and the hope implicit in our creations (including our films), while reminding us of the depths of which we are already losing sight. Our human vulnerability, they imply, *is* our superficiality, the surface-ness Baudrillard describes, the too simple view that science fiction's critics too often ascribe to the genre. We seem so vulnerable not simply because we are today everywhere exposed, deprived of some haven from others' prying eyes, but because we have, in the process of fashioning such a world, denied our interior life, our identity, a private self independent of the public and artificial one our culture defines for us. It too often seems as if there is simply nothing inside for us to show. In their images of this modern technologized body, the *Terminator* films, as paradigms of our human artifice narratives, offer us our reflection. They make our "exposed" condition "all-too-visible" and, by pushing through those surfaces, stake out a future path to recuperating the human.

· NOTES ·

An earlier version of this chapter appeared as "*The Terminator, Termina- tor 2,* and the Exposed Body" in *Journal of Popular Film and Television* 20.2 (Summer 1992): 26–34 and is reprinted with changes by permission of the Helen Dwight Reid Educational Foundation. Published by Heldref Publica- tions, 1319 18th Street, N.W., Washington, DC 20036–1802. Copyright 1992.

1. In *Forget Foucault,* Baudrillard suggests that the "obscene" destiny our culture seems to have ordained for us is *not* inevitable. He offers that we can cope with or confound it by what he calls a "reversible cycle" (43). In effect, we can "put on the act of obscenity," fashion our own "rituals of transparency" (34), and by foregrounding our "overexposure" regain a sense of self. This is the process I see being enacted in much of contemporary science fiction film.

2. In their essay "Technophobia," Michael Ryan and Douglas Kellner describe a special twist in the great number of "technophobic" films that appeared in the 1970s and 1980s, including *The Terminator.* They posit a contradiction in the era's dominant ideology, arguing that conservatism "re- quires technology for its economic programme" but "fears technological mod- ernity on a social and cultural plane" (65). The films thus hint at an ongoing cultural tension. While Ryan and Kellner questionably ascribe that tension to a contemporary clash between liberal and conservative ideologies, we should note that a similar ambivalence toward the technological runs through the whole history of the science fiction film.

3. In her feminist reading of the contemporary science fiction film, Mary Ann Doane argues that whenever the genre "envisages a new, revised body as a direct outcome of the advance of science," the question of gender con- struction naturally follows, since cultural definitions of the feminine and the maternal are "inevitably involved" ("Technophilia" 163).

4. We might see a reflexive dimension here, since these characteristics could just as easily describe the persona of these films' star attraction, Arnold Schwarzenegger. He too, after a fashion, speaks our language, crudely fol- lows our customs, and "acts" in roughly effective ways. Moreover, in a man- ner that some must surely find disconcerting, for all of his differences he has managed to blend right into the contemporary American scene.

5. Sarah's motorbike provides a telling link between *The Terminator* and *Terminator 2.* In the latter film we first see her son John working on his own motorbike, demonstrating his mastery over this piece of technology. When the Terminator acquires transportation, it is fittingly a motorcycle, a larger, adult version of John's vehicle that points toward his eventual, fatherly rela- tionship with the boy. While Sarah and John depend to some degree on the

technological, they also show their control over it through their masterly riding of these vehicles in the chase scenes.

6. We should note how both films use culturally overdetermined images—punk muggers, bikers—to introduce and *trouble* our initial perception of Schwarzenegger's Terminator. On the level of cultural wish fulfillment, the cyborg's routing of these menacing types must satisfy many viewers. But that enjoyment is compromised by the escalating violence in these scenes and, especially in the first film, by a sense that *we* are on the human side, allied with the prey of this technological menace. Both films seem intent on evoking this complex pattern of response, a kind of "guilty pleasure," in part to lay bare our own level of inhumanity, and at the same time our own uneasy place vis-à-vis the technological. Furthermore, these scenes prove disturbing precisely insofar as they imply a certain level of violence is not only justified but even necessary if we are to control our lives, maintain our identities, direct our destinies.

7. It is worth noting the extent to which heat and cold become emblematic conditions here. Sarah, we note, is noticeably "cold" toward her son. Since his birth, she has apparently been afraid to let herself feel or express any human warmth; thus she has gone from one brief relationship to another. That coldness is a possible way of steeling oneself against the impending threat of the machines. In fact, the first time the T-1000 is stopped, it occurs, suitably, thanks to a very literal coldness; he is doused with liquid nitrogen. However, that solution proves only temporary, and he is finally destroyed thanks to the fires of the steel mill—a destruction that follows from Sarah's and the Terminator's increasing displays of "warmth," of personal caring for young John.

8. We might read in this context of opening up and penetration the scene in which Sarah uncovers the arsenal she has been hoarding in anticipation of the coming war with the machines. As John and the Terminator descend into the underground bunker and inspect the variety of weapons there, they discuss Sarah and the boy tries to explain—*to* the Terminator but more *for* himself—why she has all these things and why she is the way she is. It is a very literal depth analysis, a penetration beneath the hard desert surface, accompanied by an effort to penetrate the cold, hard surface Sarah has cultivated.

Conclusion: An Overview

In Jack Arnold's classic science fiction film *The Incredible Shrinking Man* (1957), a young man sunbathing on a boat is suddenly showered by a cloud of radioactive dust—presumably the fallout from recent atomic testing. Several months later, he discovers he is shrinking at a rate of about an inch a week. As he grows ever smaller, his daily routine, his marriage, and finally the very nature of his life disintegrate, and he finds that just to exist he must battle a variety of unanticipated menaces: his "pet" cat, a spider in his basement, and his own despairing psyche, among others. As he continues shrinking, he eventually becomes invisible to the normal world. No larger than a dust mite, he crawls through a ventilator and finds himself in the world outside his former home. It is a world that, thanks to its vast scale, he finds frightening yet at the same time strangely reassuring. For here there is no human mismeasure: no outsized furniture, no unwieldy doors and windows, no humbling, gigantic wife, only the natural world in which there are always things larger and smaller, an infinite scale in which, whatever further changes he might endure, he could still find a place.

Carlos Clarens has suggested that this film introduced "a very different type of fear" into the movies of the cold war era, not one of "instant annihilation," as was then so very commonplace in the science fiction genre, but rather a kind of existential anxiety, that of "a gradual inexorable descent into nothingness" (133). While this "nothingness" does imply a type of annihilation, a literal disappearance of the individual from the Earth, it also suggests another, and far more subtle, fear that would increasingly become a hallmark of the genre and that seems an all-too-familiar dimension of postmodern culture—a terror at the unstable, constantly shifting measure of what it means to be a human being, in fact, the virtual disappearance of measure itself in the face of a technology that has seemed to render everything, including the human, open to alteration. For the various physical obstacles the shrinking man has to contend with finally only metaphorize a far larger problem he embodies: how to cope with a world and a self that no longer have a common or consistent measure, in which the very way we think about or define the self has so radically shifted that we are no longer sure just what we are—or if we are anything more than cosmic dust mites, essentially invisible and insignificant in the general scale of the universe.

Such a fear is hardly unique to this movie, nor, as the preceding chapters have suggested, to the science fiction films that followed it. The shrinking man, a product of our technology, stands not so much as a warning but as a basic metaphor of the postmodern condition—and, while not quite a human artifice story itself, this film rather neatly binds up, in a nearly allegorical way, the thrust of all such tales. For in these narratives, the various images of *imagined,* crafted, constructed beings challenge our sense of what we *really* are; their embodiments of alternate versions of the self leave our common measure of human being— even humanity itself—open to recalculation. In effect, their presence cannot help but make us consider whether we are ourselves shrinking; or as O. B. Hardison, Jr., puts it, "disappearing through the skylight" of our technological constructs (xi); or as Gabriele Schwab more darkly suggests, "destroying us as the subjects we thought ourselves to be when we took refuge in technological projects and dreams" (81).

That troubling position into which we have "thought ourselves" seems to have become a kind of defining circumstance for modern being. As Larry McCaffery has remarked, it is certainly a "spectre haunting nearly all postmodern" art (15). The works of "cyberpunk" writers like William Gibson and Bruce Sterling, mainstream figures like William S. Burroughs, Thomas Pynchon, and Don DeLillo, various industrial sculptors and performance artists, as well as most contemporary science fiction films, he suggests, all strike a common note: "the uneasy recognition that our primal urge to replicate our consciousness and physical beings (into images, words, machine replicants, computer symbols) is *not* leading us closer to the dream of immortality, but is creating merely a pathetic parody, a metaexistence or simulacra of our essences that is supplanting us, literally taking over our physical space and our roles with admirable proficiency and without the drawbacks of human error and waste" (15– 16). Here again we note not only that anxiety of disappearance but, more precisely, a questioning of the very "thought," the rationale propelling our technologically generated simulacra. In this widespread attitude McCaffery senses, on the one hand, a general cultural recoil from what he terms "the powerful and troubling technological logic that underlies the postmodern condition" (16), and on the other, an ongoing effort, throughout our popular culture, to confront that disturbing "logic."

Both the "technological logic" itself and the nature of our ongoing confrontation with it thus deserve our consideration. In fact, the very turn toward science fiction, what McCaffery describes as the tendency of much postmodern art "to borrow" the motifs, language, images, and subjects of the genre (10), seems telling. For if science fiction has come to provide us with a common and, as George Slusser in his essay "Literary MTV" neatly puts it, "correct vector" for dealing meaningfully with "our technocentury," or at least for recognizing its "troubling" portents (335), it is because of that special "logic" which is so central to the genre, its persistent focus on how we think of or measure ourselves. In our films of human artifice, dating from the very origins of the cinema, that ongoing fascination with the measure of the self moves to the foreground and lets us immediately interrogate just what sort of "subjects we [have] thought ourselves to be" in the course of this century that has been so dominated by technological development.

At the same time, as *The Incredible Shrinking Man* further implies, these films manage to locate a hope in that logic, a sense not simply that we are in the process of creating our replacements, assisting in our own extinction, but that we are also reframing and reaffirming our humanity. Certainly, Arnold's film is disconcerting enough; its image of unstable human being obviously an anxious response of cold war America to the destructive technology it had created and unleashed. It illustrated—quite literally—the sort of "fallout" already blowing our way from the arms race and development of ever more destructive weaponry, as it suggested how such technological consequences might alter our very being. Yet its conclusion also affirmed our ability to face such a radical transformation, and even to gain a kind of victory over it. Like other science fiction films, it deployed the latest scientific and technological developments as a lever, to pry loose our modern identity—as technological beings who drive compulsively to alter the world and the self, even to the point of our potential disappearance—and it found in that identity (one might argue, out of some ideological necessity) a flexibility to cope with those circumstances.

That same flexibility marks the larger body of human artifice films as well, which by turns appear to express great anxiety and yet sound a note of affirmation. Nearly every image of the robot, android, or cyborg as menace or monster seems balanced by similar figures cast in harmless, helpful, and, most recently, even *redemptive* roles. The plotting android Ash of *Alien* (1979) gives way to the self-sacrificing Bishop of *Aliens* (1986); the killer cyborg of *The Terminator* (1984) comes back as the father-figure cyborg of *Terminator 2* (1991); and the cyborg Murphy of the *Robocop* films (1987, 1990, 1993) repeatedly battles and overcomes monstrous robotic creations in the course of upholding the law—and rule—of humans. In these films that "primal urge to replicate," as McCaffery puts it, ends not calamitously but with an affirmation of the human spirit and a suggestion that our technological likenesses are not so much our *replacements* as our *extensions,* not really our *mismeasure* but in some way an *expansion* of the human measure.

In this regard, moreover, those likenesses shed light on another sort of replication; they point to the inherently reflexive nature of these narratives. Every movie about human artifice bears the potential of turning itself inside out, of resembling a kind of Möbius strip, as it invokes the movies' very nature. A product of our technology, the movies serve that urge to replicate by crafting images in our own likeness, images not bound by time or space or subject to normal human limitations, and images that provide us with a new measure of what we might be. In effect, every film is, at its base, a story of human artifice, and every human artifice story is, on one level, a tale of the movies.[1]

Like the robot Maria of *Metropolis,* our movies' images exercise a most seductive pull. It is, after all, quite easy for audiences to live in and through those images, to give themselves over to an imaginary world and self, to let it, after a fashion, do our "work" for us. And indeed, the movies have always been viewed suspiciously and even attacked precisely for exercising such power. But in this subtly reflexive turn, that power seems to be employed in our service. A film like *Robocop,* for example, not only shows through its transformed Murphy how our efforts at human artifice might affect us but it also, through its numerous sendups of newscasts and television advertisements, indicates how the mass media already wield a shaping, even controlling, influence over us. It thereby offers us some awareness of and perhaps even power over the manipulations that abound within that realm Baudrillard describes as "the ecstasy of communication."

Cop menaced by remotely controlled robotic spiders in *Runaway.*

The artificial being destroys its maker in *Android.*

The temporary imprint of the shape-changing alien of *The Thing.*

Of course, whether these films can truly subvert the manipulations and ongoing transformations of the self worked by the modern media environment is a difficult, probably unanswerable question. Understanding the complex economy of the mass media hardly constitutes a freedom from it. But in that reflexive moment, our films of human artifice at least sketch the dimensions of those inevitable and anxiety-laden interworkings of the human and the technological: as we build an ever more complex world, as we fashion perhaps helpful mechanical versions of the self, even as we go about making our movies (using more complex, computer-assisted, practically robotic components).

Having pushed in that speculative direction, I also want to rein in the broader claims of this book. I do not mean to suggest that the particular view of the science fiction film offered here is the most accurate one, the only correct one, a critical reduction that will provide us with the one true view of the genre. There is, of course, no such "one true view," even though every account would implicitly suggest as much. Certainly, most commentators on the genre seem to have seized, in much the way I have

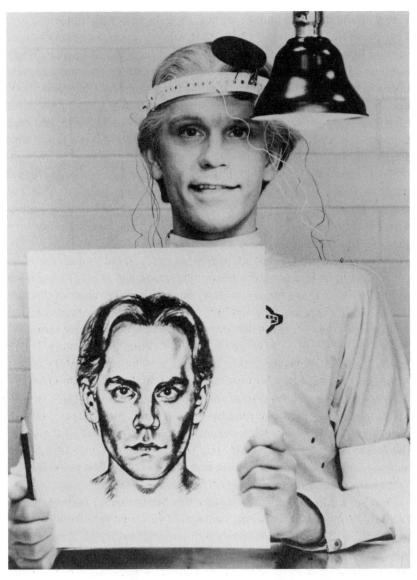

Making Mr. Right: Man made in his own image—only better.

here with the image of human artifice, on a single key phenomenon as a kind of tool of revelation, a lever that will pry open the secret box of science fiction. Perhaps the most often cited piece on this genre, Susan Sontag's "The Imagination of Disaster," observed the great wave of alien invasion and world catastrophe films appearing in the 1950s and 1960s and discerned in them a singular driving impulse. She suggested that all of science fiction was in fact propelled by a fascination with our own capacity for destruction. Similarly, Margaret Tarratt in her essay "Monsters from the Id" discerns, throughout the genre's repeated confrontations of reason and science with human emotions, a highly charged sexual imagery. Based on that recurrent imagery, she then suggests that the science fiction film is, in effect, *about* sexual repression. Numerous other articles, including some of my own, follow this same essentialist pattern in trying to parse out the genre's "truth."

In approach, the present study differs mainly in the partialness of its claims and in its bias toward a historical accounting. While I have tried to isolate the image of human artifice, trace its key appearances through the history of the science fiction film, and draw out of that image varying reflections of the genre's crucial concerns, this volume also stops short—as history, as explication of the genre, and as cultural commentary. It can finally claim to be no more than a partial and inflected history of the genre, a kind of lengthy footnote to Vivian Sobchack's essential survey *Screening Space* or John Baxter's earlier *Science Fiction in the Cinema*. My emphasis on—and enthronement of—a single phenomenon clearly shortchanges others deserving concerns, such as the image of the alien, the futuristic city, or space and time travel.[2] And the level of cultural analysis I offer tends to swerve a bit from the sort of explicit politicization that marks much current writing on film and technology.

And yet for all of these limitations, this book offers, I believe, a particularly fitting and even *useful* vantage, in fact, one that could help us sort out the historical developments in our science fiction films, correlate them to the developments in our culture, especially its confrontation with the potentials of technology for altering, completely transforming, or even destroying the self, and come to a better understanding of why this genre has proven so accommodating to the exploration of many of our most pressing contemporary concerns. That is, from the perspective afforded by that image of human artifice we might appreciate why science fiction may well be the best generic *fit* or "correct vector" for exploring postmodern culture and the absence of measure that seems to be its most disturbing fallout.

Certainly, the contemporary science fiction film invites us to catalogue our culture's major anxieties. Here issues of race (*Blade Runner, The Brother from Another Planet*), gender (*Aliens, The Handmaid's Tale*), sexuality (*Cherry 2000, Liquid Sky*), and international politics (*Robot Jox, Robot Wars*) seem to find ready expression in narratives we at one time slightingly described as "space operas." These films can accommodate such diverse concerns, though, because the genre has always bracketed off a special *kind of space*—a space wherein technology and humanity interact, as each helps to measure and evaluate the other, a space precisely occupied by those artificial beings that so abound in today's science fiction films. The genre has obviously staked out as its special territory the latest possibilities for artifice, and it has done so typically through the very latest technological developments of the cinema—computer animation, blue-screen techniques, morphing, and so on. And yet artifice finally seems to be less its end than its method, like our films, simply a most effective way we have developed for gauging the human.

· NOTES ·

1. It should be argued as well that every film about artifice also provides us with a new measure of what the movies might be. In their increasing reliance on computer-assisted animation and modeling, our artifice films also expand our very conception of film, advance a further step toward integrating the cinematic with the electronic, linking the recording capacity of film with the creative power of the multimedia computer workstation.

2. Treatments of the various semantic and syntactic components of the science fiction genre are almost too numerous to mention here. For its discussion of the alien, though, I would single out Patrick Lucanio's *Them or Us: Archetypal Interpretations of Fifties Alien Invasion Films;* for his treatment of the genre's almost inevitably dystopian future, note H. Bruce Franklin's "Don't Look Where We're Going: Visions of the Future in Science Fiction Films, 1970–1982"; and for her analysis of varieties of time travel, I recommend Constance Markey's "Birth and Rebirth in Current Fantasy Films."

Selected Filmography: Robot, Android, Human Duplication Films

What follows is a select listing of films that address, in various ways, the notion of the artificial human or human duplication. This list is by no means a comprehensive survey of the topic, nor is it strictly limited to what are usually considered to be science fiction films. However, this filmography does sketch the broad outlines of the topic in film and thus marks off the territory covered by this study, while also suggesting directions one might look in beginning further exploration of the topic.

Alien (1979) 20th Century-Fox. Dir.: Ridley Scott. Prod.: Gordon Carroll. Scr.: Dan O'Bannon. Music: Jerry Goldsmith. Cast: Tom Skerritt, Sigourney Weaver, Ian Holm, John Hurt. 116 min.

Aliens (1986) 20th Century-Fox. Dir.: James Cameron. Prod.: Gale Ann Hurd. Scr.: Cameron. Designer: Peter Lamont. Ed.: Ray Lovejoy. Special Effects: Stan Winston. Music: James Horner. Cin.: Adrian Biddle. Cast: Sigourney Weaver, Michael Biehn, Paul Reiser, Carrie Henn. 138 min.

American Cyborg (1994) Cannon Pictures. Dir.: Boaz Davidson. Prod.: Mati Raz. Scr.: Brent Friedman, Bill Crounse, Don Pequignot. Cin.: Avi Karpick. Ed.: Alain Jakubowicz. Cast: Joe Lara, Nicole Hansen, John Ryan. 95 min.

Android (1982) New World. Dir.: Aaron Lipstadt. Scr.: James Reigle, Don Opper. Cin.: Tim Suhrstedt. Ed.: Andy Horvitch. Cast: Klaus Kinski, Norbert Weisser, Don Opper, Brie Howard. 80 min.

Attack of the Puppet People (1958) American International. Dir.: Bert I. Gordon. Scr.: George Worthing Yates. Cin.: Ernest Laszlo. Ed.: Ronald

Sinclair. Cast: John Agar, John Hoyt, June Kenney, Marlene Willis. 78 min.

Barbarella (1968) Paramount. Dir.: Roger Vadim. Scr.: Terry Southern, Vadim et al. Cin.: Claude Renoir. Design: Mario Garbuglia. Cast: Jane Fonda, John Phillip Law, Milo O'Shea, David Hemmings. 98 min.

The Black Hole (1979) Disney. Dir.: Gary Nelson. Prod.: Ron Miller. Scr.: Jeb Rosebrook, Gerry Day. Design and Special Effects: Peter Ellenshaw. Cast: Maximilian Schell, Anthony Perkins, Robert Forster, Yvette Mimieux. 97 min.

Blade Runner (1982) Ladd Co./Warner Bros. Dir.: Ridley Scott. Prod.: Michael Deeley. Scr.: Hampton Fanchen, David Peoples. Cin.: Jordan Cronenweth. Ed.: Terry Stallings. Design: Lawrence G. Paull. Music: Vangelis. Cast: Harrison Ford, Rutger Hauer, Sean Young. 124 min.

The Bride of Frankenstein (1935) Universal. Dir.: James Whale. Scr.: John L. Balderston, William Hurlbut. Cin.: John D. Mescall. Music: Franz Waxman. Cast: Boris Karloff, Colin Clive, Ernest Thesiger, Elsa Lanchester. 75 min.

Cherry 2000 (1988) Orion. Dir.: Steve De Jarnatt. Designer: John J. Moore. Cin.: Jacques Haitkin. Scr.: Michael Almereyda. Cast: Melanie Griffith, David Andrews, Ben Johnson, Tim Thomerson. 93 min.

Circuitry Man (1989) IRS Media. Dir.: Steven Long. Scr.: Steven Long, Robert Long. Art Direction: Chris Neely, Royce Matthews. Cast: Jim Metzler, Dana Wheeler-Nicholson, Vernon Wells, Dennis Christopher. 95 min.

The Clones (1973) Premiere International. Dir.: Paul Hunt, Lamar Card. Scr.: Steve Fisher. Cin.: Gary Grover. Cast: Michael Green, Gregory Sierra, Susan Hunt. 90 min.

The Colossus of New York (1958) Paramount. Dir.: Eugene Lourie. Scr.: Thelma Schnee. Cin.: John F. Warren. Design: Hal Pereira, John Goodman. Ed.: Floyd Knudtson. Cast: Ross Martin, Mala Powers, Otto Kruger. 70 min.

Crash and Burn (1990) Paramount. Dir.: Charles Band. Prod.: David Decoteau, John Schonweiler. Scr.: J. S. Cardone. Cin.: Mac Ahlberg. Ed.: Ted Nicolaou. Design: Kathleen Coates. Music: Richard Band. Cast: Paul Ganus, Megan Ward, Ralph Waite, Bill Mosely, Eva Larue. 90 min.

Creation of the Humanoids (1963) Genie Productions. Dir.: Wesley E. Barry. Scr.: Jay Simms. Cin.: Hal Mohr. Cast: Don Megowan, Erica Elliot, Frances McCann. 75 min.

Creator (1985) Universal. Dir.: Ivan Passer. Cast: Peter O'Toole, Vincent Spano, Mariel Hemingway, Virginia Madsen. 107 min.

The Creature Walks among Us (1956) Universal-International. Dir.: John Sherwood. Scr.: Arthur Ross. Cin.: Maury Gertsman. Ed.: Edward Curtiss.

Design: Alexander Golitzen, Robert E. Smith. Cast: Jeff Morrow, Rex Reason, Leigh Snowden. 78 min.

The Curse of Frankenstein (1957) Hammer. Dir.: Terence Fisher. Scr.: Jimmy Sangster. Cin.: Jack Asher. Ed.: James Needs. Cast: Peter Cushing, Christopher Lee, Hazel Court. 83 min.

Cyborg (1989) Canon. Dir.: Albert Pyun. Prod.: Menahem Golan, Yoram Globus. Scr.: Kitty Chalmers. Cin.: Philip Alan Waters. Design: Douglas Leonard. Music: Kevin Bassinson. Cast: Jean-Claude Van Damme, Deborah Richter, Vincent Klyn, Alex Daniels. 86 min.

Cyborg Cop (1993) NuWorld. Dir.: Sam Firstenberg. Prod.: Greg Latter. Scr.: Greg Latter. Cin.: Joseph Wein. Ed.: Alan Patillo. Cast: David Bradley, John Rhys-Davies. 97 min.

Cyborg 2 (1993) Vidmark. Dir.: Michael Schroeder. Prod.: Raju Patel, Alain Silver. Scr.: Mark Goldman, Ron Yanover, Michael Schroeder. Cin.: Jamie Thompson. Cast: Elias Koteas, Jack Palance, Angeline Jolie. 99 min.

Cyborg 2087 (1966) Republic. Dir.: Franklin Adreon. Prod.: Earle Lyon. Scr.: Arthur C. Pierce. Cin.: Alan Stensvold. Ed.: Frank P. Keller. Music: Paul Dunlap. Cast: Michael Rennie, Karen Steele, Warren Stevens. 86 min.

D.A.R.Y.L. (1985) Paramount. Dir.: Simon Wincer. Prod.: John Heyman. Scr.: David Ambrose, Allan Scott, Jeffrey Ellis. Music: Marvin Hamlisch. Cast: Barret Oliver, Mary Beth Hurt, Michael McKean. 100 min.

The Day Mars Invaded Earth (1963) 20th Century-Fox. Dir.: Maury Dexter. Prod.: Dexter. Scr.: Harry Spaulding. Cin.: John Nikolaus, Jr. Music: Richard LaSalle. Cast: Kent Taylor, Marie Windsor, William Mims. 70 min.

The Day the Earth Stood Still (1951) 20th Century-Fox. Dir.: Robert Wise. Scr.: Edmund North. Cin.: Leo Tover. Music: Bernard Herrmann. Ed.: William Reynolds. Design: Lyle Wheeler, Addison Hehr. Cast: Michael Rennie, Patricia Neal, Sam Jaffe, Billy Gray. 92 min.

Deadly Friend (1986) Warner Bros. Dir.: Wes Craven. Prod.: Robert M. Sherman. Scr.: Bruce Joel Rubin. Music: Charles Bernstein. Cast: Matthew Laborteaux, Kristy Swanson, Michael Sharrett, Russ Marin. 91 min.

Demon Seed (1977) MGM. Dir.: Donald Cammell. Prod.: Herb Joffe. Scr.: Robert Jaffe, Roger O. Hirson (based on Dean R. Koontz's novel). Cast: Julie Christie, Fritz Weaver, Gerrit Graham. 97 min.

The Devil Doll (1936) MGM. Dir.: Tod Browning. Scr.: Browning, Garrett Ford, Guy Endore, Erich von Stroheim. Cin.: Leonard Smith. Cast: Lionel Barrymore, Maureen O'Sullivan, Frank Lawton. 79 min.

Edward Scissorhands (1991) 20th Century-Fox. Dir.: Tim Burton. Prod.: Denise Di Novi. Scr.: Caroline Thompson. Cin.: Stefan Czapsky. Ed.: Richard Halsey. Cast: Johnny Depp, Winona Ryder, Dianne Wiest, Vincent Price. 100 min.

The Empire Strikes Back (1980) 20th Century-Fox. Dir.: Irvin Kershner. Prod.: Gary Kurtz. Scr.: Leigh Brackett, Lawrence Kasdan. Story: George Lucas. Cin.: Peter Suschitzky. Design: Norman Reynolds. Ed.: Paul Hirsch. Music: John Williams. Cast: Mark Hamill, Harrison Ford, Carrie Fisher, Billy Dee Williams. 124 min.

Eve of Destruction (1991) Orion. Dir.: Duncan Gibbins. Prod.: David Madden. Scr.: Duncan Gibbins, Yale Udoff. Cin.: Alan Hume. Ed.: Caroline Biggerstaff. Design: Peter Lamont. Cast: Gregory Hines, Renee Soutendijk. 101 min.

Flash Gordon (1936) Universal. Dir.: Frederick Stephani, Ray Taylor. Prod.: Henry MacRae. Scr.: Stephani, George Plympton, Basil Dickey, Ella O'Neill (based on Alex Raymond's comic strip). Cin.: Jerome H. Ash, Richard Fryer. Art Direction: Ralph Berger. Cast: Larry "Buster" Crabbe, Jean Rogers, Charles Middleton, Frank Shannon. Serial in thirteen chapters.

Flash Gordon Conquers the Universe (1940) Universal. Dir.: Ford Beebe, Ray Taylor. Prod.: Henry MacRae. Scr.: George Plympton, Basil Dickey, Barry Shipman (based on Alex Raymond's comic strip). Cin.: Jerome H. Ash, William Sickner. Art Direction: Harold H. MacArthur. Cast: Larry "Buster" Crabbe, Carol Hughes, Charles Middleton, Frank Shannon. Serial in twelve chapters.

Flash Gordon's Trip to Mars (1938) Universal. Dir.: Ford Beebe, Robert S. Hill. Prod.: Barney Sarecky. Scr.: Windham Gittens, Norman S. Hall, Ray Trampe, Herbert Dalmas (based on Alex Raymond's comic strip). Cin.: Jerome H. Ash. Art Direction: Ralph Delacy. Cast: Larry "Buster" Crabbe, Jean Rogers, Charles Middleton, Frank Shannon. Serial in fifteen chapters.

The Fly (1958) 20th Century-Fox. Dir.: Kurt Neumann. Scr.: James Cavell. Cin.: Karl Struss. Ed.: Merril G. White. Design: Lyle R. Wheeler, Theobold Holsopple. Cast: Al Hedison, Patricia Owens, Vincent Price. 94 min.

The Fly (1986) 20th Century-Fox. Dir.: David Cronenberg. Prod.: Stuart Cornfeld. Scr.: Charles Edward Pogue. Cast: Jeff Goldblum, Geena Davis, John Getz. 100 min.

Forbidden Planet (1956) MGM. Dir.: Fred McLeod Wilcox. Scr.: Cyril Hume. Cin.: George Folsey. Design: Cedric Gibbons, Arthur Lonergan. Cast: Walter Pidgeon, Leslie Nielsen, Anne Francis, Warren Stevens. 98 min.

The 4-D Man (1959) Universal-International. Dir.: Irvin Shortess Yeaworth, Jr. Scr.: Theodore Simonson, Cy Chermak. Cin.: Theodore J. Pahle. Ed.: William B. Murphy. Design: William Jersey. Cast: Robert Lansing, Lee Meriwether, James Congdon. 85 min.

Frankenhooker (1990) SGE Entertainment. Dir.: Frank Henenlotter. Prod.: Edgar Iovens. Scr.: Robert Marti, Frank Henenlotter. Cin.: Robert M. Baldwin. Ed.: Kevin Tent. Music: Joe Renzetti. Cast: Patty Mullen, James Lorinz, Louise Lasser, Vicki Darnell. 80 min.

Frankenstein (1931) Universal. Dir.: James Whale. Scr.: Garrett Fort, Francis Edward Farogh. Cin.: Arthur Edeson. Cast: Boris Karloff, Colin Clive,

Mae Clarke, Edward Van Sloan. 71 min.
Frankenstein Unbound (1990) Twentieth Century-Fox. Dir.: Roger Corman.
Prod.: Corman, Thom Mount, Kobi Jaeger. Scr.: Corman, F. X. Feeney.
Cast: John Hurt, Raul Julia, Bridget Fonda. 85 min.
Future Cop (1976). Dir.: Jud Taylor. Cast: Ernest Borgnine, Michael Shannon,
John Amos. 78 min.
Futureworld (1976) American International. Dir.: Richard T. Heffron. Cin.:
Howard Schwartz, Gene Polito. Scr.: Mayo Simon, George Schenck. Ed.:
James Mitchell. Cast: Peter Fonda, Blythe Danner, Arthur Hill, Yul Brynner.
104 min.
Galaxina (1980) Crown International. Dir.: William Sachs. Scr.: Sachs. Cast:
Stephen Macht, Dorothy Stratten, Avery Schreiber. 96 min.
Generation (1985) Embassy. Dir.: Michael Tuchner. Prod.: Bill Finnegan,
Pat Finnegan. Scr.: Gerald DiPego. Cin.: Robert E. Collins. Ed.: Carl
Kress, Randy D. Thornton. Design: William Sandell. Music: Charles
Bernstein. Cast: Richard Beymer, Hannah Cutrona, Marta Dubois, Drake
Hogestyn. 100 min.
Gog (1954) United Artists. Dir.: Herbert L. Strock. Prod.: Ivan Tors. Scr.:
Tom Taggart, Richard G. Taylor. Cin.: Lothrop Worth. Ed.: Herbert L.
Strock. Design: William Ferrari. Cast: Herbert Marshall, Richard Egan,
Constance Dowling. 82 min.
Der Golem (1920) UFA. Dir.: Paul Wegener, Carl Boese. Scr.: Wegener,
Henrik Galeen. Cin.: Karl Freund. Design: Hans Poelzig. Cast: Wegener,
Albert Steinruck, Ernst Dietsch. 93 min.
Le Golem (1936) Metropolis Pictures. Dir.: Julien Duvivier. Scr.: Andre-
Paul Antoine. Cin.: Vich, Stalich. Cast: Harry Bauer, Roger Karl, Gaston
Jacquet. 97 min.
The Guyver (1992) New Line. Dir.: Screaming Mad George, Steve Wang.
Prod.: Brian Yuzma. Cin.: Levie Isaacks. Ed.: Andy Horvitch. Design: Mat-
thew C. Jacobs. Cast: Mark Hamill, Vivian Wu, Jack Armstrong. 92 min.
Hardware (1990) Millimeter Films. Dir.: Richard Stanley. Prod.: Paul Tryghts,
Joanne Sella. Scr.: Richard Stanley. Cin.: Steven Chivers. Ed.: Derek Trigg.
Design: Joseph Bennett. Cast: Dylan McDermott, Stacey Travis, John
Lynch, William Hootkin, Iggy Pop. 92 min.
The Hidden (1987) New Line. Dir.: Jack Sholder. Scr.: Bob Hunt. Cin.:
Jacques Haitkin. Ed.: Michael Knue. Music: Michael Convertino. Cast:
Michael Nouri, Kyle MacLachlan. 98 min.
The H–Man (1959) Toho. Dir.: Inoshiro Honda. Scr.: Takeshi Kimura. Cin.:
Hajime Koizumi. Design: Takeo Kita. Cast: Kenji Sahara, Yumi Shirakawa.
79 min.
The Human Duplicators (1965) Allied Artists. Dir.: Hugo Grimaldi. Scr.:
Arthur C. Pierce. Cin.: Monroe Askins. Cast: George Nader, Barbara
Nichols, George Macready. 82 min.

Humanoid Defender (1985) MCA. Dir.: Ron Satloff. Prod.: Stephen P. Caldwell. Scr.: Nicholas Corea. Cast: Terence Knox, Garry Kasper, Aimee Eccles. 94 min.

I Married a Monster from Outer Space (1958) Paramount. Dir.: Gene Fowler, Jr. Scr.: Louis Vittes. Cin.: Haskell Boggs. Ed.: George Tomasini. Design: Jal Pereira, Henry Bumstead. Cast: Tom Tryon, Gloria Talbott, Ken Lynch. 78 min.

Invaders from Mars (1953) 20th Century-Fox. Dir.: William Cameron Menzies. Scr.: Richard Blake (and John Tucker Battle). Cin.: John Seitz. Ed.: Arthur Roberts. Design: Menzies. Cast: Helena Carter, Arthur Franz, Jimmy Hunt. 78 min.

Invaders from Mars (1986) Cannon. Dir.: Tobe Hooper. Prod.: Menahem Golan, Yoram Globus. Cin.: Daniel Pearl. Ed.: Alain Jakubowicz. Scr.: Dan O'Bannon, Don Jakoby. Special Effects: Stan Winston. Cast: Karen Black, Hunter Carson, Timothy Bottoms. 102 min.

Invasion of the Body Snatchers (1956) Allied Artists. Dir.: Don Siegel. Scr.: Daniel Mainwaring. Cin.: Ellsworth Fredericks. Design: Edward Haworth. Cast: Kevin McCarthy, Dana Winter, King Donovan, Carolyn Jones. 80 min.

Invasion of the Body Snatchers (1978) United Artists. Dir.: Philip Kaufman. Prod.: Robert H. Solo. Scr.: W. D. Richter (and Kaufman). Cin.: Michael Chapman. Ed.: Douglas Stewart. Design: Charles Rosen. Cast: Donald Sutherland, Brooke Adams, Leonard Nimoy, Jeff Goldblum, Veronica Cartwright. 115 min.

The Invisible Boy (1957) MGM. Dir.: Herman Hoffman. Scr.: Cyril Hume. Cin.: Harold Wellman. Ed.: John Faure. Design: Merrill Pye. Cast: Richard Eyer, Diane Brewster, Philip Abbot. 90 min.

Island of Dr. Moreau (1977) Orion. Dir.: Don Taylor. Prod.: John Temple Smith, Skip Steloff. Scr.: John Herman Shaner, Al Ramrus. Music: Laurence Rosenthal. Cast: Burt Lancaster, Michael York, Barbara Carrera, Richard Basehart. 104 min.

Island of Lost Souls (1933) Paramount. Dir.: Erle C. Kenton. Scr.: Waldemar Young, Philip Wylie. Cin.: Karl Struss. Cast: Charles Laughton, Richard Arlen, Leila Hyams. 70 min.

It Came from Outer Space (1953) Universal-International. Dir.: Jack Arnold. Scr.: Harry Essex. Cin.: Clifford Stine. Design: Bernard Herzbrun, Robert Boyle. Ed.: Paul Weatherwax. Cast: Richard Carlson, Barbara Rush, Charles Drake, Joe Sawyer. 81 min.

Killbots (1986, retitled *Chopping Mall*) Trinity Pictures. Dir.: Jim Wynorski. Cast: Kelli Maroney, Tony O'Dell, Russell Todd, Paul Bartel, Mary Woronov. 76 min.

The Lawnmower Man (1992) New Line. Dir.: Brett Leonard. Prod.: Gimel

Everett. Scr.: Leonard, Everett. Cin.: Russell Carpenter. Ed.: Alan Baumgarten. Design: Alex McDowell. Cast: Jeff Fahey, Peirce Brosnan, Jenny Wright. 108 min.

Logan's Run (1976) MGM/UA. Dir.: Michael Anderson. Prod.: Saul David. Scr.: David Zelag Goodman (based on William F. Nolan and George Clayton Johnson's novel). Cast: Michael York, Jenny Agutter, Peter Ustinov. 118 min.

Looker (1981) Warner Bros. Dir.: Michael Crichton. Prod.: Howard Jeffrey. Scr.: Michael Crichton. Music: Barry Devorzon. Cast: Albert Finney, James Coburn, Susan Dey. 93 min.

Mad Love (1935) MGM. Dir.: Karl Freund. Scr.: Guy Endore, P. J. Wolfson, John Balderston. Cin.: Chester Lyons, Gregg Toland. Cast: Colin Clive, Peter Lorre, Frances Drake. 83 min.

Making Mr. Right (1987) Orion. Dir.: Susan Seidelman. Scr.: Floyd Byars, Laurie Frank. Cast: John Malkovic, Ann Magnuson, Glenne Headly. 98 min.

The Man Who Turned to Stone (1957) Columbia. Dir.: Leslie Kardos. Scr.: Raymond T. Marcus. Cin.: Benjamin H. Kline. Ed.: Charles Nelson. Design: Paul Palmentola. Cast: Victor Jory, Charlotte Austin, William Hudson. 71 min.

Metropolis (1926) UFA. Dir.: Fritz Lang. Scr.: Lang, Thea von Harbou. Cin.: Karl Freund, Günther Rittau. Design: Otto Hunte, Erich Kettelhut, Karl Vollbrecht. Special Effects: Eugene Schüfftan. Cast: Brigitte Helm, Alfred Abel, Rudolf Klein-Rogge, Gustav Fröelich. 120 min.

Mysterious Doctor Satan (1940, retitled *Doctor Satan's Robot*) Republic. Dir.: William Witney, John English. Cast: Robert Wilcox, Eduardo Ciannelli, Ella Neal, William Newell. Serial in fifteen chapters.

Nightflyers (1987) New Century/Vista. Dir.: T. C. Blake. Prod.: Robert Jaffe. Scr.: Robert Jaffe. Music: Doug Tamm. Cast: Lisa Blount, Catherine Mary Stewart, Michael Praed. 88 min.

Peacemaker (1990) Fries Entertainment. Dir.: Kevin S. Tenney. Prod.: Andrew Lane, Wayne Crawford. Scr.: Kevin S. Tenney. Cin.: Thomas Jewett. Ed.: Daniel Duncan. Design: Robert Sissman. Cast: Robert Forster, Lance Edwards, Hilary Shepard. 85 min.

The Perfect Woman (1949) Two Cities. Dir.: Bernard Knowles. Scr.: Knowles, George Black. Cin.: Jack Hildyard. Design: J. Elder Wills. Cast: Patricia Roc, Stanley Holloway, Nigel Patrick, Pamela Davis. 89 min.

The Phantom Creeps (1939) Universal. Dir.: Ford Beebe, Saul Goodkind. Cast: Bela Lugosi, Robert Kent, Dorothy Arnold. Serial in twelve chapters.

The Phantom Empire (1935) Mascot. Dir.: B. Reeves Eason, Otto Brower. Prod.: Armand Schaefer. Scr.: Wallace MacDonald, Gerald Geraghty, H. Freedman. Cast: Gene Autry, Smiley Burnette, Frankie Darro, Betsy Ross King. Serial in twelve episodes.

The Questor Tapes (1974) Universal. Dir.: Richard A. Colla. Prod.: Howie Horwitz. Scr.: Gene Roddenberry, Gene L. Coon. Cin.: Michael Margulies. Ed.: Robert L. Kimble, J. Terry Williams. Music: Gil Melle. Cast: Robert Foxworth, Mike Farrell, Lew Ayres, Dana Wynter. 97 min.

Radar Men from the Moon (1951, reedited as *Retik, the Moon Menace*) Republic. Dir.: Fred C. Brannon. Scr.: Ronald Davidson. Cin.: John MacBurnie. Ed.: Cliff Bell. Design: Fred Ritter. Cast: Roy Barcroft, George Wallace, Aline Towne. Serial in twelve chapters.

The Retaliator (1987) Trans World. Dir.: Allan Holzman. Scr.: Robert Short. Cin.: Alex Nissim. Ed.: Michael Kelly. Cast: Robert Ginty, Sandahl Bergman, Alex Courtney. 100 min.

The Return of the Fly (1959) 20th Century-Fox. Dir.: Edward L. Bernds. Scr.: Bernds. Cin.: Brydon Baker. Ed.: Richard C. Meyer. Design: Lyle R. Wheeler, John Mansbridge. Cast: Vincent Price, Brett Halsey, David Frankham. 78 min.

Return of the Jedi (1983) 20th Century-Fox. Dir.: Richard Marquand. Scr.: Lawrence Kasdan, George Lucas. Cin.: Alan Hume. Ed.: Sean Barton, Marcia Lucas, Duwayne Dunham. Design: Norman Reynolds. Music: John Williams. Cast: Mark Hamill, Harrison Ford, Carrie Fisher, Billy Dee Williams. 133 min.

Revenge of Frankenstein (1958) Hammer. Dir.: Terence Fisher. Scr.: Jimmy Sangster. Cin.: Jack Asher. Ed.: James Needs. Design: Bernard Robinson. Cast: Peter Cushing, Francis Matthews, Michael Gwynn. 91 min.

Revenge of the Stepford Wives (1980) Embassy. Dir.: Robert Fuest. Prod.: Scott Rudin. Scr.: David Wiltse. Cin.: Ric Waite. Ed.: Jerrold Ludwig. Cast: Sharon Gless, Julie Kavner, Don Johnson, Arthur Hill. 100 min.

Robocop (1987) Orion. Dir.: Paul Verhoeven. Prod.: Arne Schmidt. Scr.: Edward Neumeier, Michael Miner. Cin.: Jost Vacaro. Ed.: Frank J. Urioste. Design: William Sandell. Special Effects: Peter Kuran. Music: Basil Poledouris. Cast: Peter Weller, Nancy Allen, Ronny Cox, Daniel O'Herlihy. 105 min.

Robocop 2 (1990) Orion. Dir.: Irvin Kirshner. Prod.: Jon Davison. Scr.: Frank Miller, Walon Green. Cin.: Mark Irwin. Ed.: Deborah Zeitman, Lee Smith, Armen Minasian. Design: Peter Jamison. Music: Leonard Rosenman. Cast: Peter Weller, Nancy Allen, Daniel O'Herlihy, Tom Noonan, Belinda Bauer. 116 min.

Robocop 3 (1993) Orion. Dir.: Fred Dekker. Prod.: Patrick Crowley. Scr.: Frank Miller, Fred Dekker. Cast: Robert John Burke, Nancy Allen, Rip Torn. 105 min.

Robot Jox (1990) Empire Pictures. Dir.: Stuart Gordon. Prod.: Albert Ball. Scr.: Joe Haldeman, from story by Stuart Gordon. Cin.: Marc Ahlberg. Ed.: Ted Nicolaou, Lori Scott Ball. Design: Giovanni Natalucci. Music:

Frederic Talgorn. Cast: Gary Graham, Anne-Marie Johnson, Paul Koslo, Michael Alldredge. 84 min.

Robot Monster (1953) Three Dimensional Pictures. Dir.: Phil Tucker. Prod.: Phil Tucker. Scr.: Wyatt Ordung. Cin.: Jack Greenhalgh. Ed.: Merrill White. Music: Elmer Bernstein. Cast: George Nader, Claudia Barrett, Selena Royale, John Mylong, George Barrows. 63 min.

Robot Wars (1993) Paramount. Dir.: Albert Band. Prod.: Charles Band. Scr.: Jackson Barr. Cin.: Adolfo Bartoli. Ed.: Margaret-Anne Smith. Cast: Don Michael Paul, Barbara Crampton, James Staley. 106 min.

Runaway (1984) Tri-Star. Dir.: Michael Crichton. Prod.: Michael Rachmil. Scr.: Crichton. Cin.: John A. Alonzo. Music: Jerry Goldsmith. Cast: Tom Selleck, Cynthia Rhodes, Gene Simmons. 99 min.

Saturn 3 (1980) ITC Entertainment. Dir.: Stanley Donen. Prod.: Donen. Scr.: Martin Amis. Cin.: Billy Williams. Music: Elmer Bernstein. Cast: Kirk Douglas, Farrah Fawcett, Harvey Keitel. 88 min.

Scream and Scream Again (1969) AIP. Dir.: Gordon Hessler. Scr.: Christopher Wicking. Cast: Vincent Price, Christopher Lee, Peter Cushing, Judy Huxtable. 95 min.

Seconds (1966) Paramount. Dir.: John Frankenheimer. Prod.: Edward Lewis. Scr.: Lewis John Carlino. Cin.: James Wong Howe. Design: Ted Haworth. Music: Jerry Goldsmith. Cast: Rock Hudson, John Randolph, Salome Jens, Will Geer. 106 min.

Short Circuit (1986) Tri-Star. Dir.: John Badham. Prod.: David Foster, Lawrence Turman. Scr.: S. S. Wilson, Brent Maddock. Ed.: Frank Moriss. Cast: Steven Guttenberg, Ally Sheedy, Fisher Stevens. 98 min.

Short Circuit 2 (1988) Tri-Star. Dir.: Kenneth Johnson. Prod.: David Foster. Scr.: S. S. Wilson, Brent Maddock. Ed.: Conrad Buff. Cin.: John McPherson. Cast: Fisher Stevens, Cynthia Gibb, Michael McKean. 110 min.

Silent Running (1972) Universal. Dir.: Douglas Trumbull. Scr.: Deric Washburn, Michael Cimino, Steve Bochco. Cin.: Charles F. Wheeler. Music: Peter Schickele. Cast: Bruce Dern, Cliff Potts, Ron Rifkin. 89 min.

Sleeper (1973) United Artists. Dir.: Woody Allen. Scr.: Woody Allen, Marshall Brickman. Cast: Woody Allen, Diane Keaton, John Beck, Mary Gregory. 88 min.

Star Trek—The Motion Picture (1979) Paramount. Dir.: Robert Wise. Prod.: Gene Roddenberry. Scr.: Harold Livingstone. Cast: William Shatner, Leonard Nimoy, DeForest Kelley, James Doohan, Nichelle Nichols, Persis Khambatta, Stephen Collins. 132 min.

Star Wars (1977) 20th Century-Fox. Dir.: George Lucas. Scr.: Lucas. Cin.: Gilbert Taylor. Ed.: Paul Hirsch, Marcia Lucas, Richard Chew. Design: John Barry. Special Effects: John Dykstra. Music: John Williams. Cast: Mark Hamill, Harrison Ford, Carrie Fisher, Alec Guiness. 121 min.

Steel and Lace (1990) Fries Entertainment. Dir.: Ernest Farino. Prod.: John Schouweiler, David DeCoteau. Scr.: Joseph Dougherty, Dave Edison. Cin.: Thomas L. Callaway. Cast: Bruce Davison, David Naughton, Clare Wren. 89 min.

The Stepford Children (1987) Taft Entertainment. Dir.: Alan J. Levi. Cast: Barbara Eden, Don Murray. 104 min.

The Stepford Wives (1975) Columbia. Dir.: Bryan Forbes. Prod.: Edgar J. Scherick. Scr.: William Goldman (based on Ira Levin's novel). Cin.: Owen Roizman. Design: Gene Callahan. Music: Michael Small. Cast: Katherine Ross, Paula Prentiss, Peter Masterson, Tina Louise, William Prince. 114 min.

The Terminal Man (1974) Warner Bros. Dir.: Mike Hodges. Prod.: Hodges. Scr.: Hodges (based on Michael Crichton's novel). Cast: George Segal, Joan Hackett, Richard Dysart. 107 min.

The Terminator (1984) Hemdale. Dir.: James Cameron. Prod.: Gale Anne Hurd. Cin.: Adam Greenberg. Scr.: Cameron, Hurd. Special Effects: Stan Winston. Cast: Linda Hamilton, Michael Biehn, Arnold Schwarzenegger. 108 min.

Terminator 2: Judgment Day (1991) Tri-Star/Carolco. Dir.: James Cameron. Prod.: Cameron. Scr.: Cameron, William Wisher. Cast: Linda Hamilton, Arnold Schwarzenegger, Edward Furlong, Robert Patrick. 135 min.

The Thing (1982) Universal. Dir.: John Carpenter. Scr.: Bill Lancaster (based on John W. Campbell's "Who Goes There?"). Special Effects: Rob Bottin (and Stan Winston). Cast: Kurt Russell, Wilford Brimley, Richard Dysart, Richard Masur. 127 min.

The Thing with Two Heads (1972). Dir.: Lee Frost. Cast: Ray Milland, Rosie Grier, Don Marshall. 93 min.

THX 1138 (1971) Warner Bros. Dir.: George Lucas. Scr.: Lucas, Walter Murch. Cin.: Dave Meyers, Albert Kihn. Design: Michael Haller. Music: Lalo Schifrin. Cast: Robert Duvall, Donald Pleasence, Maggie McOmie. 88 min.

Tobor the Great (1954) Republic. Dir.: Lee Sholem. Scr.: Phillip MacDonald. Cin.: John L. Russell, Jr. Ed.: Basil Wrangell. Design: Gabriel Scognamillo. Cast: Charles Drake, Billy Chapin, Taylor Holmes. 77 min.

Total Recall (1990) Tristar/Carolco. Dir.: Paul Verhoeven. Prod.: Ronald Shusett, Buzz Feitshans. Scr.: Ronald Shusett, Dan O'Bannon, Garry Goldman. Cin.: Jost Vacano. Ed.: Frank J. Urioste. Design: William Sandell. Music: Jerry Goldsmith. Cast: Arnold Schwarzenegger, Rachel Ticotin, Sharon Stone, Michael Ironside, Ronny Cox. 114 min.

Tron (1982) Disney. Dir.: Steven Lisberger. Prod.: Donald Kushner. Scr.: Lisberger. Cin.: Bruce Logan. Ed.: Jeff Gourson. Design: Dean Edward Mitzner. Music: Wendy Carlos. Cast: Jeff Bridges, Bruce Boxleitner, David Warner, Cindy Morgan. 96 min.

2001: A Space Odyssey (1968) MGM. Dir.: Stanley Kubrick. Prod.: Kubrick and Victor Lyndon. Scr.: Kubrick and Arthur C. Clarke (based on Clarke's story "The Sentinel"). Cin.: Geoffrey Unsworth and John Alcott. Ed.: Ray Lovejoy. Special Effects: Wally Veevers, Douglas Trumbull, Con Pederson, Tom Howard. Cast: Keir Dullea, Gary Lockwood, William Sylvester. 141 min.

The Undersea Kingdom (1936) Republic. Dir.: Joseph Kane, B. Reeves Eason. Prod.: Barney Sarecky. Scr.: John Rathmell, Maurice Geraghty, Oliver Drake. Cast: Ray "Crash" Corrigan, Monte Blue, Lon Chaney, Jr. Serial in twelve chapters.

The Unearthly Stranger (1963) Anglo-Amalgamated/AIP. Dir.: John Krish. Scr.: Rex Carlton. Cin.: Reg Wyler. Cast: John Neville, Gabriella Licudi, Philip Stone, Jean Marsh. 74 min.

Universal Soldier (1992) Carolco/Tri-Star. Dir.: Roland Emmerich. Design: Nelson Coates. Cast: Jean-Claude Van Damme, Dolph Lundgren, Ally Walker. 102 min.

Weird Science (1985) Universal. Dir.: John Hughes. Scr.: Hughes. Cast: Kelly LeBrock, Anthony Michael Hall, Bill Paxton. 94 min.

Westworld (1973) MGM. Dir.: Michael Crichton. Prod.: Paul N. Lazarus III. Scr.: Crichton. Cin.: Gene Polito. Design: Herman Blumenthal. Ed.: David Bretherton. Cast: Richard Benjamin, Yul Brynner, James Brolin. 88 min.

Zombies of the Stratosphere (1952, retitled *Satan's Satellites*) Republic. Dir.: Fred C. Brannon. Scr.: Ronald Davidson. Cin.: John MacBurnie. Ed.: Cliff Bell. Design: Fred Ritter. Cast: Judd Holdren, Aline Towne, Wilson Wood, Leonard Nimoy. Serial in twelve chapters.

Meriting considerable attention in this context is the large body of animated science fiction produced in Japan in recent years. These works, some done for Japanese television, others for direct-to-video distribution, are generally grouped under the heading "Anime." Unlike most of the animation with which American audiences are familiar, "anime" is extremely violent, often contains nudity and profanity, and explores various adult themes. Most significantly for this study, it seems to have a singular fascination with various forms of human artifice. The Japanese *Guyver* films, for example, which inspired a weak American imitation starring Mark Hamill, explore the plight of an individual who accidentally fuses with an alien biomechanical fighting suit that, in times of peril, takes over his human body. This subordination of the body to a technological encrustation recurs in a more positive form in the popular *Bubblegum Crisis* and *Bubblebum Crash* series, as well as the various film and television versions of *Mobile Suit Gundam,* among others. The *Bubblegum* series, along with such works as the *AD Police Files,*

Appleseed, and *Black Magic M-66,* chronicles an ongoing futuristic struggle between humans and various "bioroid" or cyborg terrorists, typically created by and working for a powerful international corporation. Those bioroids, though, often go out of control and simply attack humans for the purpose of destroying the human race.

A contrasting view of the human-robot amalgam occurs in what is justifiably the best known of the anime films, *Akira.* It is a stunning depiction of life in a postapocalyptic Japan. In the midst of squalor and devastation, technology still flourishes under the guidance of the military-industrial complex. What that complex cannot control, though, is the appearance of an advanced being, endowed with mysterious powers that surpass those of the technological world. This new sort of being, we understand, is the product of a kind of collective spiritual yearning of future humanity—a yearning for something beyond the secular/technological realm to which they seem consigned.

These animated films seem to push the subject of human artifice in many of the same directions as most American features of the past decade. They explore the destructive as well as the potentially redemptive powers of technology, reflect the increasing difficulty of and need for expressions of feeling, emphasize the many threats to identity posed by the modern technological environment. These films may ultimately prove most interesting, though, as specific cultural artifacts, illustrating Japan's growing wariness of its technological attainments and the direction those attainments seem to be marking off for this culture, as well as an anxiety over how much the traditional Japanese sense of self is being reshaped, constructed, and controlled by a bewildering variety of external forces.

Bibliography

The bibliography that follows by no means measures the extensive literature currently available on the subject of robots or human artifice. Because this topic cuts across so many disciplinary boundaries and involves large areas of ongoing research in those various disciplines, the literature practically outstrips the individual's ability to keep up with it all. The following works, consequently, only sample this wealth of material, while giving special emphasis to film and cultural criticism directly focused on the topic.

Aleksander, Igor, and Piers Burnett. *Reinventing Man: The Robot Becomes Reality.* London: Kagan Page, 1983.

Arendt, Hannah. *The Human Condition.* Chicago: University of Chicago Press, 1958.

Aristotle. "On the Art of Poetry." *Classical Literary Criticism.* Trans. T. S. Dortsch. London: Penguin, 1965. 29–75.

Ash, Brian, ed. *The Visual Encyclopedia of Science Fiction.* New York: Harmony, 1977.

Asimov, Isaac. *I, Robot.* Greenwich: Fawcett Crest, 1950.

———. *Robot Dreams.* New York: Ace, 1986.

Barbour, Alan G. *Cliffhanger: A Pictorial History of the Motion Picture Serial.* Secaucus, NJ: Citadel Press, 1977.

Barker, Francis. *The Tremulous Private Body: Essays on Subjection.* London: Methuen, 1984.

Barnouw, Erik. *The Magician and the Cinema.* New York: Oxford University Press, 1981.

Barrett, William. *Death of the Soul: From Descartes to the Computer.* Garden City: Doubleday, 1987.

Baudrillard, Jean. *America.* Trans. Chris Turner. New York: Verso, 1988.

———. *Baudrillard Live: Selected Interviews.* Ed. Mike Gane. London: Routledge, 1993.

———. *The Ecstasy of Communication.* Trans. Bernard Schutze and Caroline Schutze. New York: Semiotext(e), 1987.

———. "The Ecstasy of Communication." *The Anti-Aesthetic: Essays on Postmodern Culture.* Ed. Hal Foster. Seattle: Bay Press, 1983. 126–34. (Note: the essay in this volume is substantially the same as that in the collection cited above; the translations, however, make enough difference so that the two pieces are worth citing—and thinking about—separately.)

———. *Forget Foucault.* Trans. Nicole Dufresne. New York: Semiotext(e), 1987.

———. *Jean Baudrillard: Selected Writings.* Ed. Mark Poster. Stanford: Stanford University Press, 1988.

———. *Simulations.* Trans. Paul Foss, Paul Patton, Philip Beitchman. New York: Semiotext(e), 1983.

Baxter, John. *Science Fiction in the Cinema.* New York: Paperback Library, 1970.

Bazin, André. *What Is Cinema?* Trans. Hugh Gray. Vol. 1. Berkeley: University of California Press, 1971.

Bellour, Raymond. "On Fritz Lang." *Fritz Lang: The Image and the Look.* Ed. Stephen Jenkins. London: British Film Institute, 1981. 26–37.

Benjamin, Walter. "The Work of Art in the Age of Mechanical Reproduction." *Illuminations.* Trans. Harry Zohn. Ed. Hannah Arendt. New York: Schocken, 1969. 217–52.

Biskind, Peter. *Seeing Is Believing: How Hollywood Taught Us to Stop Worrying and Love the Fifties.* New York: Pantheon, 1983.

———. "War of the Worlds." *American Film* 9.3 (1983): 36–42.

Bolter, J. David. *Turing's Man: Western Culture in the Computer Age.* Chapel Hill: University of North Carolina Press, 1984.

Borchert, Donald M., and David Stewart, eds. *Being Human in a Technological Age.* Athens: Ohio University Press, 1982.

Brosnan, John. *Movie Magic: The Story of Special Effects in the Cinema.* New York: New American Library, 1976.

Bruno, Guiliana. "Ramble City: Postmodernism and *Blade Runner.*" *October* 41 (1987): 61–74.

Bukatman, Scott. "The Cybernetic (City) State: Terminal Space Becomes Phenomenal." *Journal of the Fantastic in the Arts* 2.2 (1989): 43–63.

Burroughs, Edgar Rice. *Synthetic Men of Mars.* New York: Ballantine, 1963.

Campbell, Jeremy. *Grammatical Man: Information, Entropy, Language, and Life.* New York: Simon & Schuster, 1982.

Capek, Karel. *R.U.R.* Trans. Paul Selver. London: Oxford University Press, 1961.

Clarens, Carlos. *An Illustrated History of the Horror Film.* New York: Capricorn, 1967.

Cohen, John. *Human Robots in Myth and Science.* Cranbury, NJ: Barnes, 1967.

Cook David A. *A History of Narrative Film.* 2d ed. New York: Norton, 1990.

Corn, Joseph J., ed. *Imagining Tomorrow: History, Technology, and the American Future.* Cambridge: MIT Press, 1986.

Creed, Barbara. "*Alien* and the Monstrous-Feminine." *Alien Zone.* Ed. Annette Kuhn. London: Verso, 1990. 128–41.

———. "Gynesis, Postmodernism and the Science Fiction Horror Film." *Alien Zone.* Ed. Annette Kuhn. London: Verso, 1990. 214–18.

Cronenworth, Brian. "Man of Iron." *American Film* 13.1 (1987): 33–35.

del Ray, Lester. *The World of Science Fiction: 1926–1976—The History of a Subculture.* New York: Garland, 1980.

Desser, David. "*Blade Runner:* Science Fiction and Transcendence." *Literature/Film Quarterly* 13.3 (1985): 172–79.

Dickstein, Morris. "The Aesthetics of Fright." *American Film* 5.10 (1980): 32–37, 56, 58–59.

Doane, Mary Ann. "Technophilia: Technology, Representation, and the Feminine." *Body/Politics: Women and the Discourse of Science.* Ed. Mary Jacobus, Evelyn Fox Keller, and Sally Shuttleworth. London: Routledge, 1990. 163–76.

Dowdy, Andrew. *The Films of the Fifties: The American State of Mind.* New York: Morrow, 1973.

Eco, Umberto. "*Casablanca* and Cult Movies as Intertextual Collage." *Travels in Hyperreality.* Trans. William Weaver. New York: Harcourt, 1986. 197–211.

Elmer-Dewitt, Philip. "Cyberpunk." *Time* Feb. 8, 1993: 58–65.

Fiedler, Jean, and Jim Mele. "Asimov's Robots." *Critical Encounters: Writers and Themes in Science Fiction.* Ed. Rick Riley. New York: Ungar, 1978. 1–22.

Foucault, Michel. *The Care of the Self.* Trans. Robert Hurley. New York: Random House, 1986.

———. *The Foucault Reader.* Ed. Paul Rabinow. New York: Random House, 1984.

———. *The Order of Things: An Archeology of the Human Sciences.* New York: Random House, 1970.

———. *Power/Knowledge: Selected Interviews and Other Writings.* Ed. Colin Gordon. New York: Pantheon, 1980.

Franklin, H. Bruce. "Don't Look Where We're Going: Visions of the Future in Science Fiction Films, 1970–1982." *Shadows of the Magic Lamp.* Ed. George E. Slusser and Eric S. Rabkin. Carbondale: Southern Illinois University Press, 1985. 73–85.

Freud, Sigmund. *Civilization and Its Discontents.* Trans. James Strachey. London: Hogarth, 1961. Vol. 21 of *The Complete Psychological Works of Sigmund Freud.*

Geduld, Harry M. "Genesis II: The Evolution of Synthetic Man." *Robots, Robots, Robots.* Ed. Harry M. Geduld and Ronald Gottesman. Boston: New York Graphic Society, 1978. 3–27.

———. "Return to Méliès: Reflections on the Science Fiction Film." *Focus on the Science Fiction Film.* Ed. William Johnson. Englewood Cliffs: Prentice-Hall, 1972. 142–47.

Gibson, William. *Neuromancer.* New York: Ace, 1984.

Glass, Fred. "Totally Recalling Arnold." *Film Quarterly* 44.1 (1990): 2–13.

Goleman, Daniel. "Feeling Unreal? Many Others Feel the Same." *New York Times* Jan. 10, 1991: B5, B8.

Gordon, Andrew. "*The Empire Strikes Back:* Monsters from the Id." *Science Fiction Studies* 7.3 (1980): 313–18.

———. "*Return of the Jedi:* The End of the Myth." *Film Criticism* 8.2 (1984): 45–54.

Goscilo, Margaret. "Deconstructing *The Terminator.*" *Film Criticism* 12.2 (1988): 37–52.

Grant, Barry K. "*Invaders from Mars* and the Science Fiction Film in the Age of Reagan." *CineAction!* 8 (1987): 77–83.

Haraway, Donna. "The Actors Are Cyborg, Nature Is Coyote, and the Geography Is Elsewhere." *Technoculture.* Ed. Constance Penley and Andrew Ross. Minneapolis: University of Minnesota Press, 1991. 21–26.

———. *Simians, Cyborgs, and Women: The Reinvention of Nature.* New York: Routledge, 1991.

Hardison, O. B., Jr. *Disappearing through the Skylight: Culture and Technology in the Twentieth Century.* New York: Viking, 1989.

Harmon, Jim, and Donald Glut. *The Great Movie Serials: Their Sound and Fury.* Garden City: Doubleday, 1972.

Homer. *The Iliad.* Trans. Richmond Lattimore. Chicago: University of Chicago Press, 1951.

Jensen, Paul M. *The Cinema of Fritz Lang.* New York: Barnes, 1969.

Johnson, William, ed. *Focus on the Science Fiction Film.* Englewood Cliffs: Prentice-Hall, 1972.

Jolly, John. "The Bellerophon Myth and *Forbidden Planet.*" *Extrapolation* 27.1 (1986): 84–90.

Kawin, Bruce F. "Children of the Light." *Film Genre Reader.* Ed. Barry Keith Grant. Austin: University of Texas Press, 1986. 236–57.

Kinnard, Roy. "The Flash Gordon Serials." *Films in Review* 39.4 (1988): 194–203.

Kracauer, Siegfried. *From Caligari to Hitler: A Psychological History of the German Film.* Princeton: Princeton University Press, 1947.

Krasnoff, Barbara. *Robots: Reel to Real.* New York: Arco, 1982.

Kuhn, Annette, ed. *Alien Zone: Cultural Theory and Contemporary Science Fiction Cinema.* London: Verso, 1990.

Lancashire, Anne. "*Return of the Jedi:* Once More with Feeling." *Film Criticism* 8.2 (1984): 55–66.

Landon, Brooks. "Cyberpunk." *Cinefantastique* 18.1 (1987): 27–31, 58.

Lavery, David. *Late for the Sky: The Mentality of the Space Age.* Carbondale: Southern Illinois University Press, 1992.

Lem, Stanislaw. *The Cyberiad: Tales for the Cybernetic Age.* Trans. Michael Kandel. New York: Avon, 1976.

Lucanio, Patrick. *Them or Us: Archetypal Interpretations of Fifties Alien Invasion Films.* Bloomington: Indiana University Press, 1987.

MacDonnell, Kevin. *Eadweard Muybridge.* Boston: Little, Brown, 1972.

Markey, Constance. "Birth and Rebirth in Current Fantasy Films." *Film Criticism* 7.1 (1982): 14–25.

Mast, Gerald. *A Short History of the Movies.* 4th ed. New York: Macmillan, 1986.

McCaffery, Larry. "The Desert of the Real." *Storming the Reality Studio.* Ed. Larry McCaffery. Durham: Duke University Press, 1991. 1–16.

McConnell, Frank. "Born in Fire: The Ontology of the Monster." *Shadows of the Magic Lamp: Fantasy and Science Fiction in Film.* Ed. George E. Slusser and Eric S. Rabkin. Carbondale: Southern Illinois University Press, 1985. 231–38.

Miller, Mark Crispin. "The Robot in the Western Mind." *Boxed In: The Culture of TV.* Evanston: Northwestern University Press, 1988. 285–307.

———. *Seeing through the Movies.* New York: St. Martin's, 1989.

Minsky, Marvin, ed. *Robotics.* Garden City: Doubleday, 1985.

Mizejewski, Linda. "Total Recoil: The Schwarzenegger Body on Postmodern Mars." *Post Script* 12.3 (1993): 25–34.

Moravec, Hans. *Mind Children: The Future of Robot and Human Intelligence.* Cambridge: Harvard University Press, 1988.

Necakov, Lillian. "*The Terminator:* Beyond Classical Hollywood Narrative." *CineAction!* 8 (1987): 84–86.

Orvell, Miles. *The Real Thing: Imitation and Authenticity in American Culture, 1880–1940.* Chapel Hill: University of North Carolina Press, 1989.

Patrouch, Joseph F., Jr. *The Science Fiction of Isaac Asimov.* Garden City: Doubleday, 1974.

Penley, Constance, and Andrew Ross. "Cyborgs at Large: Interview with Donna Haraway." *Technoculture.* Ed. Constance Penley and Andrew Ross. Minneapolis: University of Minnesota Press, 1991. 1–20.

Poe, Edgar Allan. *The Short Fiction of Edgar Allan Poe.* Ed. Stuart Levine and Susan Levine. Indianapolis: Bobbs-Merrill, 1976.

Pollack, David. "The Creation and Repression of Cybernetic Man: Technological Fear and the Secrecy of Narrative." *Clio* 18.1 (1988): 1–21.

Porush, David. "Reading in the Servo-Mechanical Loop." *Discourse* 9.2 (1987): 53–63.

——. *The Soft Machine: Cybernetic Fiction.* New York: Methuen, 1985.

"Prometheus." *The Oxford Classical Dictionary.* 2d ed. Ed. N. G. L. Hammond and H. H. Scullard. London: Oxford University Press, 1970. 883–84.

Regis, Ed. *Great Mambo Chicken and the Transhuman Condition.* Reading: Addison-Wesley, 1990.

Rheingold, Howard. *Virtual Reality.* New York: Summit, 1991.

Romanyshyn, Robert D. *Technology as Symptom and Dream.* London: Routledge, 1989.

Ryan, Michael, and Douglas Kellner. "Technophobia." *Alien Zone.* Ed. Annette Kuhn. London: Verso, 1990. 58–65.

Schelde, Per. *Androids, Humanoids, and Other Science Fiction Monsters: Science and Soul in Science Fiction Film.* New York: New York University Press, 1993.

Schwab, Gabriele. "Cyborgs: Postmodern Phantasms of Body and Mind." *Discourse* 9.2 (1987): 64–84.

Schwab, Martin. "In the Mirror of Technology." *Discourse* 9.2 (1987): 85–106.

Segal, Howard. "The Technological Utopians." *Imagining Tomorrow: History, Technology, and the American Future.* Ed. Joseph Corn. Cambridge: MIT Press, 1986. 119–36.

Shelley, Mary. *Frankenstein.* Ed. M. K. Joseph. New York: Oxford University Press, 1971.

Slusser, George. "Fantasy, Science Fiction, Mystery, Horror." *Shadows of the Magic Lamp: Fantasy and Science Fiction in Film.* Ed. George E. Slusser and Eric S. Rabkin. Carbondale: Southern Illinois University Press, 1985. 208–30.

——. "Literary MTV." *Storming the Reality Studio.* Ed. Larry McCaffery. Durham: Duke University Press, 1991. 334–42.

Sobchack, Vivian. *The Address of the Eye: A Phenomenology of Film Experience.* Princeton: Princeton University Press, 1992.

——. *Screening Space: The American Science Fiction Film.* 2d ed. New York: Ungar, 1987.

——. "The Virginity of Astronauts: Sex and the Science Fiction Film." *Alien Zone.* Ed. Annette Kuhn. London: Verso, 1990. 103–15.

Sontag, Susan. "The Imagination of Disaster." *Against Interpretation.* New York: Dell, 1966. 212–28.

Sterling, Bruce. "Preface from *Mirrorshades.*" *Storming the Reality Studio.* Ed. Larry McCaffery. Durham: Duke University Press, 1991. 343–48.

Stewart, Garrett. "The 'Videology' of Science Fiction." *Shadows of the Magic Lamp: Fantasy and Science Fiction in Film.* Ed. George E. Slusser and Eric S. Rabkin. Carbondale: Southern Illinois University Press, 1985. 159–207.

Strickland, A. W., and Forrest J. Ackerman, eds. *A Reference Guide to American Science Fiction Films.* Vol. 1. Bloomington: T. I. S. Publications, 1981.

Tarratt, Margaret. "Monsters from the Id." *Film Genre Reader.* Ed. Barry Keith Grant. Austin: University of Texas Press, 1986. 258–77.

Telotte, J. P. "Human Artifice and the Science Fiction Film." *Film Quarterly* 36.3 (1983): 44–51.

——. "The Ghost in the Machine: Consciousness and the Science Fiction Film." *Western Humanities Review* 42.3 (1988): 249–58.

Tichi, Cecelia. *Shifting Gears: Technology, Literature, Culture in Modernist America.* Chapel Hill: University of North Carolina Press, 1987.

Turing, Alan. "Computing Machinery and Intelligence." *Mind* 59 (1950): 433–60.

Warrick, Patricia S. *The Cybernetic Imagination in Science Fiction.* Cambridge: MIT Press, 1980.

Wiener, Norbert. *God and Golem, Inc.* Cambridge: MIT Press, 1964.

——. *The Human Use of Human Beings: Cybernetics and Society.* Garden City: Doubleday, 1954.

Williams, Tony. "Close Encounters of the Authoritarian Kind." *Wide Angle* 5.4 (1983): 22–29.

Williamson, Jack. *The Humanoids.* New York: Lancer, 1949.

Wolfe, Gary. *The Known and the Unknown: The Iconography of Science Fiction.* Kent: Kent State University Press, 1979.

Index

J. P. TELOTTE is a professor in the School of Literature, Communication, and Culture at Georgia Institute of Technology, where he teaches courses in film and drama. Co-editor of the journal *Post Script,* the has previously published books on horror, the film noir, and cult films. This book springs from his dual interests in film genres and the impact of technology on modern culture.